TECHNO-BANDITS

TECHNO-BANDITS

Linda Melvern
Nick Anning
David Hebditch

HOUGHTON MIFFLIN COMPANY
Boston 1984

Library of Congress Cataloging in Publication Data
Main entry under title:

Techno-bandits.

Bibliography: p.
Includes index.
1. Business intelligence. 2. Espionage, Russian—
United States. 3. Smuggling—United States. 4. Tech-
nology transfer—Soviet Union. 5. Technology transfer—
United States. I. Melvern, Linda. II. Title: Technology
bandits.
HD38.7.T43 1984 364.1′68 84-9090
ISBN 0-395-36066-8

Printed in the United States of America

P 10 9 8 7 6 5 4 3 2 1

ACKNOWLEDGMENTS

THE AUTHORS of this book were privileged to benefit from the practical support and encouragement of many professional writers and researchers on both sides of the Atlantic. In particular, Celina Bledowska and Kevin Cahill in London and Cynthia Jabs in Washington responded proficiently to an unreasonable flow of equally unreasonable inquiries.

Advice, encouragement, and practical help came at many crucial stages from Paul Eddy, David May, Sara Vernon, and Magnus Linklater.

For help in the early stages of the research, our thanks go to Robert Fink in Washington, D.C., Philip H. Dorn in New York, Paul Tate in London, and Maureen O'Gara in Cologne. We have also drawn on the special expertise and contacts of Robin Clark, Paddy French, Professor Martin Healey, Steve Hirsch, Mark Kuchment, Andreas Orth, Henk Ruysenaars, Michael Siegert, Paul Walton, and Andrew Weir.

For their tolerance, understanding, and personal support, we owe many debts to long-suffering friends and relations: Nick Ashford, Mark Bomster, Bill Wesbrooks, and Debrah Kasouf looked after us in Washington, D.C.; Kikanne and Temple Williams did a similar job in New York; and in London Dennis Muirhead provided much needed advice. Nick Anning would like to say a special thank-you to Jill Simpson. David Hebditch doubts he would have made it without the support of Pat Gregory and the understanding of Daniel Hebditch during the long absences "on the road." It is sad that this book will not be read by Patsy Hubble, who died shortly after telling us his story. Linda Melvern would like to pay a grateful tribute to Jim, Mavius, and Richard Melvern.

This book is based on many hundreds of interviews with people who, in some way or other, are involved in the international trade in high technology. Regardless of whether they wanted to stop the trade, encourage it, or were active participants, few we approached refused to talk to us. Some did so at personal risk. For those interviews that were "on the record," sources have been cited in the footnotes; our thanks to all those individuals. We are equally grateful to the many others whom we cannot name: Customs agents, government officials, lawyers, intelligence agents, politicians, technologists, law enforcement officers, academics throughout Europe and the United States, and, of course, the businessmen who are based in the Soviet Union or who travel to the Eastern bloc.

The authors acknowledge the unusual support of Mark Hosenball at critical stages in the production of the book and thank him for finding time in a busy schedule to help with the research in Washington, D.C., New York City, and California.

We were lucky to have Frances L. Apt as manuscript editor, and we are indebted to her for her extraordinary care and perception. Robie Macauley is any author's ideal editor: from beginning to end his advice and commitment have been invaluable. Finally, we are grateful to our agent, Maria Carvainis, for her faith in the book and for her patience and diplomacy when it was most needed.

CONTENTS

TECHNO-BANDITS

INTRODUCTION

"ITS IMPORTANCE can hardly be exaggerated. It has been the most jealously guarded of all government secrets.... The plans, which are exceedingly intricate, comprising some thirty separate patents, each essential to the working of the whole, are kept in an elaborate safe in a confidential office adjoining the arsenal, with burglar-proof doors and windows. Under no conceivable circumstance were the plans to be taken from the office.... And yet here we find them in the pocket of a dead junior clerk in the heart of London."

Some things have changed and some things remain very much the same as they were in 1895, when the Bruce-Partington Plans were stolen in Sir Arthur Conan Doyle's story. But the Soviet acquisition of American high technology has indeed an "importance that can hardly be exaggerated." It is probably the single most significant action in the silent war of the 1980s. In the colorless language of bureaucracy, it is called "technology transfer."

At its most extreme, it is a matter of classic espionage: someone with the right access takes the secret technology of a satellite or a nuclear warhead or a missile and sells it to an agent of a Soviet bloc country. But the Bruce-Partington Plans sort of case now forms just a small percentage of the enormous drain. The rapid advances of technology and its dispersion throughout the civilian economy have blurred the classic definition of espionage. Technological secrets that twenty years ago were locked away in Fort Meade's National Security Agency headquarters are now part of a personal computer on sale in a local store. The mainframe computer that is used in a business office or a hospital in the West might, when exported, become a part of Soviet military hardware.

Ever since the 1940s, there has been an American effort (sometimes shared by the Europeans and sometimes not) to deny sophisticated technology with weapons potential to the Communist countries. Such an effort comes into conflict with the old Western allegiance to free trade — and the old desire of Western businessmen to make a buck. Inevitably, this dilemma has been exploited by a new breed of international brokers and salesmen — the techno-bandits.

They operate in a gray area. Most are not quite spies, because what they sell to the East in secret is openly available on the market in the West. They break no laws against treason; they simply avoid export control regulations. They think of themselves as akin to the black marketeers of the 1940s and fifties. But along with the techno-bandits, there *are* the real spies, who knowingly steal and sell highly classified technology.

The new element in the 1980s is that the United States has grown much more serious about putting a stop to all of these activities. The Reagan administration is determined to stem what it considers a massive "hemorrhage" of technology. It has tightened export controls, increased enforcement, made the problem a priority for the Intelligence agencies. The allies have been told that they must step into line with American policy.

And yet — as even the enforcement agencies privately admit — it is almost impossible to know the true extent of techno-banditry, and it is impossible to stop it altogether. This multimillion-dollar underground trade uses all the techniques of respectable business. The operators create dummy corporations in various countries, disguise their goods under false export declarations, move offices from country to country, and sometimes actually carry prohibited goods across national borders in their suitcases.

There is the American who masterminded the scheme to export illegally a multispectral scanner (a device used in satellite systems).

He used his private plane to fly the shipment to Mexico City, from where it was to go to Holland by commercial airliner and thence behind the Iron Curtain. There is the Belgian caught trying to bribe an American software house to sell him a computer code. There is the mysterious "Mr. Millions," who, operating from South Africa, has made a fortune by selling computers to the Soviets. There is the American export consultant who hired a Swiss to carry surveillance equipment out of the country in two suitcases. And there is the Silicon Valley engineer who sold secrets of the Minuteman missile to a Polish Intelligence officer in disguise.

Our story of the techno-bandits begins with "Andrew Benson." His name has been changed, but his story, based on extensive interviews, is true. He has never been caught. He is one of a certain type of techno-bandit, and his story starts in Moscow in 1982.

1

MOSCOW AND PARIS

ANDREW BENSON stared out the window of his third-story room in the Soyuz Two hotel and watched the machines at work on a construction site beneath him. He was bored, hot, and annoyed. In this September of 1982, Moscow was enjoying a spell of unusually warm weather, and for some minutes he had been debating the choice of closing the window and suffocating in the dismal "office" or leaving the window open to the noise and dirt. He stood there a few moments longer, following the progress of a pair of heavy trucks bucking along a potholed access road. The only spot of color in the monotonous cityscape before him was a banner hanging above the entrance to a large factory in the distance. Its uninspiring message was "We shall fulfill the decisions of the 26th Congress." It did not say when.

He was saved from further boredom by the ring of the telephone — an instrument of a rather incongruous pale blue — and he replied to his caller with some interest. Indeed, he said, he'd be delighted to have lunch. The Mezh in about half an hour? Of course. As he spoke, he lighted up one of the last Marlboros in his pack in an effort to combat the stink of the exhaust from the low-octane gas used by the construction trucks. He made a mental note to stop at one of the Beryozka hard-currency shops for more cigarettes. Just now, he was looking forward to lunch with Marty Prince. It would brighten things up a bit; he still had a week to go before returning to London.

Benson genuinely liked Marty, as did most of the men in the Western business colony here, even though Prince had arrived as the Moscow manager of one of the largest East-West trading companies only a short time before. The businessmen made up a close-knit little society, well known for its parties. Prince's predecessor had been driving home from one of those parties when he fell asleep at the wheel. When the militia woke him up, he was parked on the wrong side of Komsomolsky Prospekt. A policeman suggested that he was drunk. This inspired him to take a swing at the policeman. Within a few days, he was back in the United States, and Marty Prince had replaced him.

Benson locked his door and walked down the stairs to the lobby. Some day, he reflected, the future would bring the marvels of air conditioning and elevators to the Soyuz Two — but not this year. He got into his white Lada (a Soviet-built Fiat) and began to weave his way around the craters in the hotel's entrance driveway. After a few minutes, he was on the smoother surface of Krasnogvardeysky Street and headed for the International Trade Center.

Called the Mezh by the English-speaking businessmen, it is a complex of offices, hotel accommodations, bars, restaurants, and conference facilities. Much American know-how went into its design and building; it was completed at the inauspicious moment when the United States pulled out of the 1980 Olympic Games in protest at the Soviet invasion of Afghanistan. In the parking lot there are always many cars with yellow H501 series registration plates. Those are rental cars.

The lobby, which Benson was now entering, is fairly impressive. It is called the Atrium and is nine stories high. Some American visitors even pay it the compliment of comparing it with the Hyatt Regency Hotel in San Francisco. It does, in fact, resemble a great many modern structures throughout the world. Except for the bloody clock, Benson reflected.

The Mezh was busy this noon, and Benson nodded in greeting to several familiar faces as he made his way across the lobby to the Atrium bar. Prince was sitting at a table, glaring up at the huge cockerel's head.

"Can you figure the genius who invented that thing?" he asked. "I guess it's meant to give time a bad name. I took the liberty of grabbing a waiter and ordering two large Scotches. Otherwise, we might not see him until after the damned twenty-*seventh* Congress. Don't expect soda, though. I've got you a mineral water."

"Some day I'll persuade someone here to buy a soda fountain." Benson nodded toward the cockerel: "I take it they've got it mended again."

"Sure did. And it's almost showtime." They both stared at the thirty-foot monstrosity immediately in front of the bank of elevators. They waited as the minute hand clicked up to twelve and the massive cockerel on top of its column lurched to life, drew back, and uttered a strangled squawk.

Prince slapped his forehead and said, "Jesus, only a Russian would cross a cuckoo with a chicken and give the bastard a dose of steroids."

"I don't know if you've ever watched the local sport," Benson said. "Late at night, some of the blokes who live here try to fire champagne corks into its mouth. It doesn't digest corks very well. But when it breaks down, the Russians get it working again in minutes — best-maintained piece of equipment in the Soviet Union, I should say. A big problem from both mechanical and diplomatic angles. A genius of a manager will hit on a brilliant solution some day: stop selling champagne by the bottle."

Benson, like Prince, had a room here at the Mezh during his stays in Moscow; it was his office that was in the dingy converted student hostel called the Soyuz Two. Accreditation for capitalist traders allowed for the lease of offices at the trade center, but that seal of approval cost $250,000, and Benson had never convinced himself the price was worth it.

Prince and Benson, having finished their drinks, moved on to the Continental Restaurant, where the maitre d'hôtel found a quiet table for them, and they began to talk about more serious things. Benson wanted to know what information Prince had about the trade embargo the Reagan administration had laid down after martial law was declared in Poland.

"Let's see — it's been in effect about ten months now. But it's been pretty much ignored outside the U.S. Some of the companies that do big trade here — like Occidental and Control Data — have been lobbying to get it lifted. The word is they'll get their way by the end of the year."

"That sounds good. I could do without the hassle." Benson depended on American companies for many of the computer products he sold in Russia.

"Yeah, but don't get too excited. That Exodus team set up by U.S. Customs is beginning to carry some weight."

"Could they be much of a problem?"

"Well, in theory they'll give you trouble only if you're trying to export without a license from the Commerce Department; they're just supposed to beef up the Export Administration Act. But Exodus could give heartburn to a lot of guys in the business."

When the food arrived, Benson changed the subject. "Marty, do you know a guy called Ivanov?"

"You bet. About two hundred of them."

"Sergey Pavlovich Ivanov. He works for Mashpriborintorg."

"New one to me. What's the deal?"

Benson shook his head. "Oh, just that I got a call from him this morning." He left the matter at that, and Marty asked no more.

Lunch took about two hours. After he'd said goodbye to Prince, Benson walked through the lobby and past the bar again, noticing that the lunchtime crowd had gone and the most conspicuous customers were a couple of prostitutes. The initiated Western businessmen knew well enough to leave them alone; if they were working a hard-currency bar, it was a sure sign that they reported to the KGB.

Back in his office, Benson read again the notes he had made during the conversation with Ivanov. A meeting? Perhaps tomorrow for lunch? Very good — a car would pick Benson up at eleven-thirty in the morning. The license plate would be MOC 7525. (The MOC registration suggested a bureaucrat fairly high in the official hierarchy.) Benson was both curious and puzzled. It wasn't usual for a Russian trade official to approach a Westerner this way. And Ivanov had sounded unusually urgent. Very odd, all of it.

Benson spent the night with his girlfriend Sashka in her two-room apartment in the Yugozapadny district near the Olympic Village. She was fourth in the series of girls he'd had since he started coming to Moscow at the age of twenty-six, seven years ago. He'd known enough to avoid the prostitutes even then, and he also knew that a regular supply of English and French clothes, perfume, and shoes produced true love. Or a reasonable facsimile.

In the morning, he went to the Mezh, where he changed into a conservative English business suit. Then he drove to the Soyuz Two to collect his briefcase. He had been standing on the stone steps outside for less than a minute when the new-model, black Volga limousine arrived. He put his head through the open passenger window and said, "Benson." The driver nodded.

For the first few minutes, Benson could not guess where they were headed, but when they turned left onto the Krasnaya Presnya stretch of the Moskva River embankment, he glimpsed the unmistakable wedding cake architecture of the Ukraina Hotel on the other bank. Then up the hill, a turn away from the Kalinin Prospekt, past the headquarters of the Council for Mutual Economic Assistance and the new American embassy — by this time Benson was convinced that he was indeed on his way to the Ministry of Foreign Trade.

As they neared the Moscow Zoo, heading for the older part of the city, the driver eased the car into the left lane and waited for the traffic light to turn green. The Volga rumbled across the cobblestone square into Bolshaya Gruzinskaya Street.

"We're not going to the ministry, then?" Benson asked in Russian.

"*Nye-aa,*" said the driver with a shrug.

"*Tak kuda?* So where are we going?" Benson was getting irritated.

"*Seichas priyedem.* We'll be there soon," the driver insisted.

The Volga continued past the West German and Polish embassies toward the Belorussky railway station and then crossed Gorky Street into a residential area of narrow roads. At this point, Benson became totally lost. After a few more minutes, the car turned through an arch into a courtyard and stopped. Here, children were playing under the watch of old women in black dresses and kerchiefs who sat gossiping in the midday sun.

They left the car, and the driver silently preceded Benson through doorway number three. They rode an old elevator to the fourth floor and then walked up one more level. The driver rang the bell of an apartment door. Benson had been nervous in Moscow before, but never so much as now.

When the door opened, he was astonished. The woman who stood there, her fat face plastered with make-up, looked like a stage comedy whore. "Good afternoon, Mr. Benson," she said in lightly accented English. "Come in, please." He walked through the door into the most striking apartment he had yet seen in Moscow. It had wall-to-wall carpeting of a sage-green color that was matched with a vinyl wallpaper. The normal Soviet home with some pretensions has polished parquet floors; the best-quality carpets are hung on the walls to save wear. The furniture here was modern Scandinavian in design, though Benson suspected that it had been made in East Germany.

He followed the woman down a long corridor to a comfortably furnished living room. "Please help yourself to a drink. Mr. Ivanov will be here in a minute," she said as she left. Bottles, glasses, even a bowl of ice, were arrayed on a smoked-glass table in the middle of the room. He poured himself a Johnny Walker Black Label. The door opened and a man came into the room.

"Ah, Mr. Benson. I am glad that you are making yourself at home. I am Sergey Ivanov." Benson put down his glass and they shook hands. "Also my favorite whiskey," the Russian said, pouring himself a double shot, with ice. He fitted into the surroundings. His manner was smooth, and the expensive lightweight suit he wore had not been tailored this side of the Iron Curtain. He raised his glass. "Cheers! Also, please have a cigarette. I think those are Dunhills in the box.

"Please accept our apologies for calling this meeting at such short notice," he went on urbanely. "We appreciate your agreeing to come."

For a few minutes, the talk was casual. Then Ivanov set down his glass, stood up, and opened a double door at the end of the room. Beyond was a dining room, where two older men were waiting for them.

Ivanov introduced them in Russian, which was a signal: senior members of the Soviet bureaucracy usually do not speak much English. And when they went through the ritual of exchanging business cards, the signal was confirmed. The men were members of the

Soviet State Committee on Science and Technology. Benson was impressed. Compared with his usual Soviet contacts, these were top brass.

The mahogany dining room table groaned under a full spread of zakuski, the traditional Russian hors d'oeuvres. There were plates of the black sevruga caviar and the red zubatka ranged alongside white sturgeon, smoked balyk, crab salad, roast pork, ham, and beef. Bottles of Russian champagne stood in ice buckets, and there was even a bottle of the new vodka, Zolotoye Kolsto, Golden Ring, which was not yet to be found in the stores. In the middle of the display was a huge bowl of carnations.

The meal began with the customary toast. Indeed, as Benson knew, the whole meal would be punctuated with toasts, and he realized that his hollow-leg talents were going to be tested.

As they filled their plates, one of the older men spoke to him in Russian. "We congratulate you on your contribution to the development of Anglo-Soviet cooperation." Any excuse for another drink, Benson thought. He had recently been given an award from the Soviet Chamber of Commerce.

"Is this your tenth?" the other asked. Benson raised his eyebrows. He'd had only two drinks.

"The award. Have you received others?"

"Yes, but this one was just the ninth." They seemed to get the joke and they laughed. But why the hell don't they get on with it? Benson wondered.

It was only after two more hours that Ivanov got to the question. "Is your company satisfied with the contract they signed with Mashpriborintorg?" He was referring to a recent deal Benson had made to supply five Wang word processors. Benson dutifully said that it was an excellent deal and that he and his partner were quite pleased.

Ivanov continued, "I am sure that you are aware of the important role our committee plays in the Soviet economy. But, to be quite honest, we have recently experienced certain problems, and we are at a loss as to how to solve them."

"What problems?" Benson asked on cue.

"We wish to computerize office work in one of our ministries, and we lack some of the essential elements. With your desire for economic trade cooperation, you may be able to help us." Benson was used to the Russian circumlocutions and had long ago inured himself to this kind of boredom.

"What exactly are the essential elements you need?" he asked patiently, although he had already guessed and now was trying to estimate the number.

Ivanov reached down to his briefcase resting against the leg of the table and produced a single sheet of paper. It was a detailed diagram of the IBM Personal Computer, along with a list of special features and software packages.

"How many do you need?"

"Fifty," said Ivanov. "Would that be a problem?"

The Englishman shook his head. "Well, it *is* a new product. I'll have to check. . . . Also, I'm not sure that these machines have the right circuits for your alphabet."

"Do not worry about that — we shall make a special fix."

"That's fine. But about the price — "

"We are prepared to pay you ten thousand English pounds for each machine."

Benson was stunned with the good luck. Unless prices had changed recently, these small, desktop machines sold on the market for less than £3000. With bulk purchase, he might even be able to get a discount. He decided to push his luck just a bit. "Is that price FOB or CIF?"

"FOB," said Ivanov.

Great! The Russians would even pay the freight and insurance costs.

It all ended, of course, with another toast. The contract would be drafted and signed the following day. After all the eating, drinking, and cautious preliminaries, this was the quickest conclusion Benson had ever been involved in. Sometimes it took him longer to get a drink in the Atrium bar.

Benson went back to London a day early to spend the weekend with his wife, Paula, and their two children. They had a very good house, in the north London suburb of Radlett, that had cost him about £100,000. On Monday, he started out early. At the local newsstand, he bought copies of *Personal Computer World, Practical Computing,* and *Which Computer?* From these he drew up a list of all the London-area retail outlets that sold the IBM PC. Then he called the Union Bank of Switzerland in Zürich and arranged for a sum equal to £125,000 to be transferred by telex to one of his U.K. bank accounts. He spent the morning telephoning dealers to find out how many IBM machines they had in stock or on order. To avoid attracting attention, he bought no more than ten from any one company.

He collected the computers personally in an Avis rental truck and paid for them in cash. Within two weeks, he had delivered all of them to a well-established shipping company outside London. While they were being packed into a container for shipping via Harwich and the Hook of Holland to Schiphol Airport in Amsterdam, Benson was in the West End of London, shopping for clothes for Sashka. On previous trips, he had taken the risk of carrying pornographic videotapes as gifts for his Russian business contacts, but that was no longer necessary. In 1981, the Georgian *videonshchiki* had started their own lucrative skinflick industry. Instead, Benson bought five innocuous Western movies as gifts.

When he returned to Moscow, he found to his satisfaction that the computers had arrived in Russia and that the Russian letter-of-credit payment had already been posted to his Midland Bank account in the City of London.

On June 17, 1983, Andrew Benson was sitting in his Soyuz Two office talking with Marty Prince about a terrible thing that had just happened. Early that day, a senior Midland Bank employee named Dennis Skinner had fallen from the window of his eleventh-floor apartment at 148 Leninsky Prospekt. A colleague from the bank had found the body near the car park at the back of the building. A tracksuit top was wrapped around the head.

Prince said, "Somebody in our embassy claims he did it because he was going to be arrested by the Ks." (K was the nickname for the KGB.)

"That's crap," said Benson. "He was already holding an exit visa. If the Ks were going to arrest him, they'd not have approved the visa. If they'd had something on him, they'd have sealed off the building as soon as he was found. But he wasn't a suicidal type."

Skinner was well known among the Westerners in Moscow. He had not been a career banker; he had worked as a technical consultant in the Soviet office of the British computer company ICL for several years. His death was deeply disturbing to both men.

"Why did he do it, then?" asked Prince.

"Money problems? It's quite likely we'll never know." Just then, the pale blue telephone rang.

"Good morning, Mr. Benson. Ivanov here," came the voice. "You remember that we had lunch together last year?"

"Yes, Mr. Ivanov. How are you?"

"I am very fine. I would like to fix a meeting with you again. Tomorrow would be good."

"Of course. Is there anything wrong?"

"Absolutely not. We were so pleased with the last contract that we should like to talk some more. Our car will be at the Soyuz Two at eleven-thirty. Agreed?"

The lunch was a replay of the one nine months before: the same apartment, the same array of food and drink, the same senior officials from the State Committee on Science and Technology — a replay except for the ending. From the briefcase Ivanov produced a list of high-tech equipment that was all unfamiliar to Benson. It seemed to have something to do with "image enhancement."

Benson pleaded difficulties and asked for time to do some research on availability. Under the circumstances, he said, it would not be right for him to sign the contract. The Russians were affable, but this time the toasts were less elaborate.

In London, later that month, Benson passed the list to one of his business associates. The colleague's face began to show alarm as he read through the document. "Andrew," he said, "this is thorny. Every item on the list is embargoed sensitive equipment. You'll never get export licenses from the U.S. Commerce Department."

"I suspected as much. But that applied equally to the IBM computers, you know. All we have to do is to find a way of getting them from the United States to the U.K. The rest will be easy."

On a hot day in July, Benson arrived back in his room at the Soyuz Two and opened the window. Very little seemed to have changed at the construction site; the same trucks were churning the same dust into the heavy air. He had two tries at the horrid blue Polish telephone before he could get through.

"*Slushayu* . . ."

"Sergey Pavlovich?" Benson was now on a first-name basis with Ivanov.

"Andrew! Welcome back. We expected you sooner. Are there problems?"

"Not if you agree to the price."

"Ha! You English and your famous humor!" Ivanov laughed. Benson did not feel like laughing. He was beginning to wonder what he was getting into. That summer Skinner's death had caused unease in the business community. A Midland Bank investigating team had flown out and had taken two days to get access to Skinner's flat, which by then appeared to have been cleaned up.

Benson's unease was well founded. In a British coroner's court a year later it was revealed that Skinner had first been approached by the KGB more than ten years before while working as a computer salesman. He had also been used by MI6, Britain's Intelligence service. More chilling, the court found Skinner's death had been "unlawful killing," not suicide.

The secret briefing in Paris was about to start, and the chairman rose to his feet. The furniture of the COCOM committee room at the 58B rue de la Boëtie annex of the American embassy in Paris had been rearranged, because the delegates were going to watch a slide show. On the secretariat table between the open ends of the U was a stand with a Carousel slide projector. Behind their name plates on the table sat representatives of the United States, the United Kingdom, France, the Federal Republic of Germany, Japan, Italy, Belgium, the Netherlands, Luxembourg, Canada, Norway, Greece, and Turkey. As usual, Portugal was absent. The room quickly fell silent as the elderly interpreter pulled her chair forward between the two French delegates and prepared to translate the English-language proceedings.

COCOM, the Coordinating Committee for Multilateral Export Controls, is essentially a handshake affair, the result of a gentleman's agreement. It came into effect on January 1, 1950; its first meeting in Paris ran from January 9 to January 20 of that year. It was not established under any formal treaty, and its durability rests mainly on a permanent secretariat that draws up lists of advanced technologies and goods that must not be exported to Communist bloc countries. In short, a manufacturer who wants to ship an order to Warsaw or Leningrad must get a COCOM clearance. But there are some troublesome gaps in the fence. COCOM members are able to classify certain shipments as "national exceptions," and this leeway has been the cause of considerable irritation. With the election of President Reagan in 1980, the United States became more sharply concerned with the whole question of technology export to the Iron Curtain countries. Now, the American delegation had requested that COCOM representatives meet in order to hear a CIA briefing on just how the Soviets were by-passing their controls.

After the chairman had opened the meeting, William Root took over. Root was the director of the Office of East-West Trade at the State Department, an experienced diplomat, and the head of the American COCOM delegation. He had the kindly, somewhat harried manner of a teacher coming before the school board to explain a worrisome disciplinary problem in the twelfth grade. After a few words, he introduced the two principal speakers: Dr. Stephen Bryen of the Pentagon, and a senior intelligence officer from the CIA. Dr. Bryen was a Deputy Assistant Defense Secretary.

He was short, slim, and beginning to go bald. He was definitely natty this morning, having dressed for the occasion in a dark blazer and gray slacks. From the start, he struck his listeners as more assertive than Root, with important information to relay. First, he said, he would describe the technology the Russians had copied. Then he would describe the technology the Americans had seized before it was illegally shipped. He would also describe the Soviets' efforts and how America was attempting to counter them. He picked up the control wire, and a COCOM secretary switched on the machine. The first slide appeared. Black letters on a bright pink background stated, "The Threat to Western Technology."

"This slide reveals a Boeing YN 14," said Bryen. It had been developed by the United States as a short-takeoff craft. "Here is the Soviet equivalent." When he turned to point to the screen, he saw that the photographs were nothing but a light gray blur. "Mr. Chairman," he said, "I wonder whether we could turn down the lights a little."

In the back of the room, a secretary began to fumble with the switches, and suddenly the room was plunged into darkness. Root must have groaned to himself. Earlier, at the State Department, he had expressed his opposition to this whole exercise; the French and British were certain to take it as a very unsubtle kind of pressure. Now it was going haywire from the start.

After a good deal of experimentation, it was determined that if the lights were off and the shutters at the three long windows just ajar, the slides could be observed. The trouble was that Bryen now couldn't read his carefully prepared notes.

He looked pleadingly at Root, who began to search his pockets. Finally, he produced something and passed it down the table to Bryen. "It's a penlight," he said. "Press the end of it."

These absurd false starts all fitted in very well with Dr. Bryen's darkest suspicions about COCOM. He knew that it limped along on a budget of about $500,000 a year. On previous visits, he had noted that the offices were so crowded that the filing cabinets were standing in the corridors, that there were no secure communications facilities, and that, until recently, there hadn't even been a photocopier in the place. When Bryen's staff people went with him to Paris, they had to stay in flea-bag hotels in order to survive on $75 a day.

Finally, with the aid of the low-tech penlight, he proceeded with his lecture, commenting in some detail as each pair of comparison photographs appeared on the screen. "Please note the design similarities of the Soviet I1-76 heavy transport plane to those of the U.S. C-141 Starlifter." He next showed several color slides of the Russian plane with Aeroflot markings. "Note the wings," Bryen said, and went on to explain that when these planes appeared abroad, they had the distinctive civilian airline markings. But when the planes were back in Soviet territory, the markings were removed and the aircraft were used by the military. Another slide showed a satellite photograph of a massive drydock with an aircraft carrier. Two huge floating drydocks had been purchased from the West, Bryen explained, with a Soviet assurance they would be used only for civilian ships. In 1978, the Soviets had diverted one of the docks to their Pacific fleet. The other had been sent to the northern fleet in 1981.

Bryen moved on to microchips. The Russians would get hold of Western components and "reverse engineer" the chip designs. Another of their targets was microprocesssor design: the Russians had stolen eight microprocessors and the East Germans three from major American manufacturers. The bubble memories for use in "ruggedized" military computers were something garnered by the Hungarians and passed on to the Soviets.

At this point, Dr. Bryen moved into the future — in effect, to predicting what items the Soviet collection efforts would probably concentrate on. Intelligence agencies use a homely term for these items: the Soviet shopping list. The primary effort would doubtless be aimed at the huge American supercomputer, the Cray-1, which has the capability of designing weapons systems and simulating nuclear war scenarios, among other talents. Although Bryen did not mention it, two Cray-1 computers are also employed by America's supersecret National Security Agency for communications intelligence. Other targets would be new superminicomputers and high-performance microchips.

Bryen's conclusion, strongly implied throughout his talk, was clear and harsh: the only way the Russians could make up for their technological poverty was to steal the West's technological wealth. They already had a quantitative edge in strategic arms. As they acquired technology, they could make their missiles smarter and more accurate.

The Paris briefing had come about very largely at the insistence of the Central Intelligence Agency. Shortly after his election, President Ronald Reagan began to listen carefully to the Pentagon's views on the subject of high technology. The service chiefs considered the CIA's Directorate of Science and Technology "soft" on various issues, and when William J. Casey was appointed director of Central Intelligence (DCI), he began to make some changes.

As is the case with all complicated matters of intelligence policy, there is a question as to whether the Pentagon had read the situation correctly. One senior CIA intelligence officer described it as still another case of an administration making sure it heard what it wanted to hear — asking for simple conclusions about something that was a far from simple problem: "They wanted something dramatic and sexy, and all we could give them was uncertainty."[1] It struck him that the new team in the Science and Technology Directorate came to a lot of predictable conclusions: "They always came out the same door they went in."

The seventy-year-old Casey had a deep interest in intelligence operations, dating back to his wartime service as chief of Secret Intelligence for the OSS in the European Theater. As a former chairman of the Securities and Exchange Commission, Under Secretary of State for Economic Affairs, president of the Export-Import Bank, and a member of the President's Intelligence Advisory Committee, the tall multimillionaire was well known to President Reagan even before he managed the 1980 Republican presidential campaign.

After his appointment, Casey moved quickly to do something about the clandestine drain on American technological capital. He set up a database on all the methods being used by the Soviets. He started a campaign to make American think tanks and suppliers aware of the dangers. ("They responded naturally to their own security interests," he remarked later.)[2] Under him, the CIA began to regard the European members of COCOM as a source of leaks quite as serious as the traditionally suspect neutrals, like Sweden, Switzerland, and Austria. Even the Department of Commerce began to wake up as a result of the CIA reports. Assistant Secretary Lawrence J. Brady subsequently testified that "not until the fall of 1981, when we received these new analyses, did we begin to appreciate the magnitude of the Soviet activities against the West."[3]

It was because of the CIA initiative that Dr. Bryen appeared that day in 1981 to try to deliver his message to the assembled COCOM representatives: the organization had to become more effective and the intelligence gathered by its member states had to be shared with other Western governments. Above all, the COCOM nations had to understand that the problem was one they had in common; it was not simply an American problem.

So, in spite of the rather muddled start in Paris, Bryen and his colleagues polished the slide show and took it on the road. The team presented it in each of the COCOM capitals before audiences of senior trade, defense, and intelligence officials. In Washington on a visit, Michael Heseltine, newly appointed British Defence Secretary, was said to be impressed,[4] but other British officials at the presentation took a different view. They were, in fact, furious at the inclusion of a new slide that purported to show a special-purpose, computer-based "image enhancement system" that had been sold to the Institute of Geology in Moscow by a "major U.K. defense contractor." The system, which included an essential American component, is used to improve the quality and resolution of satellite photographs of the earth. Because the complete system had been assembled in the U.K., the manufacturers had requested and received an export license from the British Department of Trade in 1979.

The case came to light in a curious way. The American component, made by Comtal of Pasadena, had to be upgraded on two separate occasions, and the work had to be done at the California factory. The second time it was returned, it was brought by a Soviet engineer. There was a tip-off. The police raided Comtal and seized the unit. The British watchers were embarrassed and resentful that the matter was included in the slide show. Afterward, a senior official of Her Majesty's Government said, "What we object to is them [the United States Government] using this as a stick to beat us."[5] The incident marked the opening of one of the most serious gaps of misunderstanding between Washington and London on the technology-transfer issue.

The CIA then took the unusual action of publishing the "dog and pony show" material, in sanitized form, as a booklet.[6] It said, in part:

> The Soviets and their Warsaw Pact allies have obtained vast amounts of militarily significant Western technology through legal and illegal means. . . . [Their] intelligence organizations have been so successful at acquiring Western technology that the manpower levels they allocate to this effort have increased significantly since the 1970s to the point where there are now several thousand technology collection officers at work.[7]

It added that East European Intelligence services doing the same work gained rewards in the form of Soviet arms and equipment for their countries.

One of the most interesting sections of the report was the Soviet clandestine shopping list. Some of the items were:

> computers (all kinds),
> cryogenics,
> superconductors,
> machine tools,
> robots,
> computer software,
> satellite communications,

lasers,
fiber optics,
radio antennas,
marine systems, and
shipbuilding know-how.

Of course, it can be argued that some of these items may have peacetime, even humanitarian, uses, and the report dealt with that question:

> Because of the priority accorded to the military over the civilian sectors of the Soviet economy, Western dual-use technology — i.e., technology with both military and civilian applications — almost always finds its way first into military industries and subsequently into the civilian sector of industries that support military production. Thus, Soviet assurances that legally purchased, dual-use technology will be used solely for civilian applications can seldom be accepted at face value.[8]

What specific benefits did the Soviets reap from their acquisitions? Their lead time for research and development was shortened. The "proven" designs they bought or stole were reliable, so Soviet weapons performance could be bettered. And the imported technology contributed to countermeasures against Western weapons systems.

A notable weak spot in the report was its cursory treatment of microchip-manufacturing systems, whose technology and equipment, certainly, are all-important to the Soviets. Without them, the Russians would have grave difficulties in catching up with the West in high technology.

The CIA report concluded that the Soviet collection effort had to be stopped, but "in ways which are both effective and appropriate in our open society." This was "one of the most complex and urgent issues facing the Free World today."[9]

2

HIGH TECH, U.S.A.

SILICON VALLEY is an ill-defined area on the ten-mile-wide peninsula that lies between San Francisco Bay and the Pacific Ocean. It runs approximately forty miles south from San Mateo and the San Francisco Airport to San Jose. Here, the visitor finds exactly the California landscape he expected to see: a seemingly endless four-lane highway (with the incongruous name of El Camino Real). Motels, gas stations, liquor stores, taco joints, all stretched in intervals between shopping malls. On the left, you pass the satellite antennas of Moffett Field Naval Air Station and on the right the range of hills that mask Half Moon Bay and the ocean. San Mateo, Redwood City, Menlo Park, Palo Alto, Mountain View, Sunnyvale, and Cupertino.

Behind the cheapjack façade of El Camino Real, however, there is another world. The area is studded with the research centers, factories, laboratories, and think tanks of the silicon age. Here are the Stanford Research Institute, Intel, Amdahl, Fairchild, Motorola, Zilog, National Semiconductor, Hewlett-Packard, Tandem, Apple, Atari, Cromemco, and hundreds of others. It is not the only duchy of high tech, certainly. Just west of Boston and MIT there are such firms as Digital Equipment Corporation, Data General, and Raytheon. IBM dominates an area of upstate New York. Texas Instruments and General Dynamics are in the Dallas–Fort Worth area. There are good brandies made outside Cognac, but just as "cognac" is almost a generic name, so Silicon Valley has come to symbolize the new technology.

Some electronic firms have been established here for a long time — like Fairchild, whose spin-offspring have been called "fair-children." Another major reason for the firms' being located here is the presence of Stanford University, which began to hire technology scientists from all over the country just after World War II. Many of them made discoveries, took out patents, and started businesses in the neighborhood. One of the typical success stories of the Valley is that of Apple. In 1977, using off-the-shelf microchips and other components, two twenty-year-old Californians named Steve Jobs and Steve Wozniak worked day and night in their garage to produce a computer inexpensive enough for the home and small-business market. The rest, of course, is business history. Some time after the enormous growth of Apple began, Steve Jobs was heard to say that he feared only three companies: "IBM, IBM, and IBM."

For those with a talent for technology, this is 1849 and Silicon Valley is mother lode country. Gary Kildall is the founder of Digital Research, Inc., of Pacific Grove on the Monterey Peninsula (which is an outpost some miles south of the Valley). While still in his early twenties, Kildall wrote an operating system for microcomputers and called it CP/M. The innovative thing about Kildall's invention was that it could be used on a maximum number of the small, desktop computers. Hitherto, manufacturers of the bigger computers had written operating systems designed only for their computers. But that was too expensive for the microcomputer makers — and the great thing about CP/M was not just that it worked on many different machines but that it cost $150. When someone asked Kildall how he expected to get rich selling programs for only $150, he replied, "By selling a quarter million of them."[1] He did.

The front-page high tech of the 1980s is not limited to computers, of course, though the computer is to the high-tech era what James Watt's steam engine was to the new technology of the Industrial Revolution. In addition to them — and in conjunction with them — there are satellites, lasers, optical fibers, nuclear energy, aviation, telecommunications, various types of radio communication, and other forms of advanced electronics. There are, as well, less glamorous kinds of electronics that, usually for military reasons, are classified as the "leading edge." An example is the grinding machine used nowadays to make ball bearings. Without the near-perfection capability of this machine, a rocket steering system would not be accurate, nor could the best computer make it so.

At the very heart of high tech is the microchip. We seldom realize it is there, but in 1984 it makes function such everyday things as television sets, telephones, pocket calculators, video games, sewing machines, automatic teller terminals at your bank, digital clocks and watches, video recorders, automatic cameras, elevators, telex information service, and so on — let alone all the information-retrieval systems that are used in stores, offices, and banks.

Getting started in the business of high-volume microchip-manufacture requires three essential ingredients: money, know-how, and more money. You can set up a modest facility for $10 million, but to compete in the big leagues, you need fifty times as much. Take, for example, the experience of Her Majesty's Government.

In 1975, a group of entrepreneurs and technologists approached the Labour government with a proposal. The group included Professor Ian Barron, one of the bright young men of the British computer industry (he designed his first computer at the age of twenty), and two Americans with substantial experience in semiconductor-manufacturing. They pointed out that chip technology would soon be fundamental to the well-being of any advanced economy. All major manufacturers of chips were American, and there was a danger that Great Britain would become too dependent on the United States for this strategic resource. The government agreed. A company called INMOS (Integrated Metal Oxide Silicon) was set up and, over the next seven years, received a subsidy equal to $300 million. But by 1982, it had produced only a small volume of chips and was still operating at a loss.

One of the side benefits of INMOS was supposed to be the creation of jobs in the depressed British economy. As it turned out, the first jobs created were in Boulder, Colorado, where INMOS went to gather the specialist technicians it needed for a research, development, and prototyping center.

After a new company has the right money and the right people, it must decide on the right product for the market. The development staff will then design a chip suitable in both function and price. Next, the designer must decide how best to fit the circuit onto a chip, to get many thousands of tiny logic elements and the interconnecting links into the available space. Using computer-aided design (CAD) techniques, he can tell the computer what he wants, and the computer applies its internal logic to find the best interconnections. It usually takes a number of attempts.

Once the design looks right, the drawings are "digitized"; that is, reduced to a set of numbers that describe the layout in a form the computer can understand. This massive array of values forms the database of the chip design and from it are produced the reticles, which are the detailed schematics for each layer that will be etched on a silicon chip. The reticles are ten or twenty times the size of the final chip, and at this stage the designer has to make a meticulous comparison between the reticles and the original circuit design.

From the checked, corrected, and rechecked reticles, series of masks are made. The masks incorporate miniature copies of the circuit, reduced to exactly the size of the chip, and each mask leaves its impress on each chip layer. Usually there are up to eight layers. The actual manufacture is something like the development of photographic prints. The first mask is projected onto a chemically treated wafer. The wafers are made of silicon that is 99.999999 percent pure. Up to five hundred chips can be produced from each four-inch diameter slice. Once the mask has left its pattern on the silicon (under conditions more sterile than those of a hospital operating room), the wafers are placed in a sophisticated form of furnace and chemically treated at temperatures over 1000° C. Then the next layer is projected from the appropriate mask, and the "baking" process is repeated.

In the end, fewer than 50 percent of the chips will function properly — sometimes, with new chips, as few as 10 percent. Highly sophisticated, computer-controlled test machines prove each chip by sending many input signals into the circuit and checking the output signals. If the chip is defective, a drop of paint marks it.

Chips that pass the test are packaged in a plastic case — and here is one of the most labor-intensive parts of the whole process. The input and output leads on each tiny chip have to be connected to metal legs that project from the plastic case. Someone using a microscope and a miniature soldering iron makes the connection by means of tiny gold wires. This someone is often a worker in Taiwan, Malaysia, Singapore, or the Philippines, where the chips are flown from Silicon Valley and where wages are low.

The final stage is the assembly of chips and other electronic components on a printed circuit board (PCB). The PCB bears a series of metal tracks that connect the legs of the various components. A PCB may be as small as an envelope or as large as a file folder. With another careful soldering job, the components' legs are fixed to the PCB.

There are many types of chips beside the microprocessor kind. Memory chips store information while it is being processed and can also hold the instruction program that a computer must follow to perform a specific task. Other chips control the flow of information into and out of the computer, to the display screen, to a printer, down a telephone line, and so on. Some chips incorporate a capacity for all of these functions and can be used to control fairly complex systems — such as security and fire alarms or central heating systems. Bought in quantity, the chips may cost only a few dollars apiece. They have become the cheapest means of controlling many of our usual mechanical devices.

The progress in microchip design has been astonishing. The integrated circuits of the 1960s had fewer than ten electronic components per chip. In the next decade came the technique of chemically etching the components on silicon, which gave rise to chips with hundreds, later thousands, of components. The newest chips pack in hundreds of thousands — and they are cleverer and faster than the older kind. For some applications, speed is more important than capacity, and the new very high-speed integrated circuits (VHSIC) are the record-holders of the electronics world.

It seems likely that the next step in this technology will be the use of gallium arsenide instead of silicon for microchips. Up to now, gallium arsenide has been used for only a few military applications, but by the late 1980s and 1990s, it should be available in massive quantities.

By far the greatest use of microchips is, of course, in the manufacture of computers. And the computer has become the electronic master craftsman of our era. It can manage company accounts, teach children how to spell, aid doctors in diagnosing an illness, help to edit and produce a newspaper, tell a robot how to paint a car, schedule resources needed to build an airliner, break the telex code used by a foreign embassy, calculate a payroll, forecast the weather, bill people for electricity, play a game of chess, run a telephone exchange, control a production line, and automate the design and manufacture of more computers. Before long, it will also speak many human languages and be able to translate from one to another.

All would be well if computers' talents were applied solely to such tasks. But ever since the British creation of Colossus, the decoding machine of "the Ultra secret" fame in World War II, computers have been an important part of weaponry. They are essential to early-warning systems; they are the heart of many weapons systems; they target missiles and then guide them on their paths. Even before they play these combat roles, they participate in war games and in producing new missile designs.

This is the reason, then, that computers — and their sophisticated elements — have become such important prizes in the great game of cold war espionage. The computer revolution and the information age are Western phenomena; the West was first and most vigorous in applying the computer to war. And that is the cause of the desperate anxiety of the Communist bloc, its absolute necessity to borrow, imitate, or steal its share of the future.

Computer people like to describe their systems as developing in "generations." The computers of the 1940s and fifties were still largely dependent on vacuum tubes (or thermionic valves), which characterized the first generation. The second generation, which appeared in the late 1950s, employed the transistor. The third came along in the late 1960s, and its leap forward owed much to the use of chips that progressed eventually to "large-scale integration." The borderline between third and fourth generation is harder to define. The machines of the late seventies and early eighties are said to be fourth generation, but apart from employing the newest technology, they are very similar in design to their immediate predecessors. The titans of this world are the Cray supercomputers, whose earliest models were earmarked for the Fort Meade headquarters of NSA. A later model, the Cray XMP, can perform 200 million computations a second. This translates — for an everyday comparison — into a speed 200,000 times faster than that of the IBM Personal Computer.

The term "fifth generation" has been reserved for computers now being designed and developed to "think" as much as possible like a human being. (The malevolent HAL in Arthur C. Clarke's *2001* is its most famous projection.) No such computer has yet been built, but the Japanese have recently started to fund a massive project to produce such a computer in the early 1990s.

Computer hardware is useless without software, and this is an equally important target for espionage. Software is the set of programs, the detailed series of instructions that tell computers how to proceed with the work. In another way of looking at it, a piece of software is a self-contained system of logic. "Systems" software is a collection of programs that make the computer easier to use and to program for various jobs. "Applications" software performs the actual work of preparing invoices, guiding missiles, or doing other assigned tasks.

As a kind of side glance, it is interesting to note that the British — whatever their shortcomings with INMOS — are considered to have the best computer programmers in the world in 1984. Such American companies as IBM, Sperry, Hewlett-Packard, and Perkin-Elmer have set up software development facilities in Great Britain. A number of theories to explain this capability have been advanced, but probably the best guess is that it comes from the old British habit of making a virtue of necessity. In the United States, computer users tend to solve a problem by buying more expensive hardware. The British, on the other hand, change the program to make it work on the available hardware.

Software is easy to duplicate and steal, although it is copyrighted. Microcomputer owners do their thievery every day, and only recently have software manufacturers been incorporating protective devices. If the software is recorded on a reel of magnetic tape, a computer can make as many copies as necessary on blank reels. It is even simple to copy floppy discs on a computer. The commercial significance of this is clear when you think about a software program created to design a certain product and the effect of its theft by a competitor.

Computer people use the expressions "micro-," "mini-," and

"super-" as useful forms of shorthand. Microcomputers are compact, desktop machines used in the home and office. Minicomputers are best suited to process control and data communications work but are also used extensively for interactive commercial applications. Mainframes are general-purpose commercial computers of the IBM 360/370 type. Supercomputers are those in the Cray class.

Telecommunications networks are, arguably, quite as important to a late twentieth-century economy as computer systems. The technology of telecommunications has been comparatively slow to change, however, based as it is on transmission of an electrical picture of the human voice. For this reason, telecom systems benefit from microchips in a very limited way. Moreover, the means by which telephone calls are connected end to end are dependent on a technology nearly a hundred years old.

In the late nineteenth century, a Kansas mortician detected an unexpected drop in his business. People were still dying at a brisk rate, but they seemed to be going elsewhere to be laid out for burial. At this time, Kansas City had a manual telephone exchange. In order to be connected with another subscriber, one first had to get the operator and request her to put the call through to the other end of the line. What Mr. Strowger, the mortician, did not know was that his main competitor was having an affair with the operator. Whenever a caller asked for "the mortician," he or she would be connected with the competitor. In revenge, Mr. Strowger invented the automatic telephone exchange.

Until the 1960s, the Strowger Switch was still the most extensively installed form of telephone exchange. There has been a moderate advance in new technologies, but to date fiber optics, microwave links, lasers, and the like have influenced a relatively small part of the network. There will, indeed, have to be a fundamental change in the technology of telecom networks before they can benefit from integrated-circuit chips. The worldwide telephone system is probably the most complex machine that man has ever built, and any big changes will have to be agreed to among the nations. Even after that, thousands of exchanges will have to be replaced. Perhaps by the end of the century the system will be based on computer-controlled exchanges, satellites, and fiber-optic cables.

Efficient telecommunications are vitally important to an open society, and they have become a major adjunct of computer use. Since the late 1970s, there has been a greater volume of computer-transmitted information than of voice transmissions on American lines. Special telephone circuits link computers for what is called "networking." One airline's computers "talk" with those of another and even with your credit card company's computer.

This brief overview of the new electronic age has been meant as a bare introduction — to be followed in more detail — to a whole new order of rivalry between the West and the Communist East. For decades, the Soviet Union tried to catch up with the West's dominance in the old heavy-industry kind of technology, and its success (though a special-purpose one) was marked by the superior tanks and planes the USSR produced in the later years of World War II and after. Then came the era of atomic science and atomic energy technology. Again, by bending all talents and efforts to the job (including the work of such early Russian agents as Klaus Fuchs and Alan Nunn May), the Soviets were able to catch up. Finally, in rocketry the Soviets maintained parity and even took the lead on notable occasions. Now, in the 1980s, the Soviets are faced with another imperative to catch up. This one is much more sophisticated in that it involves many changes in all the tools of a society.

A society that is not primarily industrial can play a large role in the twentieth century, as the Russians have proved. But can it do as well in the period close to the twenty-first? Can it compete with the rival society that now produces a new generation of computers in less than a decade — and, what is more important, has made the new technology pervade almost every practical function of everyday life? For the Soviets, it is not only a matter of keeping Russia a first-rank power in weaponry; it is the bigger, more encompassing question of remaking a whole society so that it can participate in the information age.

There is the great paradox, of course. The computer is not merely an information-storing, an information-manipulating machine, but an information-furnishing machine. Can a totalitarian society live in the midst of such devices when its whole past has been based on minimal, carefully regulated information? Can a multitude of user-friendly computers have any place in a user-unfriendly society? These are questions a Marxist philosopher might ponder.

3

HIGH TECH, USSR

"WAKE UP ... wake up!" she insisted, pulling his arm. For the first time, he could hear the hammering at the door. Over her dressing gown was wrapped a faded blanket she had taken to wearing about the house. Already they could feel the onset of the cold, and their only fuel was the peat they had diligently gathered during the summer months. "Soldiers. There are Russian soldiers at the door — come quickly!" He staggered out of bed and across to the window. As he pulled the curtain back and peered down, the thumping suddenly stopped. In the half-light of the dawn and the headlights of a Soviet *gazik* (jeep) he could see the unmistakable outlines of three Russian soldiers, one of them an officer. Stepping back into view from the door was a man in civilian clothes. He waved at the man in the window, who then turned to his wife. "They've seen me. I'd better go down." He pulled on a pair of pants and tucked in his nightshirt.

His hand shook slightly as he unbolted the door and turned the key. The officer was wearing the maroon shoulder-flashes of the MVD — the Ministry of Internal Affairs, Stalin's secret police.

"Is your name —— ?" The civilian, in a heavy raincoat, looked down at a sheet of paper and read out a name. His German was bad, but the scientist had no trouble in understanding him.

"Yes." The street was suddenly lighted from the other end and a covered army truck roared to a halt in front of the jeep. The scientist could not see the soldiers in the back. Rain blew in through the door.

"Please come inside." The officer and civilian stepped in, and he took them to the small living room and closed the door. The door to the street stayed open. Nobody sat down. The man in the raincoat did the talking.

"We would like you to pack all your essential belongings, everything you can carry. The men outside will help with small items of furniture."

The German scientist could hardly talk. "I'm s-sorry. . . . Am I . . . being arrested?"

"No. You are being evacuated. You are being moved to the East, where you will be able to continue your work." Peenemünde: that is what it was all about. The scientist had, until the Russians swept into Germany at the end of the war, been a fuel specialist working on the V-2 rocket. When the Red Army captured Peenemünde on May 5, 1945, he and his wife had managed to make their way back to his father's old house, on Goethestrasse in Magdeburg. Since then he had been fortunate enough to get occasional work with a drug company that had somehow kept what little equipment it had from being confiscated by the Russians as war reparations. Their son was missing in action in Italy.

"My wife . . . ?"

"She can go too. Tell her to start packing." He looked at his watch. "We can give you an hour. We shall wait here."

As the scientist walked upstairs to the bedroom, he tried to weigh things. He was fifty-five. In East Germany, life was still a grim struggle. Food and fuel were in short supply, and essential clothing was almost impossible to find. The new Communist German government was taking over from the Russians, at least as far as the day-to-day running of the country was concerned. Things had to improve, but now there was this. His wife was sobbing gently as she sat on the edge of the bed. He placed a hand on her shoulder. "You had better get dressed."

It was October 22, 1946.[1] They would not see Germany again until the spring of 1951.

That evening, lamps burned late at the Adlershof in Soviet East Berlin. It was from here that General Ivan Serov, deputy director of

Stalin's MVD, had for the past two weeks been personally supervising a carefully coordinated mission.[2] Approval had come from the highest ranks of the *kommandatura*. Throughout the entire Soviet Zone senior staff officers were at their desks in the city halls and houses that had been requisitioned as command posts when the Red Army first overran the country.

Early that day units of Soviet soldiers, military intelligence officers, and detachments of MVD men had climbed aboard their gaziks and trucks. Each group had been given a specific task. In towns and villages across the territory that they had wrested from Nazi control the previous year the Soviet units wakened startled households. At every door that morning the instructions of the liaison officer were the same as they had been in Magdeburg's Goethestrasse: pack essential belongings for yourself and your immediate dependents. No questions. You are being evacuated. Some selected families were allowed to take their servants along. One experienced production manager was invited to take his mistress instead of his wife.

By midafternoon the first trucks and gaziks were lumbering in ones and twos over slippery cobblestones toward a number of main rail stations that had been designated as assembly points. By midnight the late arrivals from farther afield had joined the cowed throngs huddled, under guard, in the cold and the glare of searchlights on station platforms. Crammed with the human harvest, the first trains pulled out at one o'clock in the morning. From Frankfurt-am-Oder, Magdeburg, Jena, East Berlin, and the awful desolation of Dresden, they headed eastward on a journey that would last many days, taking them to uncertain destinations and even more uncertain futures inside the Soviet Union.

On that one day alone the Soviet administration, working from Serov's meticulously compiled lists, forcibly evacuated several thousand German scientists, technicians, engineers, and designers. With them went thousands more of their family dependents. Most of them would not be permitted to return home until the early 1950s. By the end of the year no fewer than ninety-two special trains loaded with this unique human freight had passed through the Soviet border checkpoint and rail terminus at Brest-Litovsk. The final total exceeded six thousand specialists and twenty thousand dependents.

But this was not simply conscript labor; General Serov's lists contained the names of men with very specific skills, men who had worked in the aircraft or automobile factories of the Third Reich, its steel or chemical plants, or who had been involved in developing the top secret V-2 rocket, the Nazi chemical warfare programs, or the crash project to design an atomic bomb.

The Kremlin had called on General Ivan Serov's special skills in "relocating" whole communities and groups of people with what for them was good cause: the recovery of the Soviet Union's heavy industry from the devastation of war. The Nazis, at the height of their 1941 advance, had seized the Ukraine, the industrial Donbas, and parts of the Caucasus in the course of a sweep that had their troops knocking at the gates of Leningrad and Moscow. When the Wehrmacht was finally pushed back, it left a landscape of human misery and destruction. For the American economy, World War II was a time of expansion, and few people in the West fully understand the scale of the German scorched earth retreat. According to a 1948 assessment:

> On the territory that had been occupied by the Germans in November 1941 lived about 40 percent of the whole Soviet population. About 65 percent of the whole prewar output of coal had come from there, 68 percent of all pig iron, 58 percent of all steel, 60 percent of aluminum, 38 percent of the grain, 84 percent of sugar ... 41 percent of all the railroad lines of the USSR.[3]

And no fewer than twenty million people died.

The Soviet government was determined to rebuild the shattered economy, and their former enemies would be made to pay much toward this effort. Charged with the job was Anastas Mikoyan, a leading administrator of the West's wartime Lend-Lease aid program and one of Stalin's right-hand men. Mikoyan's plan was simple in the extreme: every piece of plant and machinery — even entire factories — found on territory regained from the Nazis would be dismantled and shipped back to the Soviet Union. Everything. Soon after the German surrender, "Mikoyan Groups" systematically denuded Eastern Europe of its industrial facilities and shipped them east. Nut by nut, bolt by bolt, machines were taken apart, catalogued, loaded piecemeal onto trains, and hauled back to Russia.

In Germany alone, military and industrial plants worth more

than $10 billion were dismantled and transshipped. Several thousand factories, representing 41 percent of Germany's industrial capacity in the peak year of 1943, were removed. Under the agreement between the Allies a quarter of German industrial capacity, now sited in the U.S., British, and French occupation zones, was packed up and handed over to the Soviets. Poland, Czechoslovakia, and Hungary were stripped of metal foundries, petrochemical plants, mining and heavy engineering assemblies. The Soviet-occupied eastern zone of Austria lost $400 million in equipment and plant. Separate peace treaties with Rumania and with Finland contained clauses covering the relinquishment to the USSR of equipment estimated at $600 million. And in the Far East, following the defeat of the Japanese forces, Manchuria was stripped to the tune of nearly $900 million in industrial machinery.[4]

Among this massive haul was the whole of Berlin's electrical equipment industry, two thirds of the German aircraft manufacturing capacity, and key parts of the automotive industry. The Opel car plant at Brandenburg was removed in its entirety — a move that gave the 1947 Moskvich 401 sedan more than a passing resemblance to the 1939 Opel Kadett. In the process the Soviet victors made some rare and priceless catches, including the famous Karl Zeiss photo-optical factories in the city of Jena, two entire nerve gas–production plants at Dyhrenfurth (near what is now the Polish town of Wroclaw) and Falkenhagen,[5] and — crucial for the development of the Soviet missile and space program — the vast underground V-2 production complex at Nordhausen.

Where the Russians felt that they lacked the skilled workforce and technicians needed to run and develop their newly acquired booty, they simply conscripted them in Germany. This was what triggered the 1946 roundup of all the most useful people still living in Soviet-occupied territory. The whole campaign was an extreme example of what we have now come to call "technology transfer."

"... shest ... pyat ... chetyre ..." White clouds of fuel vented from the base of the rocket. The countdown squawked out of the speakers as everyone looked hard against the evening sky; the scientists, the technicians — even the zeks' uniformed guards — ignored their charges in favor of seeing a semyorka leap into the sky. "... tri ...

dva... odin... OGON!" Suddenly, flames leaped from the deflectors in the concrete stand. This was always the critical moment; already that year two of the powerful R-7 rockets had exploded before they were more than a few feet off the ground. But this one looked good. The blockhouse shuddered with the raw energy as the silver tube lifted. Ten feet. Then a hundred, accelerating all the time. Still nobody said anything.

By 10:30 P.M. Moscow time on October 4, 1957, the steady *beep, beep* of Sputnik-1 was being picked up around the world. The world's first artificial satellite was no more than a tiny short-wave radio transmitter linked to a thermometer and powered by a set of flashlight batteries. But from two hundred miles above the earth, and traveling at a speed of eighteen thousand miles per hour, its message was clear enough; it was not empty bragging on the part of the Soviet leader, Khrushchev, when he talked of intercontinental missiles armed with nuclear warheads. The Russians had a lead in the missile and space race that would take the United States more than a decade to close. The story of that achievement is the story of Sergey Korolyov.

Sergey Petrovich Korolyov, or Starik SP — Old Man SP — as everyone called him, would not have heard the zeks even if they had been cheering. The construction of the Tyuratam rocket test site owed a great deal to the use of conscripts from the Soviet labor camps. Zek is from the Russian word for convict, *zaklyuchënny*. Korolyov's fellow scientists slapped him on the back and shook his hand. Perhaps the zeks would have joined in the celebration too, penned in their barracks some way back from the launch pad. After all, Starik SP was still one of them.[6]

Korolyov's life, as one of his more candid biographers has noted, reads like a parable of the Soviet era. Trained as an aeronautics engineer and working with the great aircraft designer A. N. Tupolev, Korolyov seemed set on the road to success. He showed early interest in rocketry, and this brought him to the attention, in 1934, of Marshal Mikhail Tukhachevsky, the Soviet Armaments Minister. Korolyov was granted an army commission and allocated funds to enable him to work on early rocket prototypes, but in June 1937 his world suddenly collapsed. His mentor, Tukhachevsky, and almost all the senior Red Army officer corps were arrested, accused of trea-

son, and shot or sent to the camps of Stalin's *gulag*. Korolyov, as a
protégé of Tukhachevsky, was also arrested, interrogated by the
NKVD, and eventually sent to the gold mines of Kolyma in the Far
East labor camp complex. The early Soviet rocket program was
snuffed out with his life sentence.

Korolyov was saved by the intervention of his former boss, Tupolev, who also had been imprisoned. With most of his staff Tupolev
was interned in one of the "special prisons," a *sharashka,* where
the inmates had certain minimal but lifesaving advantages over the
camps, slightly better living conditions, and a more sustaining diet.
They were expected to continue their work while still serving draco-
nian sentences under the supervision of the secret police.

Tupolev had orders to retrieve all the staff he could for his team,
and after a year in the Kolyma, Korolyov was brought back to join
Tupolev in Moscow as an aviation scientist. In 1941, as Hitler's
Panzer divisions approached Moscow, Tupolev and his entire team
were evacuated east, to the town of Omsk. There, Korolyov was
transferred to another sharashka, where he worked on projects to
develop rocket-assisted takeoff for aircraft, rocket projectiles, and
pure rocket and jet engines. Officially still a prisoner and an "enemy
of the people," Korolyov stayed with this group for four years until
early in 1946, when he was once again transferred, this time to a
newly formed rocket development group. Within weeks he was
taken under close secret police escort to the Soviet zone of Germany
to study the haul of V-2 equipment that had been captured the previous year.

Korolyov stayed for some time in East Germany, supervising the
restoration of a damaged underground V-2 factory at Niedersach-
senwerfen and helping to coordinate the work of transshipping
rockets from the repaired Peenemünde *Zentralwerke* back to the
Soviet Union. He accompanied the final shipment back that summer and took charge of some test firings of V-2s at the upgraded
army firing range at Kapustin Yar in the Lower Volga.

Then he was sent back to East Germany, still under secret police
escort, where he carried out a series of interviews with every former
V-2 engineer and technician the Soviet authorities could locate. This
task was greatly aided by a German electronics engineer, Helmut
Gröttrup, who had helped to contact over two hundred of his former

colleagues in the V-2 program and, in 1945, persuade them to work for the Russians. He himself had originally fled to the West and then returned for a mixture of personal and political reasons. In spite of the fact that he got a good deal from the Russians — four times the comparable Soviet pay, a five room *dacha,* and his own car and driver — he still protested at the way in which the other German scientists were being rounded up. A reply suggesting alternative employment with the Ministry of Mines seemed to quell the objections. Meanwhile, Korolyov was preparing a long list of those Germans who he thought could make a contribution to the Soviet rocket program. It was handed to General Ivan Serov for action. It is a supreme irony that the mind behind the Sputnik was enrolled by one of the two branches of Stalin's secret police, the MVD, to conscript rocket scientists into forced labor while he himself was in the continuing custody of the other branch, the MGB — the Ministry of State Security and the forerunner of today's infamous KGB.

With the newly installed German teams feeding and corroborating the work of Korolyov's group, and with the captured V-2s converted into medium-range missiles, Korolyov pressed ahead with his project. In late 1947 the first Soviet-designed ballistic missile, the R-1, went through a series of successful test flights. Korolyov, still with his life sentence hanging over him, was called to the Kremlin to brief Stalin personally on the feasibility of a Soviet military missile program. Early Soviet atomic weapons, just like their Western counterparts, were cumbersome and weighty. Tupolev's Tu-4, a revamped design of the American B-29, did not have sufficient range to fly intercontinental bombing missions and still get back to base.[7] The Soviet Air Force did not perfect in-flight refueling until the mid-1950s.

It soon became clear that high-powered rockets would be required to lift the new payload and deliver it any significant distance. Stalin and the leadership were impressed with Korolyov's progress and approved a full-scale program for his proposed strategic missile. The go-ahead for the Soviet ICBM, which was finally given in 1948, coincided with the decision of the United States to downgrade its own rocket experiments — carried out with the active participation of its own team of German scientists, led by Werner von Braun and Hermann Oberth, and also relying on captured, intact V-2s. For the

next decade the United States and its NATO allies based their nuclear strike capability on long-range bombers, like the B-36, the B-
47, and the B-52. The British had their own "V-Bombers" — the
Valiant, the Victor, and the Vulcan.

Both sides lost out because of their respective decisions. The West
lost impetus in its rocket technology and surrendered the lead in
space exploration for more than ten years. But the Soviet loss,
though less overt, was much deeper and of longer duration. In the
1950s, Khrushchev was fond of saying that the Soviet Union would
"overtake the West." Proving it, however, was another matter. The
Kremlin needed a spectacular propaganda success, and Korolyov
and his team were going to provide it. When Malenkov, Bulganin,
Zhukov, and Khrushchev himself took over power after the death of
Stalin, in 1953, Starik SP was summoned to the Kremlin to address
the Politburo and present a progress report. Everything was a bit
high tech for the old men of the party, so Korolyov invited them to
see one of his rockets. Khrushchev recalled the occasion:

> When he showed us one of his rockets we thought it looked like noth-
> ing but a huge cigar-shaped tube and we didn't believe it would fly.
> Korolyov took us on a tour of the launching pad and tried to explain to
> us how a rocket worked. We were like peasants in a market place. We
> walked around the rocket, touching it, tapping it to see if it was sturdy
> enough — we did everything but lick it to see how it tasted.[8]

It certainly was "sturdy enough"; that was the very problem. With
one million pounds of thrust the R-7 — nicknamed Semyorka, or
Number Seven — was easily three times more powerful than the
American Atlas. Khrushchev's propaganda coup was almost as hol-
low as the Sputnik itself. The rockets based on the R-7 could carry
conventional vacuum tube–based guidance and communication
gear whose bulk and weight could easily fit into the space allocated
for the nuclear warhead. No special modifications or newly designed equipment would be needed. Similarly, Soviet ground tracking stations had radar that was adequate for the job of following
missile test flights. There was no immediate pressure for vital advances to be made in the field of electronics. The Soviet military
machine could see no immediate application for a small device that
came off the laboratory benches at Bell Laboratories in the United

States at the end of 1947 and was now going into volume production: the transistor, the first stage in a process of miniaturization that would eventually lead to the microchip. The results of this lack of foresight were to become all too apparent in the 1960s, not just in the field of missiles and space exploration, but in another key area — computers.

The Soviet failure to get in at the start of the silicon age may well be an accident of history. However, attempts to close the technology gap were not aided by the nature of the USSR's system and some of the decisions made by its leaders in the critical postwar period. From 1945 on, two major strategic decisions by Stalin and his Politburo became realities.[9] The Soviet Union would reconstruct its industrial base out of the devastation left by the invading Nazis, giving heavy industry and the military sector the highest priorities. And the Soviet Union would do this under its own steam; it would rely on its own monolithic, centrally planned economy and would accept no aid from its wartime Western Allies in the fight with Hitler. Both of these decisions resulted from Stalin's deep-seated belief that the Soviet Union should never become dependent on the West for financial aid, raw materials, or technology. This conviction was undoubtedly shared by a large cross section of the leadership, whose view was reinforced by a feeling that the Soviet Union had proved itself as a nation, against all the odds, by its huge contribution to the fall of Hitler.

During the war the Lend-Lease program of food, hardware, equipment, and ammunition, much of it financed on long-term credit, had played a significant role in helping the Red Army turn the tide against the Nazis. But after 1945, United States financial support, in the form of Marshall Plan aid, appeared to Soviet eyes to be too much like a velvet glove on the iron hand of capitalism. Stalin, ever mindful that he had already built up a huge debt on Lend-Lease, was opposed to accepting further aid, fearing that it might be used as a lever against him, particularly when any pressure could be backed up by the threat of America's growing atomic arsenal.

The newfound Soviet confidence in the immediate postwar years contributed to the widening gulf between the USSR and the West in certain key technologies over the next two decades. Since the German invasion in 1941, the Soviets' beleaguered heavy industry had managed to recover and to produce tanks, transport, armaments, and ammunition in sufficient quantity and quality to supply the Red Army for its decisive drive against Hitler following Stalingrad and the battle at Kursk. Soviet weaponry, planes, and engines had proved a match for German technology under the most extreme and taxing conditions imaginable. The Soviet rail system, so vital in a country with such a huge land mass, had been upgraded and restored in the west, where war damage had been at its worst, with modern track, rolling stock, and signaling and communications equipment.

To Stalin, the Soviet victory over Hitler was also a vindication of the heavily centralized planning and command structure, which had been tested to the very limit since 1941. Now the Soviet Union would continue to rely on that same centralized chain of command, with the party in ultimate control and Stalin handing down the decisions from Moscow. The economy would be administered under the State Planning Committee, GOSPLAN, with a series of new Five Year Plans. The inherent inefficiencies of such a system were not immediately apparent in 1946, when the fourth Five Year Plan for industry was launched. The pyramid-planning and decision-making process was even duplicated with some success in high-priority research ventures, such as the one to produce Soviet atomic and hydrogen bombs, and the ballistic missile project, where acknowledged Soviet experts were given charge of extensive facilities to pursue their aims. By contrast, progress in such specialized fields as radio technology, radar, and the infant science of computing was less spectacular. And this was to have serious long-term repercussions.

Nor, in some important respects, did the Soviet Union of 1945 come off its war footing. It remained a highly militarized, heavily disciplined society. It had taken a massive pounding. Millions had been mobilized into the armed forces or other branches of the war effort, and the Red Army kept large numbers of its men tied down on garrison duty in occupied Eastern Europe. With a weighty portion of its national budget committed to military expenditures, the Soviet Union inevitably developed a tendency to view the demands of the military machine as top priorities.

This was also the case to a certain extent in the West, with one essential difference. There, the growing role of a private consumer sector helped to offset the rise in military expenditures as postwar economic prosperity returned. On the other hand, until Stalin's death, and indeed for some years after 1953, Soviet consumer industry was minimal. More crucial than that in the long run was that, unlike the competitive and materialistic West, the Soviet system had no mechanism for sampling or assessing consumer demand. Without that, there was no way to cater directly to the private need for such common items as clothing, shoes, household appliances, and food. And if that was true of the essentials, it applied even more to the luxury items, which were soon considered to be standard in the West: radios, television sets, stereo systems, refrigerators, washing machines — and, of course, the flagship of the American dream, the private automobile.

As long as Stalin's Russia concentrated its efforts on re-establishing its coal and oil industries, its heavy metal and bulk chemical production, and its national electricity program — all based on a state planning strategy that emphasized production in quantity under the "norm" or quota system — it would face a growing problem. When the need for innovation and change became vital, its ability to absorb new technology and new production techniques would be very low.

But Soviet ability to learn from the experience of the country's ideological rivals in the capitalist Western world was further diminished by the onset of the cold war in 1947 and the consolidation of the Iron Curtain across Eastern Europe. With Communist regimes established in East Germany, Poland, Bulgaria, Hungary, Rumania, and finally, in 1948, Czechoslovakia, Stalin set about the task of binding the satellite states more firmly into the sphere of the Soviet Union. (The Russians did not leave their sector of Austria until 1954, under a treaty stipulating continued Austrian neutrality.) Since their access to Marshall Plan aid was politically unacceptable, the Soviet bloc nations founded the Council for Mutual Economic Assistance (CMEA), often referred to in the West as COMECON.

For their part, the countries of the North Atlantic Treaty Organization soon agreed that it was against their interests to allow items of strategic military importance to reach the Eastern bloc, and for that reason they set up COCOM in 1950. Strategic considerations apart — and following the Berlin blockade and airlift of 1948–1949 there seemed little chance of rapprochement between Stalin and the West — COCOM drew some of its raison d'être from the increasing Western awareness that Soviet intelligence was making inroads into some of its most cherished secrets.

Not least among these was the detailed information about the atomic bomb that had been obtained very recently by Soviet espionage agents. Once the Soviet Union exploded its own atomic bomb, in 1949, it would be only a matter of time before it achieved an H-bomb as well. The United States, concerned over the victory of Mao Tse-tung's revolution in China that same year, was in the grip of anti-Communist fervor at home that resulted in the rise of Senator Joseph McCarthy's crusade. Like its NATO partners, the United States was naturally disinclined to provide any encouragement to the Soviet military effort by trading critical technologies. The first COCOM embargo lists were drawn up in 1950, following the U.S. Export Control Act of 1949.

The key decisions made by Stalin at the end of the war built into the Soviet system blocking mechanisms and points of inertia that were gradually to increase the disparity between the Soviet and the Western technologies. But even though the Soviet Union was unable to match its rivals in the scope of their industrial range and output, Russian research ability and strength in the theoretical sciences was undoubted. Indeed, as their atomic research, missile, and rocket programs were soon to demonstrate, they were able, at least at first appearances, to emulate and in some cases outdo the West. Considering that the United States and, to a lesser extent, Britain, had not had to deal with the aftereffects of a massively damaging invasion of their territory when they made the switch from a war footing to peacetime industry, the Soviet achievements in high-priority projects were all the more impressive.

There is a side to Soviet technology that could be described as the "abacus syndrome"; it is a tendency to rely on well-tested workhorse models of particular pieces of equipment for familiar uses. The abacus counting frame was, until comparatively recently, an everyday sight in the Soviet Union, especially in stores and cafés, but also in banks and offices. No great priority was given to the development of electronic cash registers, calculators, or electronic scales when traditional manual methods would do just as well, because the Soviet attitude toward manufacturing production was "We don't have a special need for this; let someone else make it." If a Soviet industrial plant can make a reliable line in bulk, it has no incentive to come up with new models or improvements. Such changes incur the risk of disrupting production, failing to meet state-determined production norms, and losing bonuses for both the workforce and management. Experimental and innovative diversity, therefore, has never been at a premium, as it is in the West. The demarkation between design and production is often a deep trench. The exception to this set-up is the military *voenpred* system, where military representatives (*voennye predstaviteli*) follow both design and production work on key projects.

Even so, the military sector has been affected by the same conservative thinking that governs consumer-goods production. Filling the demand for standard items in an efficient and cost-effective manner may take precedence over advancing the development of a gun or tank. And it may mean that research is put off in the face of competing demands from other areas of the economy. An example is the case of the solidly reliable infantry rifle, the Avtomat Kalashnikov, which in its 1947 configuration, known all over the world as the AK-47, has lasted, virtually unmodified, to the beginning of the 1980s and is still standard issue in the Red Army. It is simply made, from simple materials. It is easily assembled and repaired, and the spares are readily available. It works under the harshest conditions and, above all, it is inexpensive. Yet for a long time Soviet specialist armament lacked the more sophisticated options made possible by advances in machine-tooling, alloy technology, and, in more recent years, computer-aided design.[10]

If the Soviet attitude is "If it works, leave it alone," the prevailing Western attitude is "If it works, it must be obsolete." The net effect for the Soviet Union is a stubborn inability to absorb new technology into its products and its means of manufacture.

The early history of Soviet computers illustrates the abacus syndrome at work. The Russians were undoubtedly aware of the work in the United States during World War II to produce a vacuum tube–based computer that would calculate the trajectory of an artillery shell. Though initially carried out in strict military secrecy at the Moore School of Electrical Engineering for the U.S. Army Ordnance Department and then transferred to the Ballistics Research Laboratory at the Aberdeen Proving Ground, in Maryland, this work led to the development of Eniac, the first American electronic computer, which was operational by early 1946. Soviet intelligence may also have picked up rumors of the top secret Colossus computer developed by the British to crack German Enigma codes. Articles appeared in scientific journals on the successful progress being made in peacetime at two British centers, the universities of Cambridge and Manchester. By 1948 the first general-purpose stored-program computers were becoming operational. First-generation computers had become a reality in the West.

Meanwhile, in the Soviet Union there was strong opposition, not only to the idea of cybernetics as a science, but also to committing to it research effort as well as scarce financial and material resources. The view was that the tasks performed by computers could be carried out by familiar and established punch-card-tabulating machines and differential analyzers. The Soviet revitalized rail network, for example, used tabulating machines for freight dispatch, route management, and rolling-stock control. That this initial opposition was overcome at all was a triumph for a number of far-sighted people working against the odds in the same way that Korolyov had.

Immediately after the war, Mikhail A. Lavrentyev, a distinguished professor of mathematics and physics, was vice-president of the Ukrainian Academy of Sciences. It was through his efforts that the academy agreed to fund and support a laboratory to design the first Soviet computer. It was to be based at Feofaniya, on the outskirts of the Ukrainian capital of Kiev.[11] At Feofaniya, Lavrentyev assembled a young and enthusiastic research team, which included the man who was to take over much of the active design work on the new computer, S. A. Lebedev.

Despite shortage of material, the design work went ahead, but one crucial area was hampered by the lack of essential vacuum tubes. They were required in large numbers for the prototype, and their relatively short life made regular supplies essential. Bottlenecks in the production of tubes were eased by the intervention of Aksel Berg, a colorful ex-submarine commander turned engineer. The former admiral was an early and influential convert to the science of cybernetics, in spite of ideological disapproval. He was later appointed to the Soviet Academy of Sciences and in the post-Stalin era became head of the Council of Cybernetics. In the late 1940s, Berg, as deputy head of the Council on Radio Location, was well placed to help Lavrentyev. The tens of thousands of tubes needed for the Kiev prototype computer were diverted from the manufacture of radio systems. Work on the Ukrainian computer, the MESM, began in 1948 and was completed in 1951, not long after the first Univac-1 prototypes were on line in the United States.

The Feofaniya laboratory eventually grew into the Kiev Institute for Cybernetics and Computer Sciences and has remained an influential focus of Soviet computer research to the present day. Academician Viktor Glushkov, the leading Soviet computer theoretician, was a member of its staff. Lebedev, who was also made an academy member for his contribution to the birth of the Soviet computer, was transferred to Moscow when the MESM prototype was completed. As head of the Institute of Precise Mechanics and Computer Engineering, his first task was to refine and expand the original Kiev design. In 1952 he completed the first BESM-1, the original in a family that is still thriving.

It is possible that the BESM-1 was used in design work on the Soviet H-bombs. It would clearly have had applications in the calculations of orbits for spacecraft, but the Sputnik shot was still to come. The infant Soviet computer industry really began to grow only after the death of Stalin. Then research started at the Academy of Sciences' Institute of Electronic Control Computers and at the Radio Ministry's Institute of Mechanics and Instrument Design.

From the available evidence there is little doubt that in the 1950s the Soviet Union gave its early computer and electronics industry much less priority than its nuclear and space research programs. This, combined with the absence of the commercial drive to produce computers for the nonmilitary market, meant that there was no surge of development equivalent to that experienced in the United States and Europe. The development of the USSR's first generation was not so late that it could not have caught up. The lack of awareness of the pace of developments is typified by the fact that no special provision was made for the design and construction of computers until the creation of the Ministry of Electronics in 1965; until then, computer production was overseen by a relatively unimportant section of the Radio Ministry. By this time, the West had already gone through the second generation of transistorized computers, and the previous year IBM had announced the System/360, the first commercially available third-generation machine. Simple, small-scale integrated circuits were used in its construction.

In contrast to the unplanned growth of Silicon Valley, the development of Zelenograd, the USSR's high-tech capital, was planned to the last inch.[12] In the spring of 1963, the old village of Kryukovo was invaded by some strange, new forces. Kryukovo was a village in the *podmoskovye,* the environs of the capital, and it lay close to the Leningrad highway out of Moscow. It was a stop on the *elecktrichka* fast-transit railway.

Nobody in Kryukovo was much surprised when great blocks of anonymous apartment houses began to go up; living space to accommodate the spillover of workers from the city was always needed in this area. What did seem odd was the number of visitors who came all the way from Leningrad to inspect the old school building after a new and larger school had been built. Soon, the citizens of Kryukovo saw the old school building being converted to offices, and they heard that some government bureau was acquiring land in the vicinity.

Then the land was cleared and construction workers moved in. The large structures that began to rise were not the usual prefabricated kind but something of better quality. The people were given no clue as to the intended use of the buildings; all they knew was that the work never seemed to stop. Eventually, they found their old settlement swallowed up in a vast complex that included three huge construction plants, eight institutes, and a college that was called a "study institute." The apartment developments had grown large enough to house most of the fifty thousand people who had come here to work in the new facilities.

It was clear that the newcomers were privileged. The new shops that opened were like those in the center of Moscow itself. Each new arrival carried a Moscow *propiska* — the internal passport that dictates where a Soviet citizen may live — that allowed him or her to live either in Moscow or Zelenograd. The villagers of Kryukovo, after a time, began to get used to the new name for the town. And the newcomers were different in other ways as well. They seemed better educated than average workers; the work they were doing seemed to have some high priority; they exuded an air of confidence and importance.

By 1972, Zelenograd had become the Silicon Valley of the Soviet Union. The site is ideal for quick transit and communication with Moscow. The train journey by elektrichka is about fifty minutes — thirty-five minutes on the rush-hour express trains — and it is easy enough to live in Moscow or at least spend evenings there.

The journey from the center of Moscow takes a visitor from Red Square out to the Leningrad highway, past the massive Khimki Reservoir, and eventually past a huge red-painted structure — a World War II tank trap left intact to remind travelers just how close the German Army got to Moscow. Some ten kilometers farther on, you pass the road leading to the nearby Sheremetyevo International Airport; then another ten kilometers through a gentle countryside with stands of birch trees, and Zelenograd, among its pine forests, comes into view.

It in no way appears to be a secret city. Parking is easy, and the traveler can walk about the center of town and visit shops freely. It is only at the gates or entrances of buildings that security men (the "first section" of each institute — retired KGB men or officers on detached service) bar the way.

Here, in one town, is everything needed for the research, development, and production of microchips. In the early years, however, the Soviet military machine had no intense interest in Zelenograd. The Russian defense oligarchy is probably one of the most conservative parts of Soviet society, and it was slow to recognize the long-term potential for integrated circuits. Chips that could operate at very low temperatures — an important consideration for Russians — were not yet a practical proposition. As the technology advanced and became more "ruggedized," this view would change, and the general staff would take a closer look at Zelenograd. But that did not happen until the 1970s.

Beginning in 1973 and 1974, the staff at Zelenograd began to notice a change in policy about the acquisition of essential items of technology from the West. The planning engineers had failed to anticipate a heavy demand for photoelectric repeaters, and they sent out a call for help. Soviet trade officials in countries of the West soon identified the best source as the David Mann Company in the United States. The Soviets made contact with Western middlemen to act as their brokers. They, in turn, established front companies in Yugoslavia, Switzerland, and West Germany and began to buy embargoed photorepeaters from the unsuspecting American company. Some middlemen even set up special facilities — which the Americans were allowed to inspect — and then shipped their purchases on to Russia. This experience was obviously a valuable lesson for the Soviets — and they were full of praise for the techno-bandits they had discovered.

Zelenograd was to become a coordinating center for both home-grown and acquired technology, and it would establish liaison with other centers of expertise set up in the capitals of all the major Soviet republics — Riga in Latvia, Minsk in Byelorussia, Tallinn in Estonia, Yerevan in Armenia, and Tbilisi in Georgia.

The chief designer of the Zelenograd complex was an American electronics engineer named Alfred Sarant. Known in Russia as Filipp Staros, this fascinating character was also a founding father of the whole Soviet semiconductor industry.

If the claims of Harvard University's Mark Kuchment are true, then this is one of the most bizarre cases of high-tech transfer in postwar years.[13] Staros first appeared in the Soviet Union in 1955. He had been living in Czechoslovakia for the previous five years. Opinions on how he was persuaded to move to the Soviet Union vary, but he may have been recruited on the initiative of Dmitry Ustinov, a friend who at the time was Minister of Defense Industries. During a project that involved the debriefing of several hundred émigré electronic engineers, stories emerged about the role of Staros in the establishment of the Soviet's post-Stalin computer capability. An émigré Soviet scientist himself, Mark Kuchment was fascinated by the claims of Staros's former colleagues that he was an American of Greek extraction. When *Izvestiya* published his obituary, on March 17, 1979, it said that Professor Filipp Staros had graduated from the University of Toronto in 1941.

The investigation made progress only when Kuchment compared what little was known of the early life of "Staros" with that of Alfred Sarant. Sarant, who had a Greek father, was a graduate of Cooper Union and had worked for both Westinghouse and Western Union as an electronics engineer. He was a friend of the Rosenbergs, the couple convicted as Soviet spies, and in 1949 he disappeared from the United States after being interviewed by the FBI. Shortly after, Staros appeared in Prague. When Kuchment showed photographs of Staros to people who had known Sarant in the 1940s, they confirmed the suspicions: it was the same man.

Whatever the reasons for his appearance in the Soviet Union or the secrets of his identity, Staros was immediately made head of a new laboratory at a secret military research institute. This was an institute *s yashchikom,* that is, with a box. It had, in other words, a front in the form of a post office box number, in this case number 155, Leningrad. Staros was given a high salary and extraordinary facilities; he also received top Soviet security clearance. His research area was computers and electronics, and he became a consultant to the all-powerful VPK (Voenno-Promyshlennaya Kommissiya), the Military-Industrial Commission. The VPK is a top-level interface between the government, defense industries, and the scientific world. Its membership comprises some of the Soviet Union's senior military personnel, leading academicians from the State Committee on Science and Technology, and the most influential politicians.

In late 1958 Staros presented a report to a conference of the principal designers and managers in the electronics industry. The report advocated a new commitment on their part to accelerate research and development in microelectronics. He was clearly an expert in his field, and his American education and training gave him a unique understanding of the advances being made in Western electronics and of the kind of organization and corporate structures that were producing them. His report was accepted.

He also had the support of the Soviet defense oligarchy. The military had been impressed by Staros's early work, and with their continued backing the Leningrad Design Bureau expanded from a dozen people to a large organization that played a leading role in early Soviet computer development. Soon it was employing several hundred and work was under way on a pilot semiconductor production plant. The growing awareness that the Soviet Union was trailing behind the West in microelectronics led to the creation in 1961 of the State Committee on the Electronics Industry. A leading light on this body was Alexander Shokin, who had had many years experience in the defense industry. At the time, Shokin was Deputy Minister of Radio Technology. The main task of the radio industry was to produce basic electronic components for radar and communications equipment. Shokin and others of the same mind saw the advantage in setting up their own production facilities for semiconductors, transistors, and the new integrated circuits being pioneered in the West. Staros, who had been avidly following Western developments, was given the task of planning a complete and self-contained Soviet semiconductor research and development plant, to be based just outside Moscow.

According to one scientist who took part in this project:

All development of the project on the center of microelectronics was undertaken by a group of five to ten people under the direction of Staros. Our project was not based on wishful thinking. It was meticulous throughout. We were young and enthusiastic. Staros knew all the people who counted, enjoyed high authority, and had carte blanche from Khrushchev. Khrushchev visited our place in 1962 and saw for himself what possibilities the development of microelectronics could open.[14]

Clearly, Khrushchev had given his blessing, and in the early 1960s a series of secret edicts from the Central Committee and the Council of Ministers gave the go-ahead to a number of projects on the development, production, and application of computers in both the military and civilian sectors.

Staros's brainchild grew into the full-fledged Center for Microelectronics at Zelenograd. Yet despite the pressure of work there, he still found time to prosper in his other job as head of the Leningrad Bureau, which produced for the military the UM-1, a second-generation, transistor-based process control computer. Staros and the Leningrad team received a state prize for one of these, the UM-1 NKh, in 1964. It was installed in a steel-rolling mill. The initials NKh gave rise to jokes about Staros's patronage by the leadership; the initials are the same as Nikita Khrushchev's. The truth was less exotic: they actually stood for "national economy" to indicate the source of the funding. The first Soviet-made integrated circuits began to appear in 1963, and the Leningrad Design Bureau first used them in the Elektronika-200, made in 1964.

In spite of the resounding successes of Staros, all was not sweetness and light for the expatriate American. For many years his merit-based recruitment policy had upset the bosses of the Leningrad Regional Party Committee. They disliked his propensity for recruiting only the best people he could find, regardless of all other considerations; complaints were made that his staff at this prestigious and top secret institute included Jews and non-party members. They also resented the fact that he was a foreigner who resisted their attempts to force favored people on him. In desperation, he wrote to Khrushchev about the problem. The letter outlined his grievances against the powerful Leningrad party and complained that he had not received support in resolving the problem from Shokin at the State Committee on the Electronics Industry.

Unfortunately, Staros's timing could not have been worse. The letter was sent early in October 1964; on the fourteenth of that month Khrushchev was ousted from power. It seems that the letter was found in his safe and, because it referred to electronics, was sent to none other than Shokin. Shokin was less than pleased, and Staros was summoned from Leningrad. What he said to Staros typifies the environment the American had to work in:

"Filipp Georgyevich, it seems to me that you have the strange fantasy that you are the founder of Soviet microelectronics. That is all wrong. The Communist Party created Soviet microelectronics, and the sooner you realize this fact, the better it will be for you." In 1965, Staros was removed from his post as the associate director general of research at Zelenograd and told to return to his less glamorous work in Leningrad.

If nothing else, Nikita Khrushchev had brought some degree of peasant humor to the Soviet leadership after the traumatic years of Stalin's lengthy reign. The leaders who took over after his downfall in 1964 had little to offer in terms of personality but at least had some experience in the administration of the economy and the running of Soviet industrial enterprises.

Having taken power, they were quick to emphasize the collective nature of the new leadership and made an early start in identifying the hitherto unrecognized middle-ranking administrators as being key to the success of the Soviet economy. This heralded the new era of "managerial Communism," which, it was claimed, would solve many of the problems associated with the USSR's catching up with the West in the volume and quality of the goods and technology. Perhaps the biggest single challenge to face managerial Communism from the late 1960s through the 1970s was closing the growing gap in electronics and computer technology. The flagship of the new venture was to be the Soviet Unified Series.

"The Soviet Union has been forced to develop all aspects of the computer business relying exclusively on its own intellectual and technical resources." These were the brave but suspect words of Professor A. P. Ershov, a leading Soviet computer scientist and a Fellow of the British Computer Society. They are quoted from Ershov's article in the September 1975 issue of the American trade magazine *Datamation*.[15] A look at Soviet developments since the 1960s, however, suggests that he was not quite telling the truth.

One of the great announcements in computer history came in 1964: IBM was about to introduce the System/360 range of mainframes. They were the first third-generation computers to be made in high volume, and they were to become pacesetters. Other manufacturers could only shake their heads and try to emulate. To avoid infringement of patents, other new computers — the RCA Spectra 70 Series, for example — could operate the same way but had to have different engineering. The Soviet Union, unhampered by a respect for patents, joined the emulators.[16]

The big Soviet announcement came in January 1972. The Ryad-1 Series[17] was being introduced. It bore a remarkable resemblance to the IBM 360s, but the project had taken eight years, and by that date IBM had already released its advanced System/370 Series. It was back to the drawing board again, and the Soviet Ryad-2, inspired by the 370, was announced in 1978.[18] All this Russian effort would have taken even longer had they tried to develop their own systems software (operating systems, utility programs, and so on). But by this time they had learned the lessons of desperation: find some techno-bandits to help you and then steal what you need from IBM.

Until the advent of the Ryad-1 Series, Soviet computing had depended on a hodgepodge of obsolescent (by Western standards) machines from many different Soviet factories. The Minsk Ordz-honikidze plant, run by the Radio Ministry, produced a range that included the Minsk-2 and the Minsk-22. These were quite limited, because they depended on crude magnetic tape drives for bulk storage and offered no capabilities for multiprogramming, time-sharing, or data communications. Even the improved Minsk-32 of 1968–1975 was far behind its Western contemporaries. Of the two thousand or so Minsk computers manufactured, most were shipped to the East European satellite countries.

At its plant in Kazan, the Radio Ministry produced the computers for military and space programs. This was the M Series, direct descendents of the earliest Soviet computers, the MESM and the BESM family, and there were various upgradings (M-20, M-220, and M-222) through 1969. Most of the computers in this series, like the Minsk-produced machines, are still in use.

There were also some notable failures. A whole series of process control machines made at Severodonetsk, in an attempt to achieve IBM compatability, was a wash. Similarly, the Ural range, five hundred machines made in Penza in 1969, finally found a niche in the Soviet railway system.

Russian computer development has been continuously handicapped by a lack of adequate "peripherals." Peripherals include such important functions as data storage, printing, and communications. Each of these requires specialized technology in manufacturing. In the West, for instance, only specialist firms produce magnetic disc storage devices. The USSR is at least ten years behind in this area. There is a scarcity of modems to connect computer terminals with phone lines, and, worse, the Soviet telephone system is far from first rate. That often means using the slower telex or telegraph lines assigned for computer communication. A proposed COMECON computer network has been announced, but there is little evidence that it has become an operational reality.

The very first foreshadowing of that big January 1972 announcement was made by Deputy Minister of the Radio Industry, G. Kazansky, in December 1967:

We are working on the so-called "third generation" with respect to machine capacity. They will operate with integrated circuits. The so-called "series" (*ryad*) of four such machines is being developed. They will have the same internal structure and mathematical capability and will operate at 20, 100, 5000, and 2 million arithmetical operations a second, respectively.[19]

The unspoken part of Kazansky's message was that the "internal structure" would be copied from the IBM 360.

The program was a massive one, and it was decided to recruit the East European satellites as participants. Some — like the Poles, Czechs, and Rumanians — preferred to continue their own computer development programs, but all finally fell in line. The new range of machines was called the Edinënnaya Sistema (Unified System), or ES.[20]

The Moscow Scientific Research Center for Electronic Computing Technology, which took on the job of coordinating ES development, gave each country its assignment on a fairly arbitrary basis, ignoring individual assets. Hungary had developed an expertise in software, and several of the others had a West-influenced sophistication that the Soviet Union had not managed to acquire. The East Germans, avid imitators of IBM, had a large contribution to make. (Their Robotron of the 1960s was based on the IBM 1401; their R Series culminated in the R-40 in 1968 and was aimed at IBM 360 compatibility.) The assignments from Moscow were nevertheless given out country by country. Hungary got the ES-1010 to build, Czechoslovakia the ES-1021, Poland (and the USSR) the ES-1030, and so on through seven models.

The result was that the five most powerful machines (from the ES-1020 to ES-1060) could claim compatibility with the IBM. In addition, the ES-1050, designed by the Moscow Calculating Machines Factory, had years of production problems and finally limped into volume production in 1976. The Hungarian and the Czech machines turned out to be fairly strange mutations. The Bulgarian-Soviet ES-1020 ran into manufacturing difficulties and many delays. And even after all this massive effort and expense, the Unified System computers cannot be considered to have 100 percent program compatibility with the IBM 360.

One of the few Ryad computers in Western hands belongs to the Control Data Corporation of Minneapolis (CDC). CDC is one of the world's largest suppliers of peripheral devices. In 1975, when the company was trying to get East European contracts to supply peripherals to the ES line, it bought an East German–built ES-1040 to check some CDC products. CDC assessed the machine's performance as somewhere between the IBM models 50 and 60 (in the 360 range). It was a reliable machine, though hardly state-of-the-art even for its time. The old-fashioned core memory (256,000 characters) and a heating problem caused it to run slowly, although it was capable of taking modern Western peripherals.

In 1970, IBM announced the introduction of the 370 series; it was the beginning of the rapidly growing employment of integrated-circuit chips. The smaller machines were in the 4300 series and the larger were the 303X and (in 1980) the 308X.

The Eastern bloc countries remained about eight years behind. After a series of interim computers developed in Bulgaria, Hungary, Poland, and the USSR, the bloc announced a new effort to catch up: it was to be the Ryad-2, based on the IBM 370. But even in this determined attempt, a good many compromises were accepted. The new models (ES numbers 1025, 1055, and 1065) retained the IBM 360 instruction set, with only some of the 370 instructions included in the design. Because of that, the Ryad-2s still had to use the old IBM 360 software.

Soviet hardware problems — in reliability and maintenance — are grave. Repair centers have been established, and there have been efforts to see that well-trained engineers are on hand when needed, but they do little good when production planning has broken down and spare parts are simply unavailable. Sometimes computers have been installed in rooms without dust filters and air conditioning. One whole factory system was installed under a hole in the roof, got rained on, and was ruined. An agriculture institute in Uzbekistan reported that its computers averaged three hours a day "up" time during the course of a year.

But an even bigger problem was the software. IBM had assigned hundreds of programmers to the job of creating the software for the 360s — to the dismay of their Western competitors, who had to duplicate the effort for their own machines. But the Soviets, as one of the first big acts in the era of techno-piracy, simply stole some of the 360s' operating systems. The functionality of the Soviet systems introduced in 1976 and 1977 was identical with that of the IBMs. The dead giveaway is that the instructions were in English and were word for word the same as those of IBM.

The scene of the crime was the Scientific Research Institute for Electronic Computers at Minsk, which, after 1976, became a ready customer for IBM 370 computers and software brought in by the techno-bandits of the world.

How useful are computers to the Soviet military and the civilian economy? Probably the most that can be said about the military is that Soviet defense systems and the KGB are the first-line customers for the latest in computer technology. There is not enough information to be able to make any intelligent comparison between Western and Eastern capabilities.

In the civilian sector, the greatest limitation is not in hardware or software but in the Soviet mind itself. The Soviet economy works on the production quota system. Good production brings a bonus in the pay envelope at the end of the week. So what more natural use for the computer — in the eyes of the Soviet manager — than payroll records and personnel files?

Soviet managers seem to be older and more inhibited than their American opposite numbers, and so they tend to ignore the possibilities of using computer techniques for decision analysis and modeling management problems. The system in which they work demands straightforward production rather than innovation and marketing decisions. When the Soviets *do* go in for economic modeling or simulation, as they have in the State Planning Committee, GOSPLAN, it isn't to look for general or unexpected possibilities in a problem situation; it is to reach a "correct Socialist solution."

There is, moreover, a strong suspicion that Soviet managers often keep a double set of books. Soviet industry has learned to distrust its own statistics — so what does one do with a computer system for the "official" operational management of an enterprise when the actual practice is different? Dare a manager use the computer to keep the records of "expediter" slush funds or under-the-counter deals with other firms?

Managers and workers everywhere, of course, have some built-in resistance to change. By 1984, however, the computer has become such a part of our lives that we have accumulated a lot of knowledge about the practicalities of computer system planning, and jokes are no longer current.

But they may be in the USSR, where the unreliability of the Soviet computers probably produces the same mixture of suspicion and derision we once had.

The vital need to compete with the West *should* have produced at least some sign that Professor Ershov's words have a potential for truth. But the facts, according to the CIA's experts on Soviet acquisition of high tech, are these: "Since our past is, to a considerable extent, their future, they should be able to look ahead to further accelerate and overlap the various stages. However, their efforts to do so have not been successful."[21]

4

THE TRADER-SPIES

THE TURNING POINT was 1975. The USSR was just beginning to learn how far behind the West it was in two critical areas — the manufacture of integrated circuits and the construction of advanced computer systems. The related deficiencies in these areas would affect both the military and the civilian economic sectors. The solution was obvious: they would have to take a short cut through the lengthy and expensive process of research and development by buying technology and products from the West. Information technology was advancing so rapidly that unless drastic measures were taken, the USSR might never catch up. The 1972 trade agreement between the United States and the Soviet Union would be the vehicle through which they could buy complete semiconductor manufacturing plants from companies like Fairchild, computers from IBM, CDC, and Honeywell, and other components from Texas Instruments and General Electric.

After all, Prime Minister A. N. Kosygin had paved the way in his keynote address to the 23rd Party Congress in 1966, when he had stressed the need to import technology from abroad, not simply to improve performance in industry and agriculture but also to save millions of roubles in research and development costs. It was significant that Kosygin's son-in-law, Dzherman Gvishiani, continued to be an outspoken supporter of such views from his top-ranking position as deputy director responsible for foreign technical imports at the State Committee on Science and Technology. Equally useful were the precedents. In the same year as Kosygin's speech, 1966, the first steps were taken to improve Soviet production of private cars. The deal involved Italy's Fiat car company in a $363 million contract to construct an entirely new production plant at the specially built town of Togliattigrad on the River Volga. The Zhiguli compact sedan, a Soviet version of the Fiat 124, went into production in 1972. A similar deal with the French firm Renault soon followed; a complete "turnkey" factory was commissioned. Even later came the Kama River truck plant. The automotive industry had paved the way.

But there were problems. Senator Henry (Scoop) Jackson of Washington State, influenced by a young aide, Richard Perle, proposed that the United States put pressure on the USSR through his amendment to the 1972 trade agreement: benefits to the Soviets would be in proportion to the number of exit visas awarded its citizens. The USSR responded to the pressure by cancelling the agreement. This happened in 1975 and firmly closed the door on any prospect of repeating the Fiat and Renault deals in the area of information technology. The Soviets had to find another way.

Appointed by the Supreme Soviet, the Council of Ministers supervises the day-to-day activities of the sixty-six ministries that form the administrative heart of the Soviet government. Immediately below the council are the various state committees and commissions that oversee specific areas. The most interesting of these groups are the all-pervasive Committee of State Security (the KGB), the State Committee on Science and Technology (the GKNT), the State Planning Committee (GOSPLAN, responsible for the implementation of the Five Year Plans), and the Military-Industrial Commission (the VPK, charged with, among other things, imposing on the ministries the requirements of the military oligarchy).

At a lower level, but still under the direct control of the Council of Ministers, are the various ministries and other bodies of a similar rank. These include the Ministry of Defense, which is the home of the GRU. The GRU — the Intelligence Division of the General

Staff—participates officially in the GKNT and has agents in the foreign trade organizations (FTOs) to ensure that the interests of the military are represented in technology acquisition exercises. The USSR Academy of Sciences is the prestigious assembly of the country's most honored and distinguished scientists. The ultimate accolade for the Soviet scientist is to be elected an academician, but the influence of the body is not limited just to the power of its individual membership. From the custom-built city-sized think tank at Akademgorodok, outside Novosibirsk in Siberia, to the special training schools for gifted children in various locations throughout the USSR, the power of the Academy of Sciences makes itself felt in all walks of Soviet life.

There are three ministries that have been essential to the growing electronics and computer industries. The Radio Ministry is responsible for complete systems, such as the ES and SM ranges. The Electronics Ministry handles the manufacture of integrated circuits and other components. Finally, there is the Ministry of Instrument Building, which produces electrical and electronic instruments and process control systems. Essentially, these three are among the main customers of the foreign trade organizations.[1] The VPK is, in turn, the main customer for goods and systems that are destined for use by what are nicknamed "the eight sisters"—the major defense-related ministries that service the Soviet military machine.

The Ministries of Foreign Trade oversee the activities of the foreign trade organizations. These will play leading roles in the story of the techno-bandits. Although there are more than sixty, only four will feature prominently: Technopromimport, Mashpriborintorg, Techmashimport, and Elektronorgtekhnika (or Elorg, as it is more commonly known). Technopromimport imports equipment for Soviet industrial concerns, a wide range of capital goods from medical equipment to combine harvesters. Mashpriborintorg specializes in machine tools for industry. Techmashimport is concerned with all other machines of a technical nature. It deals with the chemical and rubber industries, alcohol, soap, pharmaceuticals, synthetic fibers, industrial and commercial refrigeration plants, and optical systems and products, including lasers. Elorg is responsible for international trade in electronics and computers. It also runs a network of sales outlets in Finland, Sweden, Holland, Belgium, and other European countries.[2]

What does not appear on the organization chart for the upper echelons of the Soviet Government is the influence of the Communist Party. The very ways in which the party works make it difficult to place this power structure on the same chart as the one outlining the formal administrative structure. There are a number of factors that relate to the paramount influence of the party, whose membership comprises eighteen million citizens.

By adapting Heisenberg's Principle of Indeterminacy, one could say that even if you know what a party member's position is, you cannot automatically say what he does; if you know what he does, you cannot automatically say what his position is. It is safe to assume that all senior members of the ministries and the FTOs are members of the party. If the Central Committee issues an edict, the administration will be bound to act on it. The party structure will, by its very nature, ensure that policy directives originating in the Central Committee and the Politburo will be expedited. Also, there are channels of communication within the party quite separate from those imposed by the administration.

The Russians have a word for it. *Nomenklatura* refers to the system of patronage whereby senior party members try to ensure that supporters are placed in key positions below them in the hierarchy. Of course, this happens in Western organizations, but probably not in so well refined a way. The ponderous Soviet system is further lubricated by a network of fixers, or *tolkachi.* The Russian people are used to dealing with tolkachi, who are well placed to make things happen — as long as the roubles are there. A tolkach can arrange for that new apartment, see that there are spare parts for your car, make available a pair of Western jeans, foreign currency, and so forth. FTO officials, therefore, view the techno-bandits as the tolkachi of foreign trade, the fellows who can get you anything from an illicit Digital VAX superminicomputer to a complete semiconductor plant.

A British Intelligence report prepared in 1976, stated:

> It is . . . contrary to Soviet policy to rely on foreign sources of supply; this applies particularly to the electronics industry, which is very much geared to the production of military equipment. There are no signs of change in this over-riding policy, and the Soviet Union's need for

Western technology in the electronics field will therefore be limited to the following fields:

a. Electronic equipment filling gaps in the civilian sector which otherwise involve the diversion of resources from military production.
b. One-off items of electronic equipment required for technical exploitation and the associated acquisition of technical "know-how."
c. Some sophisticated production machinery and associated "know-how" especially for the manufacture of advanced semiconductor devices and automation equipment.[3]

At the time that it was written, it was a reasonable assessment of the Soviet position. Ever since the rule of Stalin, the USSR had been determined to become as self-sufficient as possible in its electronics industry. But the portent was not good; although it produced some $22 billion worth of goods per annum, by the mid-1970s the industry was still inefficient by Western standards and was able to make the more advanced high-quality components only in limited quantities for its military customers. Key projects in Zelenograd, Moscow, Minsk, and Leningrad were behind schedule, forcing the technology gap to widen even further.

The British report makes no reference to the fact that contacts had already been made with the techno-bandits who were to help in the critical task of equipping the silicon chip–manufacturing plants. Indeed, only months earlier, U.S. federal agents had successfully smashed one of the earliest smuggling rings that shipped the critical hardware to Moscow.

By 1978 it was clear to the Soviet leadership that since the end of détente in 1975, the techno-bandits had become their main source of supply from the United States. The foreign trade organizations were geared to the legal acquisition of technology within a framework of the good relations and trade treaties that no longer existed. The FTOs were not geared to the new environment and had to be changed; the KGB and the GRU military intelligence people would play a more direct and formal role in the matter of technology imports.

At the May 1978 meeting of the Central Committee of the Communist Party of the Soviet Union, the subject of the FTOs was second only to the perennial problem of agricultural production. A decree was signed on May 31 by Prime Minister Alexey Kosygin and Minister of Administration Mikhail S. Smirtyukov. It called for the reorganization of the FTOs during 1978 and 1979. In a memorandum from the British embassy to the Foreign Office in Whitehall, the most important changes were listed:

> Emphasis is placed . . . on a more thorough use of market research into goods on the world market . . . [and] the importance of a thorough study of available Western technology and equipment. . . . [It] sets out the need for the ministries and administrations to be involved in discussions on major contracts and also lays down that the State Committee on Science and Technology should be consulted on questions relating to technology . . . permits the formation of "specialized firms and other organizations" within the framework of the re-organized FTO.[4]

By April of 1979 the nature of the changes initiated by the edict became public: there was a radical restructuring, and many new faces appeared in the more senior positions. In the January issue of the Soviet magazine *Foreign Trade,* the new constitution of Elorg was published.[5] Beneath a central board of directors were nine specialist firms, which the Soviet magazine described:

"Elorg-ES, the subject of whose activities shall be the export of multipurpose Unified System computers and peripherals thereto." Director Vladimir Plakhov was appointed in April 1979.

"Elorg-SM, the subject of whose activities shall be the export and import of minicomputers and SM peripheral devices." Also appointed that April was Yevgeny Gorlenko, a forty-eight-year-old graduate of the Bauman Technical School and a probable KGB agent. The purpose of Elorg-ES was straightforward enough: the sale of Soviet-built Ryads to the Eastern bloc. The brief for Elorg-SM did not include just the sale of the PDP-11–compatible Sistema Mikro (SM) series, but also the import of other minicomputers, PDP-11 peripherals, and actual PDP-11 systems from the West. In this way, the deficiencies in the SM range were to be corrected.

The division of responsibility among the other firms was less clear-cut. The *Foreign Trade* article continued to describe their various roles:

"Elorgsistema, the subject of whose activities shall be the import of multipurpose computers, accessories thereto, and storage devices." Appointed director was one of Elorg's younger men, Vladimir Usanov. Previously director of Elorg's Technical Center in Budapest, he did not start his new job until April 1981.

"Elorgkomplekt, the subject of whose activities shall be the import of peripherals to multipurpose computers." Taking up the position of director in April 1979 was another Bauman graduate, Igor Samkov.

"Elorgmash, the subject of whose activities shall be the export and import of office electronic equipment." Yury Kotsonis, another relative youngster of forty-two, became director of this office-automation group at the end of 1979. He is a chemical engineer who had previously served in France.

"Elorgintegral, the subject of whose activities is the export and import of active electronic components;

"Elorgkomponent, the subject of whose activities shall be the export and import of passive electronic components." This is a roundabout way of saying that Elorgintegral will deal with integrated circuits (microchips) and that Elorgkomponent will handle other, simpler electronic devices, such as resistors and capacitors. Vladimir Sokolovsky and Fridrikh Vissart were appointed the respective directors in April 1979.

"Elorgdetal, the subject of whose activities shall be the export and import of spare parts, component blocks, and maintenance of computer equipment." The youngest of all the new appointees, thirty-three-year-old Valery Glazunov, was made head of the firm one year later, in April 1980. The last firm to be constituted at the beginning of 1979 was

"Elorgintech, the subject of whose activities shall be the import of computer software, special-purpose minicomputers and microcomputers, and samples of new technology." Fresh from a five-year stint as a trade representative in Afghanistan was the new director, Vladimir Yakovenko. Another firm was set up in Elorg later in the year, and still others were to follow.

In essence, the overall objectives for the reconstituted organization were

The export from and import to the USSR of mini- and microcomputers, software, office electronic equipment, active and passive electronic components, spare parts and component blocks ... the export from the USSR of multipurpose computers, accessories thereto, and SM peripheral devices ... the import to the USSR of multipurpose computers, accessories thereto and storage devices, and peripherals to multipurpose computers.[6]

Heading the management board of Elorg was General Director Yury Shcherbina. His six deputies were Valentin Antonov, Lev Arkharov, Alexey Vassilyev, Yevgeny Mikhailov, Nikolay Shishkov, and Viktor Kedrov, to whom we shall return later. The profile of these functionaries follows a familiar pattern. After graduating from college with a technical degree, each entered one of the FTOs in a minor capacity. The key to advancement to a more senior position was graduation from the All-Union (Federal) Academy of Foreign Trade, which most seemed to attend on a part-time basis. Graduation usually occurred between ten and fifteen years after the man first joined the FTO. Transfers between FTOs and other parts of the foreign service were fairly common. Each deputy speaks at least one foreign language; most of the directors speak two. English and German are the most popular. Service abroad was also helpful (apart from being an important perk). These assignments were in the Eastern bloc, third world countries, or, preferably, Western Europe or North America.

Membership of the Communist Party is a vital rung in the career ladder. Close links with the KGB or the GRU are equivalent to having access to an elevator. And such links do exist. The biography of Gorlenko, the director of Elorg-SM, a graduate of Bauman Technical School, has a four-year gap following his course at the Academy of Foreign Trade in 1966.[7] He next appears as an officer at the USSR trade delegation in London in 1970, but his first overseas appointment was a short one; the following year he was expelled, along with 104 of his colleagues, when Prime Minister Edward Heath agreed to MI5 requests for a purge of suspected intelligence officers. After a brief respite back in Moscow as an office director at Mashpriborintorg, he was sent to Helsinki to work for Koneisto, a company jointly owned with the Finns.

Deputy Director Viktor Kedrov is also suspected of being an agent of the GRU. After being based in London between 1964 and 1968, he reappeared in Copenhagen in 1971. In a combined operation with the British Intelligence Service, the Danes expelled him for high-tech espionage in 1974. In the late 1970s, he was involved with a West German businessman, Werner Bruchhausen, in a conspiracy to divert large quantities of semiconductor manufacturing equipment from California to the USSR. Kedrov disappeared from the hierarchy of Elorg toward the end of 1982.[8] Most of the other FTOs went through the same process of restructuring and the appointment of new directors as Elorg did. That organization serves here as an example.

The May 1978 edict from the Central Committee called for the greater involvement of the various ministries. They had always been involved to some degree, especially in a technical consulting capacity, but this was to be increased to ensure that the *apparatchiks* obtained the most current technology. An interesting example of this was the large number of staff members of the Ministry of Electronics who were linked in one way or another to the negotiations with Peter Gopal, a Silicon Valley specialist in "reverse engineering" who visited Moscow on a number of occasions.[9] The business cards in his possession at the time of his arrest for stealing trade secrets included those of Alexander Rubtsov (diploma engineer, semiconductors), Alexander Ivanov (manager of Special Technological Equipment Department), Leonid Dymov (chief of department), Vasily Kurdin (director of marketing), Gennady Verkhovenko (sales manager of semiconductors), and Vladimir Sokolov (diploma engineer, department of licenses, know-how, patents). The Ministry of Electronics is, of course, responsible for the manufacture of integrated circuits in the Soviet Union.

Another organization that is important in the Soviet planning of high-technology acquisition is the State Committee on Science and Technology. The Central Committee's edict of 1978 called for the GKNT to be "consulted on matters referring to technology."[10] The GKNT brings together people from the Academy of Sciences, the universities, research institutes, and the administration to oversee trade agreements, the planning of expositions, the allocation of research and development funds, and the monitoring of R and D activities in both the Soviet Union and in other countries in the Council for Mutual Economic Assistance. It is also believed to be responsible now for coordinating the participation of the KGB and GRU agents involved in the activities of the FTOs.

The Eastern bloc plays a relatively small role in international scientific conferences and trade shows in the West. The reasons are problably twofold: in most Communist nations foreign travel is viewed as a privilege, and an expensive one at that. Only one person (and perhaps his watchdog) may attend an important conference. He can make notes, and these, plus copies of the official proceedings of the event, would be given to the other interested bodies back home. From time to time, Eastern bloc countries have been known to present papers at conferences; this is particularly true of the Hungarians. Many Eastern bloc technical personnel could benefit from attendance at the staff-training seminars held in Western Europe. These, however, can be even more expensive than the conferences, and it is usually more cost-effective for the institution concerned to persuade the training company to present the same seminar for a number of people on an "in house" basis.

The least expensive way for the Russians to gather information on the advance of high technology is through the systematic reading and abstracting of the thousands of learned journals and trade publications released each day in the West. There are estimated to be thirty-five thousand of these published in no fewer than sixty-five languages each year. This yields about 1.5 million articles and papers that have to be read, assessed, summarized, and, in some cases, translated.[11] The logistics of this should not be underestimated, but the fact remains that it is the most efficient approach to the problem.

The 1960s were a low point for the Committee for State Security. From 1961 to 1967, the huge security and intelligence apparatus was headed by Vladimir Semichastny. The appointment of the former Communist Youth League bureaucrat to this important post proved to be a bad decision for the Soviet leadership. Unsubtle in manner, Semichastny was a bungling administrator; he was fired.

His replacement was a very different man. Yury Andropov had few KGB connections prior to his appointment to the post by Leonid Brezhnev, but his wide experience with the Soviet political machine equipped him well to succeed as head of this uniquely Russian organization. One of his earliest decisions was typical of his style. He took the important First Chief Directorate out of the dreary, claustrophobic Dzerzhinsky Square headquarters, which it shared with the Lubyanka Prison, and into a spanking new modern building on the Moscow ring road. But the changes were not merely cosmetic; within a few years new procedures and training methods had been introduced, and an unusual air of efficiency and confidence began to prevail.

In American terms, the KGB is a massive group that embraces the scope of both the FBI and the CIA, with a few other areas thrown in: border guards, armed forces security, protection of defense installations, approval of entry and exit visas. Apart from the 300,000 elite border guards, it was estimated in the early 1970s that the KGB included 90,000 staff officers and another hundred thousand clerical workers, building guards, and "special troops." The number of informants and spies runs into hundreds of thousands.[12] The KGB is well described as the bastion of the Soviet Communist Party.[13]

Broadly, the Second and Fifth Chief Directorates cover the same ground as the FBI. The First Chief Directorate, roughly equivalent to the CIA, is the body responsible for the KGB's involvement in the activities of the GKNT, the ministries, and of course the foreign trade organizations. The First Chief Directorate comprises a number of sections called directorates and departments. During Andropov's chairmanship, the work of these was consolidated and expanded to meet the needs of the time. Most interesting of the subdivisions is the Scientific and Technical Directorate, referred to internally as Directorate T. Created during the last years of Khrushchev's rule, Directorate T was expanded dramatically during the 1970s. Its brief was, and still is, to acquire data on space, missiles, and nuclear research and to monitor advances in such key areas as robotics, cybernetics, cryogenics, holography, and advanced industrial processes. Included in its assignment is the whole area of electronics and computers. Within the directorate, the department known as Line X is specifically responsible for field operations abroad. This, in turn, leads to its involvement with the FTOs.

The very nature of the FTOs dictates their need to have personnel based outside the USSR — in most, if not all, of the foreign capitals of the West. Inevitably this has caused the FTOs, the consulates, and the trade missions to be used as "cover" for the traditional intelligence activities of the KGB and the GRU. This should come as no surprise to Western observers; the CIA and the British Secret Intelligence Service are also known to have adopted the same approach by using both embassy trade officials and businessmen working for private companies. There was a furor in 1962 when the KGB arrested the British "businessman" Greville Wynne. He was charged with being the Moscow controller for the spy Colonel Oleg Penkovsky of the GRU, probably the highest-ranking Soviet officer to cooperate with the West, and was sent to prison for eight years. Penkovsky was shot. Wynne was exchanged in April 1964 for Konon Trofimovich Molody, alias Gordon Lonsdale. Some years later, in his autobiography, Wynne admitted that he had been a British agent and had worked for the Intelligence Service since the Second World War. Virtually everything the Russians accused him of was true.[14]

Notwithstanding this tradition of using trade officials as cover for espionage, the relationship between the KGB, the GRU, and the FTOs seems to have changed some time during the latter half of the 1970s, probably in 1978. At that point it became evident to the Soviet authorities that they would need to supplement their internal deficiencies in many areas of high technology; they would have to increase their dependency on the techno-bandits. Ensuring the best possible flow of illicit high technology would require some degree of "field craft," which was not available to the FTOs. Since these skills apparently are not taught at the Academy of Foreign Trade, the quickest way they could be injected into the trade organizations would be through the assignment of professional KGB and GRU officers. More than a few full-time trade officials were already representing the interests of the ubiquitous organizations alongside their regular duties; now the FTOs at home and abroad were to get assistance.

The 1982 CIA report (based on the Paris "dog and pony show") places much emphasis on the part played by field KGB personnel in acquiring both products and know-how and cites large numbers of successful agents.

One cannot deny the importance of the Soviet intelligence groups in the business of high-tech smuggling, but it is clear from discussions with East-West "gray" traders that the last thing these people want in the West is "help" from the KGB. First of all, once the techno-bandit gets his purchase contract from the FTO, it is unlikely that he will need the support of agents in obtaining the goods and arranging the shipment. Second, the discovery of any involvement with known KGB or GRU agents is likely to increase any subsequent charges from misdemeanors associated with licensing and Customs declarations to something closer to espionage. In any case, such an association would be bad field craft in itself; both the techno-bandit and the intelligence agent would be placed at risk. Good agents are valuable; their safety cannot be entrusted to amateurs.

Most, if not all, contact between outsiders and the KGB is limited to Moscow. Approaches at trade shows are the favored technique; the very presence of the businessman is taken as an indication that he is prepared to do some kind of selling. One California businessman who is not involved in the gray end of the trade said:

> Each year I attend half a dozen shows in Moscow and get approached on average two or three times by someone who has funny connections and is looking for something that is not licensable. When you point this out to them, they look appropriately embarrassed and apologize. It is all very polite.[15]

An Englishman who was to become involved in the sale of surveillance systems to the KGB told of the first time he was approached:

> If you are primarily involved in the legitimate trade, you will spend most of the time sitting around the waiting rooms of the FTOs, waiting for appointments. My earliest contacts in Moscow were a couple of Laurel and Hardy characters called Gregoryev and Yushkov; the fat one was the "black hat" guy, and the thin one wore the "white hat." They worked for the Ministry of Foreign Trade, ostensibly. Somehow, I must have given them the impression that I would be prepared to "do some business." A few months later I was setting up an exhibition stand at a show in Kiev. We were unloading a container of products that had been shipped over by one of the companies I represented. My associates had taken some packing cases into the exhibition hall and I was on my own in the back of the container. Someone tapped me on the shoulder; he was a short, stocky individual, clean-shaven and smartly dressed. He introduced himself as Yury and said that Gregoryev and Yushkov had given him my name and that he would like to talk to me.

"Yury," it turned out, was not the man's real name. The English businessman continued: "I said that I was busy and asked him to come back later. He was persistent, but left when his colleagues returned." It soon became apparent that Yury was to be the trader's main contact from that point on. All business was done through Yury, who took the Englishman to parties held by senior officials and generally became his *dyadya,* or "uncle," in Moscow. On one occasion, the businessman realized that his visa was about to expire before the end of a trade show. When he approached the head of the exhibition with his request for a temporary renewal, he was refused. A few hours later, after he made a telephone call to Yury, he received a new visa.

The Englishman did not have dealings with Gregoryev and Yushkov again, but he did learn that Yushkov was one of the Soviets' leading experts on bugging systems: "I only saw him again once. I was living in Luxembourg and recognized him in the street. He ignored me. This was the same year that the new European Parliament building was being constructed. I was struck by the coincidence."[16]

Although it is clear that much techno-smuggling can be initiated by the Soviets from the comfort of their own homes, a little foreign travel is sometimes involved. There is more than the routine office work in trade missions and the systematic collection of "open literature" for analysis; the work has its dangers. Once in the field, KGB and GRU agents inevitably attract the attention of the local security services.

Two Russians based at the Washington embassy of the USSR certainly attracted the attention of the FBI. The assistant director of the Intelligence Division reported to the Senate in 1982:

In October 1979, two Soviets, dressed in jeans and sports shirts, and almost 2500 miles from their posts in Washington, D.C., visited Ely, Nevada, a potential basing site for some MX missiles. They identified themselves as Vladimir Kvasov and Vladimir Militsin, listed respectively by the Soviet Embassy as a lieutenant commander/assistant military attaché and as a civilian employee of the attaché's office. The assistant librarian at the Ely Public Library was previously notified by the FBI as to a possible visit by them. They showed up at the library dressed very casual and described themselves as travelers from Washington.

The younger Russian went to the newspaper rack while his friend asked for books on industry in Las Vegas. Las Vegas is a restricted area for Soviet Embassy personnel because of its proximity to Nellis Air Force Base and the Nevada nuclear test site.

After browsing, they both came back with a book on the Nevada sites — a 300-page environmental impact statement for the Nevada site where the U.S. Government conducts underground tests of its nuclear weapons. They received permission to copy the volume, which was done at a cost of $47 at a nearby store. The Russian who did the copying identified himself as an energy engineer from Washington. The two Russians subsequently made several other stops, inquiring about the area and the kind of industry in the area.

The fate of the two diplomats is not recorded.[17]

Viktor Baryshev, a forty-seven-year-old official at the Soviet trade mission in Bangkok, managed to get his arrest by Thai security officers videotaped and photographed. On May 19, 1983, the Southeast Asia posting for Baryshev and his wife came to an abrupt end in his favorite coffee shop at the Windsor Hotel:

At 11:50 A.M. he stepped into the hotel lobby. Five minutes later a Thai in a dark blue safari suit entered. There was not a hint of recognition between the two, but within minutes they were huddled together at a corner table. . . . The waitress who served them had done so before, but the foreigner's mood, she noticed, was different. "He usually smiled," she said later, "but he looked sad that day. He ordered tea instead of his usual coffee." . . . Shortly before 12:15, Thai security men saw Baryshev's safari-suited companion pass him some papers, then leave the coffee shop. Baryshev, the papers in a trouser pocket, was on his way out of the hotel at 12:20 when a uniformed policeman stepped in front of him and announced: "You're under arrest on a charge of espionage." When the Russian tried to bluster past the policeman, protesting that he had diplomatic immunity, converging plainclothes policemen locked him by the arms. Shocked into silence for a few moments, Baryshev then agreed to be escorted — in his own Toyota Corona bearing white diplomatic plates. Declining the offer, the policemen coerced him into their own car.

Special Branch Police Major General Opas Ratanasin supervised the search personally. In the left trouser pocket of the Russian — code-named Mee-uan, or Fat Bear, by Thai counterintelligence agents — was a three-page report on military installations on the Thai border with Cambodia. But the Thai authorities were subsequently to claim that Baryshev's terms of reference did not include intelligence only on Cambodia and China; he was also responsible for "the re-export of Western and Japanese high-tech products to Moscow." Given the use of Thailand's low-cost labor in the completion of Silicon Valley–produced microchips, the use of Bangkok as a center for gathering samples of new microchips does not seem unreasonable. The following day the Russian was expelled and left with his wife on an Air Vietnam flight for Hanoi.[18]

On January 6, 1983, Vladimir Chernov finished work at his small office in London's Haymarket and walked the hundred yards to Piccadilly Circus Underground station. His coveted four-year posting as a translator at the International Wheat Council was about to come to an end.[19] He was not aware of this yet.

A mile or so to the south, in Downing Street, a top secret dossier lay on Prime Minister Margaret Thatcher's desk. It contained information from Whitehall's top Intelligence watchdog, the Joint Intelligence Committee, that left her in no doubt as to what she should do. Within days, Chernov, his wife, and young son were packing their bags for home. He would soon be back at his old job in Moscow's Foreign Trade Ministry on Pudovkin Street, another victim of the Western drive against high-tech poaching.

Chernov had played a pivotal role in briefing Moscow on the latest applications of computers in advanced agricultural research. The Wheat Council, despite its unassuming title, had been a perfect place for Chernov to harvest information about the West's most sophisticated wheat development projects and the kind of computer hardware used in agricultural genetic engineering. The information Chernov supplied was of enormous value to the Soviet economy. Despite considerable efforts over the years to increase grain production, the Soviets were still forced to rely on imports from the West. Any breakthrough that would increase wheat yields could help the Soviet Union to break free of that dependence. Chernov was not the first high-tech spy to be expelled. Nor, as it turned out, would he be the last.

The USSR had reacted to the growing gap between the West and the East in high technology by deploying its best intelligence resources in Moscow and throughout the world. But in the early 1980s the Western security agencies were alert to the problem, and in the first six months of 1983 alone as many as ninety Soviet agents were expelled from their base countries for varying degrees of intelligence-gathering activities. Forty-seven were sent home from France, four from Britain, four from Italy, eighteen from Iran, and three from the United States. There were also expulsions from Holland, Spain, West Germany, Norway, Australia, and Japan. In Denmark, Yevgeny Motorov — thought to be the local head of the KGB Directorate T's Line X — was also expelled. In Belgium, Elorg owns a company jointly with the Belgian Government. In the first half of 1983 its director general, Yevgeny Mikhailov, was invited to leave the country. His predecessor had left the same way seven years earlier.

The Soviets had reacted to the technology gap, but so had the West.

5

OPERATION EXODUS

THANKSGIVING was cold that year. In the disused control tower, Customs Agent Bob Cozzolina, wearing a heavy topcoat and gloves, huddled up to the small electric fire. This was his first major case, and he was beginning to find out just how tedious surveillance could be. There had been no action for hours; he had watched the video screen religiously and the scene had not changed. But "Cozz," an ambitious new recruit, never complained. Using the forty-foot-high airport control tower — abandoned years before — was still preferable to the original idea: setting up a hot dog stand right outside the warehouse itself.

Cozz and the other agents on the case never ceased to be amazed at the ideas of the man running the team. Dick Curci, Brooklyn-born, a Customs veteran of fifteen years' service, was known as the "Doctor," because he always made himself available to listen to everyone else's problems. The suspect company warehouse was in a quiet residential area in Farmingdale, New Jersey, on Belmar Boulevard. Any surveillance van or car would have been too conspicuous.[1] Curci had hit on the idea of approaching the owner of the bicycle shop across the street. The elderly storekeeper was left in no doubt about the seriousness of the matter, and he agreed to have the video cameras set up in his front windows. It was also Curci who had the inspiration about where the cameras could be monitored. Half a mile down the road was Monmouth Airfield. The field was still operating, but the derelict control tower was no longer occupied. Curci took over the observation deck, equipped it with a few old chairs and an electric heater, and installed his agents. The Doctor made sure there was a quick rotation — even playing poker all day palled after a while for the men.

The watch had been going on for nearly three months. By December 1978, the agents had put together a good intelligence file on the case. They knew the background and movements of the two Monmouth employees as well as the lifestyle of the American owner, who flew in once a month from his home in Germany to oversee the export operation. Curci's agents thought it was a case they could not muff. The tip-off had originally come from the Customs office in Baltimore. Because the suspect operated from Farmingdale, the tip had been passed on to Newark, New Jersey, and Curci had claimed it quickly. None of them could have realized then that the case was to become a milestone in the history of the Customs Service.

In the late summer of 1978 Microtel Corporation, a Defense contractor in Maryland, received an order for one of its most sophisticated pieces of equipment. The wide-range surveillance receiver was capable of intercepting radio signals and, if required, jamming them. Until that time, the only call for the $61,950 system had been from government agencies. A request for the receiver from the tiny Farmingdale company, Winkler Electronics, was strange, to say the least. The purchaser was told that the equipment would take several months to assemble. Soon after the order was placed, the watch on the Winkler warehouse was set up. Microtel had cooperated, promising to contact Customs again as soon as the system was ready for delivery.

In December the sensitive order was completed, and an agent traveled to the Microtel facility in Maryland. With the help of an engineer, he made the receiver partly inoperable. Next, a call was placed to Winkler Electronics: the unit was ready. One employee wanted to know whether an engineer from Microtel could deliver it and give a quick run-through to show how it should be operated. The man from Microtel agreed.

In the office next to the Winkler warehouse, the Microtel engineer and an undercover Customs agent gave a demonstration of the system. It soon became clear to them that neither of the Winkler employees present had any idea of what the receiver was used for. The equipment was left with the Winkler men, and the agent later briefed Curci on what had happened. The Doctor decided to try to get the Winkler staff on his side. When he told them that their company was being investigated by the government and the reason for the investigation, they readily agreed to cooperate. Each man was wired with a hidden radio transmitter. Again, it seemed to Cozz and the other agents that this was a case that was bound to succeed.

The next day a receiving aerial was erected on the roof of the deserted control tower. From then on, said Curci, "We had everything — audio and visual." Agents sat in the cold — and watched and listened. They were just in time. Michael Winkler telephoned from Frankfurt the following day and was told that the receiver had arrived. "Ship it out," he told his two employees. They hesitated; there would be absolutely no possibility of getting an export license, they told him. "Then I'll come over and take care of it myself," he replied. The agents in the control tower grinned; the Doctor was delighted.

Both Curci and Cozzolina had missed Thanksgiving; they hoped they were not going to miss Christmas as well. But the cards were still being dealt in their favor. Winkler seemed to be in some sort of a hurry. On December 4, 1978, he flew into JFK. He was watched by agents as he came through Immigration and Customs. He was a pudgy man in his mid-forties, balding, of medium height; he looked totally insignificant. Michael Winkler had never spent much on clothes, nor on anything else, as far as they could tell. At 3:30 P.M. he boarded New York Airways helicopter flight 947 for Newark Airport. An agent sat behind him during the flight. An hour later Winkler was in his small office, talking to his employees. In their freezing observation post in the control tower, the agents listened.

Winkler slept in the office that night. "He was a mean man. He was saving money on hotels," said Curci. The next morning, the agents continued to listen as he told his employees how the unit could be exported. "We'll just ship it out and chance it," he said. The agents, forty feet up in the observation post, also listened in as Winkler telephoned the Bayshore Air Freight Company, which serviced the south-central Jersey area. Would they come and pick up an assignment? The Bayshore truck arrived a few hours later, and, while the agents watched on the video, a packing case was put inside. Before the truck had even arrived back at the Matewan freight depot, some seven miles away, Curci had contacted Bayshore. He told them of the seriousness of the investigation and asked them for access to the box. He then carried out what was to become a Customs tradition: the switch. He took the equipment out of the crate and replaced it with sandbags of the same weight.

The district attorney then made the decision to close in. On December 7, Curci, armed with search and arrest warrants, walked into Winkler's office. Winkler was amazed, but he remained composed. When told he was being arrested for violation of munitions export control laws, Winkler admitted the offense at once to the agents. The unit was bound for a company in Vienna called Videtron, he said. One of Videtron's conditions of purchase was that the shipper's documents show a West German address. The one he had given was a phony. He had received $8,000 down payment and was to get the balance on delivery. He had not attempted to obtain an export license, because the process took too long and would have resulted in a lost sale. Neither of his employees had been involved.

The offices were searched, and Cozzolina was given the task of making out the inventory. Winkler had filled out the shipper's export declaration himself, putting the total value of $1100 and describing the component as "CPU and accessories." He had said the box was going to a company called Helmut Rentzing GmbH, of Il-gernerstrasse, Leiman, West Germany. Agents in Bonn were contacted; they told Curci they believed the equipment had been ordered by Elorg in Moscow.

Michael Winkler had spent twenty years in the U.S. Army Signal Corps. When he was demobilized, he set up the Farmingdale company, three miles from the headquarters of the Signal Corps at Fort Monmouth. Then he went to live in Heidelberg, where he established the German end of the enterprise, Winkler Electronics GmbH. Because of his army background, Customs reported the case to the FBI. "We thought he might be a spy," said Curci. The FBI interviewed Winkler at length. Three months after his arrest there was a brief hearing on the case in the Newark District Court, New

Jersey, before Judge Clarkson S. Fisher. The defendant was charged on three counts, but two were later dropped as a result of plea-bargaining. On the third, that of attempting illegal exportation and making false statements under the Export Control Act, Winkler pleaded guilty. His lawyer and the government prosecutor told the court that Winkler had passed information to the FBI. He had fully cooperated with the government and would do so again if asked. The plea-bargain, however, did not render him immune from any future espionage charges; the FBI investigation was not concluded.

Judge Fisher asked Winkler why he had done it. "We had a letter of credit," Winkler replied, "and I was overdue in shipping this shipment.... It was a stupid thing to do...." "Did you know you were misleading Customs?" the judge asked. "Yes, sir," Winkler acknowledged. He was sentenced in May 1979 to two years' imprisonment and fined $5000.[2] The prison term was reduced to three years' probation. He also lost the $60,000 worth of sophisticated equipment that he had already paid for. It was sent to Customs headquarters in Washington.

Winkler's sentence was hardly pleasing for the Customs agents involved. "I thought he should have gotten more time," said a disappointed Curci. "But he was an army veteran, he had cooperated, and he was a diabetic. It all counted in his favor. We only had one shipment and couldn't prove it was going to Moscow." And the FBI was finally satisfied that Winkler was not a spy. In the annals of U.S. Customs, the Winkler incident became a classic case. Agents were to run across the same type and the same method quite a few times again. It had a distinctive influence on the direction of Cozzolina's career as a Customs investigator. From then on, high-tech smuggling was to have a magnetic attraction for him.

"Cozzolina."

"Is that the duty agent?"

"That's right. Agent Cozzolina here."

"This is Serengetti, baggage."

"I'm sorry?"

"Serengetti, baggage handler. We've got a problem down here and they said I should call you." Cozz had been hoping for a quiet shift. He was working his way through graduate school in Newark and was hoping to spend the day studying. He pushed the textbook away from him.

"What's the problem?"

"A parrot."

"A what?"

"A parrot," said Serengetti. "We have a parrot walking around Carousel B."

By the time Cozz got down to the baggage claim area, the carousel was surrounded by passengers and airline personnel. He could not see the parrot at first, but he managed to find the baggage handler. Serengetti pushed a path through the crowd, and the two of them stood there, looking at the parrot. It was standing on the center of the carousel, just out of reach.

It took Cozz only a few seconds to make an identification. "What we have here, Serengetti, is a greater sulfur-crested cockatoo."

"Certainly looks like a parrot to me," replied the baggage handler.

"This is definitely a 'greater'; look at the feathers. I'll get someone to call the SPCA to help us catch it — this is positively an illegal immigrant."

The parrot flew off. After a couple of circuits of the terminal building, it landed on the top of one of the high metal beams in the main hall. The airport had virtually come to a standstill by this time and no one was buying or selling tickets.[3]

One of the audience claimed that he knew where to get some lettuce. A member of the airport staff rigged a net to a pole used for cleaning windows while Cozzolina and some of the others tried a variety of bird calls. The Port Authority official got a rubber band and some paper clips; he was going to try to shoot at the parrot with a makeshift slingshot. The officer of the Society for the Prevention of Cruelty to Animals finally turned up; decided that there was nothing he could do then, and went away for lunch. Cozz kept trying. He theorized that the parrot had been smuggled in a suitcase and had perhaps chewed its way out because it was hungry. Eventually the man from the SPCA returned from lunch and promptly caught the parrot. It bit him. Cozz, who by now had identified how the bird had arrived, ended his day by taking it to Baltimore and arresting the owner.

Cozzolina will always be known in the U.S. Customs Service for his parrot story. It has much to do with the way he tells it; standing, arms waving, and punctuating it with hoots of laughter. Yet he tried hard to maintain his interest in high tech, even while performing other Customs duties, which involved anything from fraud to the smuggling of endangered species. "For a time, under Carter," he said, "endangered species were a priority. I was pulling panthers out of oil cans. There were no resources for high tech and very little interest." Certainly he knew what he meant by high tech. "Guns? I thought we could forget guns. If they don't get them from us, they'll get them from somewhere. But this! This is national security!"

He and two other agents set up a short-lived team to try to put a stop to the high-tech drain, and Cozz even went to the headquarters of the National Security Agency, at Fort George Meade, in Maryland, to gather information. But there was neither manpower nor funding. And, even more important, at the Customs office in the Treasury building there was the low priority accorded to high-technology smuggling. So in July of 1980 the three-man team disbanded, and Cozzolina was sent to Newark as part of an internal Customs probe and afterward joined a team in Florida, tasked with fighting the cocaine traffic.

"Customs has always been an agency without a mission," said a senior government official. The service had, he observed, always fought everyone else in government. There is a story about the Customs Service that many old hands remember as typical of such infighting. In 1974, Customs officials began patrolling the Mexican border. The Immigration and Naturalization Service had been active on the same border for very much longer, and the Immigration men began to declare that Customs was so badly prepared that they did not even know where the border actually was. The Customs agents could not speak Spanish. The radios carried by the agencies worked on different frequencies. Matters came to a head when there was a shoot-out, not with illegal immigrants or smugglers, but between men of the two agencies.[4]

Founded under the aegis of the Treasury Department in 1789 as America's first federal law enforcement agency, the Customs Service saved the nation from bankruptcy in the early years by collecting import duties. Customs revenue paid the Revolutionary War debt and for nearly 125 years provided the only source of income for the government. Even in its early days, the duties of the U.S. Customs Service were varied. It allocated pensions for the military, recorded statistics on imports and exports, and collected hospital fees for sick and disabled seamen. In 1870 the Special Agency Service — the forerunner of the Customs Office of Investigations — was formed. From then on, the prevention and detection of fraud was among its assignments.

The prevention of smuggling had been one of its very first tasks. The job became enormous during Prohibition, but Customs lost the assignment in 1933, when Prohibition was repealed. During the 1960s, the service launched the war against drugs, but in 1973 President Richard Nixon, under a reorganization plan, set up the Drug Enforcement Administration and relieved the service of one of its most important assignments — as well as five hundred agents. Customs was ordered not to investigate any major cases; all the important leads and information had to be passed to the new agency. The move still causes some bitterness.

In addition to its own statutes, Customs enforces more than four hundred provisions of law on behalf of forty federal agencies. It is even assigned to combat the illicit art trade. Among its more famous agents, Customs claims Herman Melville, who was an officer in New York in the middle of the nineteenth century, and Nathaniel Hawthorne, who was a Customs officer in Boston. Hawthorne seems not to have enjoyed the work. Describing his job to a friend, he wrote, "I have no reason to doubt my capacity to fulfill the duties, for I don't know what they are."

The two agents sat in the unmarked sedan and trained their binoculars on the Ilyushin passenger jet. As it turned onto its allocated stand, the blue Aeroflot insignia came into view. The sedan was parked as unobtrusively as possible, giving the agents a good view of the aircraft, though they could see little else of the vast, sprawling airfield. The agent in the driver's seat dropped the binoculars into his lap and said, "What do we do now?"

"We wait," said his superior. The Ilyushin stood in isolation, its engines still running, untroubled by the usual scurry of service vehicles. After a few minutes a forward door opened some cautious inches and then halfway. A uniformed figure peered out before disappearing again. The motor of the sedan was also running. The day was bright but bitterly cold, and the two agents had been at their observation point for nearly an hour; the Soviet jet was late. Occasionally, they would wind down the windows to demist the interior. Within seconds, they would begin to shiver and the windows would be wound back up again.[5]

The agents watched as the passengers descended the aircraft steps and got into the ground transport bus, which then shut its doors and moved slowly away in the direction of the main Dulles terminal building. Through their binoculars, the agents noticed a few more passengers coming down the aircraft steps. These got into Soviet embassy cars, which had just driven into view from a different direction. Suitcases were put into trunks; the doors closed. The cars moved away from the plane, but instead of going to the terminal building, they went toward a side entrance used only by airport service personnel.

Bill Rudman, never easily surprised, was excited by what he had just seen. He had been head of U.S. Customs at Dulles International Airport, Washington, for only a few weeks when one of his team told him that he ought to get out on the apron when the Aeroflot jet arrived and watch what was going on. "You've got to do something about it," the agent had told him. The twice-weekly Aeroflot planes had previously flown into New York, but after the invasion of Afghanistan, the unions at JFK had refused to service the jets. The Soviets then asked whether the flights could be redirected to Dulles, but none of the unions would service them there, either. So it was agreed the Soviets could service their own aircraft, using personnel from their Washington embassy. From then on, the Russian planes undertook "hot landings," which meant a quick turnaround. The engines would be kept running during the stop, and refueling would take place in Newfoundland on the way home. Because of the short time the plane was on the ground, the Soviet personnel had passes allowing them to use the service entrance to the airport. It seemed to Rudman, that cold day in November 1980, that the Soviets were making good use of them.

There were never any doubts in the minds of his colleagues that William Nicholas Rudman was heading for the top. His fellow agents were proud to have a Harvard lawyer among their number. "You'd never know it," said one; "he covers his brilliance with crudity." Rudman certainly had an unorthodox background for a Customs agent. While teaching ancient history at a Boston school, he decided to supplement his income by getting a part-time job at Boston University as a campus policeman. "I got bitten," he says. After a spell in the Bureau of Narcotics, he moved on to get a law degree at Harvard and a graduate law degree at Suffolk. Just before his Dulles posting, he spent seven years with Interpol in Paris.

With his usual forethought, Rudman decided he would not act immediately on what he had seen on the apron at Dulles. "We decided on a sudden hit, no warning. We would lull them into a false sense of security. I wanted to be sure I was covered. I wanted support." He decided to wait until after President Reagan's inauguration in January 1981. What worried Rudman was that no other government agency seemed concerned about the Soviet jet. Within a month he learned that there was, in fact, considerable interest: the plane was suspected of flying over the nuclear submarine base at Groton, Connecticut.

Tuesday, May 12, 1981, saw Bill Rudman in the Washington headquarters on the fifth floor of the Treasury building. He was with his deputy, Bill Rohde, and they were getting a briefing from a specialist on the exact status of a diplomatic pouch. They had begun preparing the ground. It was a beautiful spring day, bright and windy; they were going to enjoy the drive back to Dulles. On their way, a call came over the car radio. Would Rudman meet two men in the main airport parking lot immediately? He and Rohde lost no time. When they got to the lot the two men were waiting. The four of them walked along slowly together. "Will you do today's flight?" Rudman was asked. The men were from another government agency, with which Rudman had already been in touch. He later recalled that it was the hardest decision he had ever had to make. It was already 3:00 P.M., and the Aeroflot plane was due in half an hour. He decided to continue the walk with Rohde. They quickly went through the consequences: they would be going in blind; they did not have time to "run up the permission flag." And yet they had been told that "it would be a good day."

In less than ten minutes, Rudman had made up his mind. He walked to the terminal and found a pay phone. He rang his immediate superior in Baltimore and told him what he was going to do. "Jesus Christ!" the superior said. "Good luck!" and hung up. Rudman gathered as many agents as he could in the limited time left. Within minutes he was conducting a briefing with fifteen agents in the cramped office of the Customs inspector. He was getting lucky. The Soviet jet was late. Shortly before five, an inspector brought in the aircraft's manifest and handed it to Rudman. There were three items of interest. One piece of cargo was described as "radar receiver processing equipment," with the note "no license required." The second was a device used for measuring radioactivity. It had a commodity control number. Rudman went to check the index; there was no such number. The third item was described as a fertilizer valve.

The jet would be leaving Dulles in twenty minutes. Rudman watched the last outgoing passengers get into the bus that would take them to the plane. Then he returned to join his agents. As the bus pulled out of the bay and started toward the Ilyushin, eight cars appeared from nowhere and spread across the apron. One blocked the path of the bus, and the others headed for the jet. Pulling athwart the nose wheel, one of the sedans stopped the plane from moving. Rudman was in the lead vehicle. Before it had come to a halt, his door was open, and he ran up the aircraft steps. Rohde was behind him. Following Rohde were fourteen FBI agents from the Foreign Counterintelligence Department, some of whom were fluent in Russian.

Rohde went straight to the flight deck. The pilot stood, reached into the bulkhead, and pulled out a black automatic pistol. Rohde grabbed the man's wrist and took the gun away. An FBI agent pulled four more holstered guns out of a small cubbyhole in the bulkhead. The agent removed one from its holster; it was a black, 9-mm. 8-shot Makarov with a red star on the black handle — standard issue to Aeroflot flight crews. Inside the holster was a folded piece of paper. It was then, one agent later remembered, that "the Russians went crazy." The pilot pushed past the men and went into the toilet next to the cabin. He came back with a Russian Air Force colonel's uniform jacket and started to pull it on. He told them he used to be Khrushchev's personal pilot; he would not be treated this way.

Rudman had gone in the opposite direction from the flight deck.

The cabin crew was standing at the back of the plane, shouting loudly in Russian. Within a matter of seconds, a Soviet vice-consul (one was always present when a plane landed) pushed his way up the aisle. He was in his late thirties and wore a brown, ill-fitting polyester jacket. He was furious. He told Rudman to get off the plane, which was a diplomatic area. Rudman replied that he was aboard a commercial airliner and was conducting a routine Customs search. "I willl use force if necessary," Rudman said. The passengers had been sent back to the terminal to wait. Rudman went down to the apron. "We just pulled the cargo from the plane," one agent remembered. Nothing that had diplomatic seals was opened. There were several of these crates and boxes, and the agents speculated that they probably contained the most interesting technology. The Customs agents were faced with the task of opening more than a hundred boxes. What they did find were dozens of luxury consumer goods: food processors, electric can openers, stereo systems, and videotape players.

The cargo was spread all over the ground by the time the Soviet consul general arrived. Rudman was told that a complaint had already been lodged with the Department of State. He had created an international incident. Rudman kept on with his work. "The Russian started waving his credentials in front of Rudman's face," said one of the other agents. "He called him a thug and a bandit." Rudman looked at the Russian. Then he shouted to him to get out of the way — he was interfering with a lawful government operation.

Rudman was being harassed not by the Soviets alone. It seemed that most of the United States Government wanted to speak to him on the telephone. Calls were coming in over his personal radio, through the car radios, and to the telephone of the commercial airline building nearest the jet. Government officials had even tried calling the Baltimore Customs office, but no one there knew what was happening.

The Aeroflot jet finally left Dulles at 7:00 P.M. It had been delayed for two hours. When the time came to reload the cargo, Rudman was told by the Soviets that his agents would have to do it themselves; their own personnel would not touch it. Rudman was also told that if the cargo was loaded by amateurs, he could put the aircraft at risk. Rudman ordered his agents to start reloading.

The Soviet plane departed without the seized technology. The "radar receiver processing equipment," which the manifest had stated did not need a license, did indeed require one. It had been issued by the Department of Commerce. The problem there was sloppy paperwork. The dosimeter, used for measuring the amount of radiation picked up by workers in nuclear industries, had a commodity control number; the wrong number had been typed on the manifest. As for the "fertilizer valve," it took government experts forty-eight hours to find out that it was part of a . . . fertilizer valve. It fitted the descriptions, and no license was needed. "It was a circuit board for a gigantic valve in a fertilizer plant," said Rudman. The technology was eventually all given back to the Soviet authorities.

The State Department received a formal protest from the Soviet Government, which charged the United States with "terror and banditry." The official news agency TASS said there had been "outrageous provocation." The Soviet crew held a press conference in Moscow and accused Customs agents of endangering the jet by opening instrument panels and equipment access hatches and tampering with navigational equipment that was kept in a baggage compartment. William T. Archey, the acting head of Customs at this time, stated at a Washington press conference that his agents had acted on an inaccurate tip that material on board was defense-related. But he refused to say that the raid was a mistake.

On May 14, 1981, *Pravda* carried a story on the Aeroflot raid. It claimed that all baggage on board had been opened, even the items carrying diplomatic seals. Knives had been used and some damage was done. The paper stated that flight deck navigation panels were opened and equipment of "defense" significance had been seized, including spare navigational technology required by U.S. civil aviation regulations, which had been brought back to the United States for repair under warranty by its American supplier.

Rudman continued to defend the raid. Among its positive results, he said, was that the Russians never again used the side gate at the airport. Other agents said they believed there was a very good reason for the raid's being carried out on that particular day. Although they were not privy to everything that went on in the flight deck during the search, one senior investigator has said that the piece of paper found in the gun holster was in some way involved with the flights over the submarine base at Groton.

The day following the raid, Rudman was called to Washington headquarters. The meeting was not a confrontation. He was asked for an account of what had happened. Weeks later, he was told that Edwin Meese, then counselor to the President, had told Treasury Secretary Donald Regan that the raid was just the sort of operation the administration had been looking for. "From then on," said Rudman, "everyone became interested in the problem of high technology." The raid changed the history of the U.S. Customs Service. It created the right political climate for the birth — five months later — of Operation Exodus, Customs' counteroffensive against high-tech smuggling. The "agency without a mission" had finally found one and was going to fight to keep it.

Bill Rudman became Washington head of Operation Exodus. On his office wall hangs a framed portrait of the long-serving Soviet ambassador to Washington, Anatoly Dobrynin. Written along the top of the photograph is the sentence "Rudman, *ty sukin syn, proklyatye ruki proch ot nashego samolyota!*" It was a gift from his colleagues. The message means "Rudman, you son of a bitch, get your goddamn hands off our airplane!"

Operation Exodus began in October 1981, with a massive cargo-inspection program. In the first six months more than $20.5 million worth of goods were seized by port inspectors throughout the country. Prior to the operation, there had been little inspection of outbound cargo, but this procedure was to be the backbone of the new program. Shippers had four days after cargo left to complete their export declarations. By seizing suspect consignments, Customs could, with the help of the Department of Commerce, determine whether licenses were in order. Fraudulent declarations could be isolated. The Department of Defense, in an unusual move, financed the operation with no less than $28 million. Surveillance vehicles were purchased; secure telephones and Teletype machines and digital voice radios were installed. Customs was getting into the area of counterintelligence.

Until that time, the role of Customs had been to respond to requests from the Office of Export Administration of the Commerce Department to undertake searches, seize cargo, and make arrests.

When Cozzolina was asked for ideas on an export control program, he said that a major part of the operation should entail developing sources of information within the high-tech industry. The best approach, he suggested, would be to gain the cooperation of the industry; agents should visit manufacturers and distributors and warn about the need to look out for unusual orders. He was brought in on the new project, becoming a section chief in the New York Intelligence branch. A national campaign got under way to contact manufacturers, exporters, shippers, brokers, and freight forwarders to alert them to the possibility of diversions.

After a year of running Operation Exodus, the Customs Service concluded that the majority of diversions were then taking place through Western Europe, and the key countries were Switzerland, Austria, and Finland. Significantly, Switzerland imported five times more technology from the United States than from the Soviet Union. The next stage was to draw on the experience of Customs agents stationed abroad. While carrying out investigations, they could also establish useful contacts in European capitals.

By the end of 1983, Rudman could confidently assert that there had been a complete shift. Critical technology transfer was now "right up there with narcotics." "We had to be turned around and made to face the other way. We had always looked at what was coming in; now we're looking at what's going out." Like most Exodus agents, he uses the narcotics analogy. "There are no infinite networks, as there are with drugs. We have a finite number of manufacturers." Customs had forced the techno-bandits to become more devious. The oft-repeated criticism — taken up by industry managers tired of the delays caused by port seizures — that Customs agents did not know the difference between a microchip and a potato chip, was no longer valid. Increased training and experience had changed all that, Rudman declared. Tactics would soon change too, under a secret plan to "bug" electronic equipment leaving the country. Project Rampart, whose development cost $2 million, called for the insertion of electronic tags into high-technology products, allowing Customs agents, equipped with sensors, to detect items subject to control. The system was similar to antitheft devices used in libraries and stores. Within a few months, the operation was gaining national media attention. According to a *Time* magazine story of February 27, 1984, "Since Operation Exodus began in

1981, the Customs Service has seized 2851 illegal shipments of defense-related equipment worth $177 million. The Soviet Union is the leading destination, but U.S. officials say that smuggling to China is on the rise."

It was on January 27, 1982, that the U.S. Customs Service proudly launched the Exodus Command Center in the Treasury building on Washington's Pennsylvania Avenue. The center was one more indication of how important the offensive against the techno-bandits had become. There would, from then on, be a twenty-four-hour contact point for inspectors, who could telephone in the details of any suspect shipments they had seized. It was from here that Exodus was to be masterminded. It would provide operational guidance by special agents, inspectors, import specialists, patrol officers, and program analysts — all coordinating inspection and investigation.

Sitting and waiting for the first call to come in that Thursday was a veteran inspector, Pat O'Brien, who had lobbied hard for the new center. "We had to expand," he said. O'Brien, director of the General Investigations Division, was one of the senior officials who thought that techno-bandits were still not being given the priority they deserved. Typically, he wanted to be in the center himself to see how it operated. It was a long day and a long wait. At 11:15 P.M. an inspector called from Chicago's O'Hare Airport. He had detained a shipment that he thought very suspicious, something that appeared to be a highly intricate piece of electronics. For the very first call, it was a disappointment. When Customs eventually received the licensing information from the Department of Commerce, the shipment turned out to be integrated-circuit boards that were being shipped to Europe quite legally.

O'Brien was later to become assistant regional commissioner for enforcement in New York, a newly created position. His office in the World Trade Center, Building Six, has a telescope pointing toward the East River. A large chart of the KGB directorates stands in one corner. Earlier in his career, O'Brien had not been so enthusiastic about technology-transfer cases. He had been an agent for only two and a half years when, in 1968, he was ordered to track down a suspected techno-smuggler. He tackled the job with characteristic enthusiasm.

The operation, requested by the Department of Commerce, began on October 23. That month, O'Brien was part of a team of six agents whose assignment was to follow a wealthy businessman, a naturalized German, who lived on Long Island. "There were lots of trips to the Amityville post office. He was apparently sending out electronic equipment to West Germany through the mail," said O'Brien. It was a loophole he was to be reminded of in years to come. Up to the end of the month, two hundred man hours were spent watching the suspect. In November, Customs agents watched for a further six hundred hours, and by the end of the year, a grand total of twelve hundred man hours had been clocked up.

If there is one thing that Pat O'Brien really enjoys, it is surveillance. "It's what I like more than anything in the job, and it's what I am really good at," he says. "We were running around following him everywhere. At one point we were coming up to the Amityville rail crossing, he went across, and the gates were coming down. We nearly got hit by a Long Island train." But the case was a disappointment. Customs was told by Commerce to forget the case, and it became, as Pat O'Brien put it, "a pissing match between the two agencies." At that time he did not understand the reasons why.[6]

O'Brien is a New Yorker. It is evident in the way he talks and, like all natives of New York, it is there that he wants to be. His Irish father was a Customs inspector for thirty years, and O'Brien apparently never thought of doing anything else. It would come as some surprise to his colleagues to know that before joining the service, he had worked as a physicist. He is the sort of man who can charm the birds out of the trees. He can also put the fear of God into his agents. "He will not tolerate mistakes," said one. "One slip and you are off his team ... and it is his team, no one else's." Prematurely gray, he looks older than his forty-one years. He works, say his colleagues; he does nothing but work.

He believes that the Customs Service now has the ability to get to grips with techno-contraband. "In comparison, fraud is boring. For the first time in ten years we can command an investigation. We can give this something no one else can." Like his fellow agents he remembers the loss of five hundred people to the Drug Enforcement Administration. "For ten years with narcs it got worse and worse. We've finally found a unique role." When he briefed Cozzolina, one

of his new section chiefs, he told him, "Cozz, I want three things —
Sovs, Sovs, and Sovs."

The head of Customs, who fought for and now directs the new mission, is Commissioner William von Raab. Von Raab is credited by
agents with having made the service an up-beat agency that people
are desperately eager to join. He has given it a new and exciting
image, and he is out to change the history of the U.S. Customs Service. Von Raab, a charming and handsome man, was once described
by an agent in Silicon Valley as being "short like me — and we always see eye to eye." He believes in the direct approach: "We have
got religion on high tech," he says. Generally called by his last
name, the commissioner also has acquired a nickname among a select group of agents working on Exodus: Elephant Balls, because he
is afraid of no one. For von Raab, Exodus was a veteran combat
unit, ordered into the field.

From his large suite of offices that fits the description "mahogany
row," von Raab has a big say in how Exodus is run. He keeps
abreast of the current cases and can talk about past successes in
great detail. What he considers the "flow" of high technology to the
Soviets is first on any list of topics he agrees to discuss when interviewed by journalists. The war against narcotics is the last. In
speeches, he leaves his audience in no doubt about his priorities. In
1983, he told the Washington Rotary Club: "From where I sit, I can
see what has been happening to our nation's technological superiority. We in the U.S. and the other NATO countries are facing a serious national security threat. A threat from the most evil government
on the face of the earth, the Soviet Union. To further the development of its terrorist military machine, it is stealing some of our most
advanced weapons-systems technologies."

Von Raab was sworn in as commissioner the same month that Exodus was launched. He is a graduate of Yale and the University of
Virginia Law School. He began his career as a securities lawyer in
New York and advised the chairman of a capital management institution on strategic planning. He was also vice-president for administration and financial consultant to New York University. His
government posts have been varied. He was consultant to the director of the Bureau of East-West Trade. Later he became director of
the pay board for the Cost of Living Council. He entered Customs

after having joined a Washington law firm, Haskell, Slaughter, Young & Lewis.

Von Raab puts in long hours on the job, and he likes to know everything that is going on in the service. He usually saves the paper-work until the end of the day. When the majority of his support staff has gone, he settles down in a quiet office and works through his files. One day in early January 1983, he was doing just that when the telephone rang. The caller refused to give his name but started to tell him about some computer equipment that was about to be shipped to Bulgaria. "It was hot shit," he said later. As soon as he put down the telephone, von Raab rushed up the three flights of stairs from his office to the Exodus Command Center on the sixth floor.[7] He burst into the room — to the surprise of the agents working at their computer terminals — and waved his notes in the air.

The call resulted in an investigation known as the Printemps case, and Commissioner von Raab's name was put on the inspection report under "examining officer." The inquiry lasted ten months. On November 3, 1983, two Californians from Orange County were indicted for conspiracy, illegal exportation, and making false statement to government agencies. According to court records, the conspiracy started in June 1981, when two Bulgarians — since indicted for conspiracy but still fugitives from justice — wanted a centrifugal spinning device used to produce the magnetic coatings for computer storage discs. These were to be shipped to a disc-coating facility, DSO "ISOT" ZMD, in Pazarjik, Bulgaria. Ognian Bozarov was described as the director of a buying group called Industrial Cooperation (INCO), and Assen Koinov was described as the "project manager." They had met with one of the defendants, Edward King, aged fifty-two, the president of a Yorba Linda export company called Printemps, in Amsterdam in June of that year.[8]

Assistant U.S. Attorney William Fahey later noted that two of the devices, worth a total of $100,000, had been shipped to Bulgaria before the investigation began. Two pieces of equipment were, however, seized at Los Angeles International Airport after von Raab's tip-off. Von Raab said later: "If this guy hadn't gotten to me, the stuff would have left the country. The guy on the phone told me that he had tried to interest the Commerce Department in what was going on but no one would listen."

6

COMMERCE VS. CUSTOMS

OUT OF NOWHERE, on a plain near the banks of the Kama River, close to the western foothills of the Ural Mountains, the Soviets planned to construct the largest truck factory in the world.

It was a mammoth project, devised by Leonid Brezhnev in 1970, when he was at the height of his power in the party and the government. And this memorial to the pursuit of détente would be built with the help of American technology.

The Kama River Complex — Kama Avtozavod, or KAMAZ for short — was to incorporate a futuristic new city for the 400,000 workers who would be needed to produce 150,000 trucks and 250,000 diesel engines a year once full capacity was achieved. Naberezhnye Chelny, a small riverside town with twenty thousand inhabitants and a back-country Russian name that sounds like something out of a Slavonic equivalent of *Huckleberry Finn,* would be sacrificed. The Soviet Union had a pressing need for diesel trucks to replace its less economical gasoline models, and in quantities that would take the strain off its increasingly overloaded railroad system. When completed, the Kama plant was to be twice as large as the Ford Motor Foundry in Flat Rock, Michigan.

On the eve of the 26th Communist Party Congress in 1981, Brezhnev sent a telegram to the workers there: "Like the ploughing of the virgin lands, Kama by right will enter the annals of the outstanding achievements of the Soviet people." His words still adorn a huge billboard on a Kama highway: "Years will pass, but all Soviet people will proudly recall the feat of labor on the Kama." The portrait that went with the resounding slogan has been quietly removed.[1]

The party predictably gave the name Brezhnev to the emerging city alongside the huge forty-square-mile works, and the place soon had a reputation for well-stocked shops, ultramodern housing, and — most important — premium wages. Young workers flocked to the site faster than the planners had anticipated. The average age of the workforce is still only twenty-eight. An underlying reason for its popularity is that it is far enough away from the drudgery of Moscow to be considered intellectually free by Soviet standards.

But Kama was not without its problems. It was said to be too ambitious from the start. In 1982, output was only eighty-five thousand trucks. One of the contributory factors to this slow start was that the plant relied from the start on American cooperation. There were 250 individual contracts worth $430 million for the sale of the foundry, the engine designs, the assembly lines, and an IBM 370/158 to be used for production control.[2] In the words of Yakov S. Pessin, a Kama official who handled foreign contracts, "We've had a hell of a time keeping track of all your sanctions."[3]

In the West there had been controversy over the plant since the first Soviet request, in 1970, for American technology for Kama. Both the Ford Motor Company and the Mack Truck Company negotiated to serve as general contractors, but withdrew after Department of Defense warnings. The DOD was concerned that the trucks made there would "find their way down the Ho Chi Minh trail."[4]

The early seventies were a time of détente between the superpowers, and by 1972, when the trade agreement between the United States and the USSR was signed, both the Commerce and State Departments were encouraging U.S. firms to participate in the project. Whether there should be cooperation and to what extent was discussed at all levels of the United States Government. Eventually, the decision to approve licenses for Kama equipment was made by President Richard Nixon, a policy later sustained by President Gerald Ford.

One of the lawyers involved in drawing up the contracts between the suppliers and the Russians has said that the possibility that the trucks might be used by the military could have been a factor for consideration by the government. "The technology they wanted was available worldwide anyway," he said.[5] This was echoed by senior government officials involved in the Kama case. One explained, "Nixon decided to take the risk. Anyone giving it ten seconds' thought would realize you can't control the use of trucks in the Soviet Union anyway." He went on: "This is the difficulty with trade controls. You always have to weigh the risk. During the Nixon and Ford administrations and in the early Carter days, there was a belief that trade with the Soviets should be expanded. Hard-liners now find that unacceptable."[6] Just how unacceptable was to be made clear in the late seventies.

At 2:00 A.M. on Thursday, May 24, 1979, a tough, abrasive, and ambitious Commerce official blew the whistle on the Kama River truck plant. From a witness stand behind closed doors on Capitol Hill, he told a House Armed Services Subcommittee that the CIA had reported that Kama was already producing trucks for the military. He also accused his superiors at the Commerce Department of "covering up."[7]

Suddenly the Kama controversy was "one of the most vivid examples of U.S. commercial technology being diverted for military use in the Soviet Union."[8] It quickly became the primary illustration of the need for increased export controls and for an export policy that took into account dual-use technology — commercial equipment with military potential.

The Commerce official was Lawrence J. Brady, who had tried for the Republican nomination to the Senate from New Hampshire in 1980. He had an interesting background. He received his B.A. in political science from Catholic University in Washington and, between 1971 and 1974, was a senior staff member of the White House Council on International Economic Policy. Before that, he had been at the State Department as an economist in the Office of International Trade.

After his broadside to the House Armed Services Subcommittee, he became known as the technology-transfer whistleblower. In one afternoon, he made himself a large number of enemies and changed the course of his career. Brady had been at Commerce since 1975 and had been acting director of the Office of Export Administration. Some Washington observers theorized that his blast was in retaliation for not having been made permanent director. His superiors were staggered by his outburst. Stanley Marcuss, Deputy Assistant Secretary for Industry and Trade at the time, strenuously denied a cover-up. "We did not know about the secret intelligence reports. We were shocked that he had given the information to Congress and not to us." He added ruefully, "Brady actually signed some of the Kama licenses himself."[9]

Brady's testimony to the subcommittee is still classified. But it has emerged that he went beyond his revelations on Kama: he said that the national security export system was "a total shambles."[10] Brady now describes the reaction to his outburst as "like all hell breaking loose." He says he was told in a telephone call the next morning that he was fired. And he claims that there were attempts to push him sideways and to violate his rights as a career officer.

But Brady did not give up. In early December of 1979, he was back as a congressional witness, this time before the International Finance Subcommittee of the Senate Banking Committee. His testimony was just as explosive: "Over a period of about ten years, the system [of national security export controls] has been gradually dismantled to the point where the Soviet Union and other controlled countries are now acquiring some of the most sophisticated Western technology and diverting it to military forces." The Commerce Department, he said, had "failed to adequately protect the national security interests of the United States."[11] In a written memorandum to the committee he noted that end-use restrictions made it plain that the Kama River truck plant was going to be used only for civilian vehicles. In the face of mounting evidence the United States had not enforced available sanctions against the Soviets.

Commerce continued to assert that military use would not constitute a violation of the law, because the licenses contained no restriction about the use of the trucks or the engines. The department strenuously denied Brady's accusations about export controls and issued a statement saying his charges were false, misleading, and irresponsible. Although Commerce Department officials believed Brady had exceeded his authority by trying to shape policy rather than carry it out, they denied that he had been demoted because of it.

The Civil Service Merit Systems Protection Board recommended at the end of 1979 that Brady be restored to "full duties and responsibilities commensurate with [his] salary and grade level as a member of the Senior Executive."[12] However, on Monday, January 21, 1980, Lawrence Brady resigned. He did not go quietly. In his letter to Commerce Secretary Philip M. Klutznick, he said he had been "persecuted, demoted, and the subject of intense personal attacks," because he had spoken out over Kama. The resignation was announced at a press conference sponsored by the American Security Council, a body that advocates hard-line defense policies against the Soviets.

At the conference, Brady produced a Commerce Department internal memorandum, which he claimed would create a large loophole in President Carter's embargo. Dated Friday, January 18, it outlined five proposed "hardship exceptions" to the high-technology export ban to the Soviet Union. Exceptions included maintenance of hospital equipment and of American-built aircraft owned by Western European airlines at the Moscow airport. Also included was maintenance of computer equipment under service contracts. What had prompted his action, Brady later asserted, was what he saw as a lack of consistency in policy. Controls could not be administered by the Commerce Department because it did not have the attention and resources it needed.

The Carter administration, apart from Zbigniew Brzezinski, National Security Adviser, and one of his assistants, Major General William Odom, were not as concerned with technology-transfer problems as they should have been. Brady also charged that the President's directives were not being implemented.[13] The Department of Commerce, he claimed, had usurped congressional authority and had convinced several administrators that trade controls were impossible to implement.[14]

Détente was to blame for the downgrading of the export control department, Brady said. Licenses had been approved for technology that was being turned against national security, and the Kama truck incident was merely one case in point. He also accused the Nixon administration of having been less than frank with the U.S. allies over Kama licensing. "We told the Europeans there would be no military use when the licenses came up. If they're saying they knew about the possibility of military use, they're covering their ass. They all lost out on the deal in the early seventies." He claimed the Defense Intelligence Agency knew of military production at the plant in 1975 and in 1977, but because neither this agency nor the CIA trusted the Commerce Department, the information "never perked to the top." Even after military use was known, the administration had approved a "very large computer for the plant."[15] So concerned was he about the "total shambles," Brady said, that he became the "White House spy in the Commerce Department. The department just could not understand how the White House knew so much." President Jimmy Carter, he said, was being treated like a licensing officer. "Everyone, State, Commerce, Defense, was appealing to him on individual cases."[16]

Until this time, the various official views of export controls and the Kama controversy had remained out of the public eye, and the scandal might well have died down. Certainly, the Commerce Department did not seem eager to continue the debate on Kama. Senior officials there were accused later of having undertaken a "massive campaign" to convince Congress there was nothing improper going on.[17]

On December 14, 1979, secret CIA reports on Kama were sent to Kempton Jenkins, Deputy Assistant Secretary for East-West Trade, Commerce Department. They had been prepared by the CIA's USSR–Eastern Europe Division, Office of Economic Research. "It is seldom possible to describe a specific Soviet truck model as purely military or purely nonmilitary.... Nearly all Soviet trucks are dual-use vehicles serving both the military and civilian needs.... Most of the rural road system of the USSR is so primitive ... that during much of the year ... large sections ... are considered to be 'roadless'.... This creates a need for all-wheel drive vehicles for many civilian activities." The report went on to say that as the USSR had no privately owned trucks, all trucks were allocated by the government to industrial, agricultural, or military use. The state could mobilize civilian trucks in support of military emergencies.[18]

The controversy still did not die down; indeed, it got much worse. Fourteen days after the CIA reports had been sent to the Commerce

Department, the USSR invaded Afghanistan. It became public knowledge that among the trucks used to carry the troops were a number from the Kama River plant. The U.S. Government retaliated by suspending all licenses for Soviet exports, among them eight hundred for high-technology products, like spare parts for the IBM 370/158 production control computer at Kama.

The administration also had to make a decision about a request from the Soviet Union for two more assembly lines at the Kama River plant. The Commerce Department held that the line was old technology and did not require a license. Further, the department stated that the use of the trucks in the invasion did not mean control regulations had been violated. The only end-use restriction imposed on technology in Kama referred to the IBM computer, and that involved only its capacity and capability.[19] However, on May 6, 1980, after it had become clear that the Russians were not going to pull out of Afghanistan, the President imposed foreign policy controls on the assembly lines, which meant the loss of an $8.5 million contract for the Ingersoll-Rand Company.[20] (In January 1983, an attempt to export an assembly line illegally was foiled.[21])

The winds of change had begun to blow. The Carter administration, after months of political infighting, had finally been forced to take a tougher stance on export policy. For some, the controls were not enough. "Who are the President and the Commerce Department trying to fool?" asked Senator Jake Garn of Utah in the fall of 1980. "The new guidelines imposing sanctions on the Soviet Union are riddled with loopholes wide enough to drive a Kama River truck through.... Soviet military planners will suffer only temporary inconveniences until trade resumes; the real losers, however, will be the American people."[22] And presidential candidate Ronald Reagan had begun to use the technology-transfer issue in his campaign.

On June 13, 1981, the crusading technology whistleblower was finally given the power to carry out his mission. Lawrence Brady was named an Assistant Secretary in the department from which he had resigned eighteen months earlier. He became Commerce's senior political appointee, in charge of the Office of Trade Administration, which supervised licensing and enforcement. A determined man was back in the government department that, he had said, "will always be deficient in its implementation of long-term export control policies as mandated by the Export Administration Act." He had added, in that earlier testimony, that "one department cannot be expected to administer export promotion and control policies. . . . An official is always forced to wear two hats."[23] Just how difficult it would be to wear those hats — even within the Reagan administration, which was so sympathetic with his views — Lawrence Brady was to find out.

Technology transfer and the control of trade became subjects of heated debate during the two and a half years Brady held his post. With the Reagan administration determined to stop what it considered a massive leak of technology to the Soviet bloc, the issue became popular with the powerful and ambitious. And the department that came under the strongest attack was Commerce. There were more congressional reports on its activities than on any other department. Its current and past officials were subjected to vociferous attacks on Capitol Hill for having allowed the leakage of technology, not only by approving licenses but by failing adequately to enforce controls.

Lawrence Brady, who was dedicated to bringing about change, soon found himself at the receiving end of a barrage of criticism. Within the space of two months in the late spring of 1982, two investigative reports on the Commerce Department's activities regarding export controls were published. Both condemned licensing requirements and procedures and both criticized the department's efforts at stopping illegal transfers. A General Accounting Office report concluded that the export license applications could be eliminated without affecting national security. It also found that Commerce was not fulfilling its responsibility in ensuring that exporters abide by license conditions. There was a "backlog of unresolved cases" of intelligence investigations into illegal transfer.[24]

The second report went further. It said that the Compliance Division, the office that handled the enforcement of controls, "had no overall strategy to stop technology leakage." It had insufficient, untrained staff and inadequate management. It had no secure files, and the offices were "crowded, ill-maintained, and noisy." These problems had been pointed out before, but no one had resolved them, a fact that raised doubts about the department's commitment and ability. There were seven hundred potential violation cases sitting in files — a "severe backlog."[25]

One of Brady's ambitions was to improve enforcement. "Our objective is to get a highly professional white-collar crime outfit working with the Intelligence agencies," he told Congress.[26] It was this objective — and the tenacious belief of his colleagues — that led Commerce into direct confrontation with Customs, whose determination to be in control of technology-transfer enforcement equaled the department's.

The Commerce Department still had primary responsibility for enforcement. This entailed inspecting cargo, identifying and investigating violations, administering civil penalties, and forwarding criminal cases to the Justice Department for prosecution. But the FBI, CIA, Department of State, and Customs were part of the enforcement, too. The FBI participated in its counterintelligence role, and the CIA provided information on violations abroad. The State Department assisted with enforcement work that had to be done overseas. Until the birth of Exodus, the Customs Sevice's contribution consisted of conducting searches under warrant, seizing cargo, and making arrests — Commerce officials had no powers to do this — but after the establishment of Exodus, Customs became more involved.

The seeds of what was to become a fierce confrontation were sown in 1980, when the Carter administration decided to try to strengthen controls after the Soviet invasion of Afghanistan. In June, an interagency working group was set up at Carter's request to investigate enforcement efforts.[27] By September 11, 1980, the administration had decided that enforcement should be increased. A memorandum went from the chairman of the interagency group, Robert L. Keuch, an Associate Deputy Attorney General, to all U.S. attorneys. One of the mandates of the interagency committee, he told them, was to ensure that important cases of technology transfer received priority attention. They were asked to review their investigative and enforcement procedures. The main area for concern was the shipment of sophisticated technology, goods, and data to the Communists.[28]

Four subcommittees were set up to investigate enforcement and intelligence coordination. Their findings went to the interagency group, which, in turn, reported to the National Security Council. The final report is still classified, but one of the findings was that "much needed to be done to strengthen our combined efforts in this area."[29] Throughout the meetings, arguments were put forward that there be one agency to oversee enforcement — and that that agency should be the U.S. Customs Service. In a memorandum of February 3, 1980, to National Security Adviser Brzezinski, Deputy Treasury Secretary Robert Carswell wrote that only the Customs Service had posts abroad and criminal investigative abilities. The Justice Department, too, was in favor of Customs taking over.

A letter, dated October 30, was sent to the committee chairman by Deputy Assistant Customs Commissioner William Green, and he did not mince his words. The letter, which was to become known as the Green Memo, was damning. It accused the Commerce Department of impeding cooperation in investigations, compromising Customs and foreign government sources, and damaging Customs relationships with the allies. The Commerce Department, said the Green Memo, had contributed to problems affecting the national security.

The Department of Commerce hit back. It claimed that Customs had not always responded with help when needed, that it had initiated its own investigations without telling Commerce, and that if Customs seized shipments without proper technical knowledge to support those seizures it would be harassing legitimate exporters. Commerce stressed that all export control enforcement should be under one agency — the Commerce Department's Compliance Division, where controls were a priority. Customs was responsible for enforcing a number of laws, and its priorities were constantly being reassessed.[30]

Accusation and counteraccusation continued as, during the next few years, Congress became increasingly involved. The criticism from each side was bitter, but the most damning of all for Commerce came in May 1982, after an eighteen-month investigation by Senate staff members into the behavior of the Compliance Division. One special agent employed in the Compliance Division, who had served more than twenty years as a criminal investigator, told Senate staff that "the Kremlin's spy organization, the KGB, could not have organized the Compliance Division in a way more beneficial to Soviet interests."[31]

The Senate investigators demolished the Commerce Department's claims that the Compliance Division was competent. "Our investigation found that ... it is an understaffed, poorly equipped, and in certain instances undertrained and unqualified investigative and intelligence unit." How could it carry out its function when it was overwhelmed with work? The division did not even have a "secure" telephone. Everyone knew about the problems, the Senate staff member told his committee; it was one of the worst kept secrets in the Executive Branch. But he had found no one who would come forward and tell the truth. "The highest leaders of our nation are led to believe that we have an export control capability when, in fact, we don't."[32]

Most shocking of all to the assembled senators was a revelation by a former Compliance Division investigator that he was the only person responsible for ensuring that companies adhered to former President Carter's embargo on grain sales to the Soviet Union after the invasion of Afghanistan. Senator Sam Nunn of Georgia, a member of the Committee on Governmental Affairs, remarked; "So you have a major decision by the President of the United States on a major foreign policy issue involving the United States and the Soviet Union, involving all our allies, involving the credibility of our foreign policy and economic policy throughout the world, and you have the Commerce Department assigning one individual for enforcement purposes." Senator Nunn, who later introduced legislation to amend the Export Administration Act and transfer criminal enforcement from Commerce to Customs, said, "When [President Reagan] starts talking about the export of technical equipment that aids the Soviet Union, nobody tells him that they have eight inspectors covering all the airports and ports of the country in enforcing the Export Administration Act, do they?"[33]

The investigation met with resistance by government departments. Working agents and senior officials were candid — but insisted on anonymity. Both the FBI and the Justice Department refused to help evaluate Commerce, although there was a widespread sense throughout the affected areas of government that the Compliance Division was inadequate. Senator Nunn remarked: "So the attitude generally is what the President of the United States doesn't know about the inability of his Commerce Department to carry out his own policy doesn't hurt him, right? What the Congress doesn't know doesn't hurt them?"[34] Reports on the Commerce Department's relations with the Intelligence community were just as damning. The Senate investigation found intelligence on technology transfer to be insufficient, a commitment of needed resources lacking, and the Intelligence community not organized to use information to block prohibited transfers. Intelligence sources told the Senate investigators that they had "virtually no communication with . . . Compliance regarding ongoing investigations. . . . There is a little feedback from Commerce regarding intelligence information it provides. . . . Compliance . . . rarely seeks the expertise of the intelligence community."[35]

The friction between Commerce's Compliance Division and the Customs Service eventually led to scarcely credible behavior by government officials. "Customs is doing its thing . . . Commerce is doing its thing . . . and nobody is happy and it is costing the taxpayer over thirty million dollars," remarked Representative Don Bonker of Washington State, sponsor of the House version of the bill to amend the Export Administration Act.[36]

At the receiving end of the attack, Lawrence Brady did not flinch. The official who had said export administration was a "total shambles" was unswerving in his belief that Commerce should be the major body for enforcement of the Export Administration Act at home and abroad. In February 1983, he told skeptical senators that significant strides had been taken in correcting the deficiencies that had built up during the seventies. He now believed Commerce to be the equal of Customs in most respects. The Intelligence agencies had been asked to prepare current analyses of Soviet acquisition targets and methods: these were being read regularly by Brady and his staff. Budget and manpower had been increased; for the first time technical people were being hired as licensing officers. Commerce officials were being educated in how to use the control list, prepare license applications, and examine various licenses. Thirty-five highly trained criminal investigators had been hired, and a third of a million dollars had been spent on state-of-the-art surveillance equipment.[37]

But the main change was that a new Commerce Department office had been created. The much-criticized Compliance Division had been upgraded to office status. To head the new and expanded Office of Export Enforcement, Lawrence Brady had brought on board one of the West Coast's most renowned attorneys in the technology-transfer field, the man who had prosecuted three well-known cases.[38] Theodore Wai Wu was an assistant U.S. attorney in Los Angeles, where he was assistant chief of the Criminal Division and senior trial attorney for Customs and export control violations. Wu was not unpopular with the Customs agents with whom he had been in close contact during high-tech investigations, although one said, "He tended to get overenthusiastic." The story the agent told took place during one of the trials on technology transfer.

"He kept jumping up and down and shouting 'Objection! Objection!' The judge kept saying, 'Sustained.' At one point, Wu jumped up and shouted, 'Sustained!' 'That's my line, Mr. Wu,' the judge told him."[39]

Customs agents found him knowledgeable about technology; they admired that. And he was good at explaining technological complexities to juries. Wu was a graduate of the U.S. Naval Academy and had served on active duty in weapon and engineering assignments. He had done graduate work at Tufts University and got a J.D. at Boston University Law School.

Like Bob Cozzolina, Ted Wu believed that the first line of defense in controlling technology transfer was the private sector. "Tip-offs are critical. We rely on industry to give us leads."[40] Each of the cases he had prosecuted had been a result of information from industry. One of Ted Wu's main assets was the Commerce Department's newly acquired IBM 370 computer, storing the 300,000 existing export licenses and all the new applications. It had on-line tracking for all cases to proscribed destinations and details of computer exports to Western countries. It was to be upgraded throughout 1983 to store intelligence information and details on the foreign availability of technology. Accessible from the West Coast and New York, with eventual expansion to forty-seven cities, it would enable local investigators to check both destinations and users. Lionel Olmer, Under Secretary of Commerce for International Trade, told Congress in February 1983 that information in the computer would provide valuable help for the FBI, the CIA, and the Customs Service.[41]

But the stronger the enforcement capabilities at Commerce, the more intense became the rivalry with Customs. At the heart of the dispute was the information stored on Ted Wu's computer. Customs agents complained that they were being denied access to the wealth of information in those memory banks, and this was hampering their investigations. Commerce officials were willing to give them details only on a case-by-case basis. Congress became aware of the problem in the spring of 1983. Under Secretary Olmer claimed at Senate hearings that a memorandum of understanding on sharing the information was about to be signed. However, it was a couple of months late getting off the ground.

"I understand you are negotiating the size of the table," said a senator.

"No, I don't think so," replied Olmer. "I'm not looking for a Nobel Peace Prize."

He was told it might be worth it.

"I do not believe there are any serious issues between us that would prevent us from getting a memorandum ... signed within the next week or so," replied Olmer. But he went on: "We've been criticized ... for not giving ... Customs ... information from the private sector which is given to us in the course of ... applications for export. ... There is an awful lot of proprietary information ... and we are simply not prepared to let it go without some understanding."[42]

At the center of the controversy was a clause in the Export Administration Act that protected proprietary commercial information obtained by Commerce. Customs Commissioner von Raab told Congress that the computer was closed to his agents because "apparently it contains some business confidential information." He said the use to which *he* might put the information would not cause problems. The State Department, after all, opened its files, and the Justice Department had, in fact, ruled that information that might be closed to the public was not closed to government agencies. Now, the Commerce Secretary had ruled that the information be made available; it was junior officials who were refusing to supply the data on anything other than a case-by-case basis.[43] Congress was told that the refusal by Commerce to open its files was unique to the Reagan administration. Theodore L. Thau, who from 1961 to 1972 was executive secretary of the Export Control Administration Re-

view Board, in charge of the legal aspects of export control enforcement, had shared information with other government agencies.
Thau was "surprised and shocked" that for the first time since 1949,
when the act's confidentiality provision was adopted, the question of
sharing information had arisen.[44]

The Exodus team became desperate for the licensing details. After
shipments were seized at ports of exit, the Washington Command
Center was obliged to wait until Commerce officials told them the
licensing status of the equipment: the fact that copies of licenses
were not included with shippers' export declarations infuriated
them. Commissioner von Raab did not hesitate to express their
concern. He told Congress that to speed the work of his team he did
not need validated licenses with shipments; just photocopies. Twice
a day one of his agents was obliged to walk across Washington's
14th Street from Treasury to Commerce, carrying details of the
shipments seized by his team. "Commerce then decides what to do
with the detentions," he said.[45]

Von Raab's "veteran combat unit, ordered into the field," was
being hampered by Commerce officials. "We asked Commerce to
change regulations," he said at the end of the year. "They refused to
do this."[46] By the fall of 1983, Exodus was seizing an average of 140
shipments a month, and agents claimed that they often had to wait
nearly a month for licensing information to come back from Commerce to the Exodus Command Center in the Treasury building. A
Customs official said one shipment seized on the West Coast had
been held up for a year. "We just couldn't get the licensing details
from Commerce. It is a tactic they are using. They know when shipments are held up there will be an outrage from industry against
us."[47] Another said that getting licensing details from Commerce
was like pulling teeth. "We had people working over there in a
liaison office. They were GS-12 agents, quite senior, obliged to
behave like secretaries. When they were in licensing offices, Commerce officers were so overworked they were even answering the
telephones for them. The conditions were appalling. It was like
1925."[48]

"We are like two scorpions in a bottle," said Bill Rudman of Exodus. "We sit on our asses and wait for them to tell us about a license
and only then can we decide if we release or not." He said that 75

percent of his time was spent trying to sort out the problems with Commerce: "We tried to resolve it at the working level. Then it went to the lower managerial level. Then it went up the line and got stuck. We all run to the White House, but the White House doesn't want to piss anyone off. It's a disgraceful situation. And all the time the Russians are stealing our technology."[49]

But Customs wanted more than just information on individual license status. What the Exodus team was desperate for were details of applications that had been denied to Communist countries. They wanted to analyze the refusals so that they could work out patterns in trade with the Eastern bloc. They wanted to find out who had been dealing with proscribed countries before controls were imposed as result of the invasion of Afghanistan and the imposition of martial law in Poland. Their investigations were being hampered through lack of information — and that information was available just across the street from their command headquarters.

Secretary had written to Secretary about the problem. The Justice Department ruled that the Customs Service should have access. But Exodus was still being told that information was available only on a case-by-case basis. Eventually it chose a different tack. "I decided," said a senior Customs official, "to treat the Commerce Department like a suspect."[50]

The determination of the Exodus agents to collect their own intelligence data first became evident in April 1983. The New York office sent in a procurement request to the Census Bureau for all shippers' export declarations for fiscal year 1982. Although it is part of the Commerce Department, the bureau cooperated. "The request was handled by administrators," said Pat O'Brien, disparagingly. The shippers' declarations are used by the Census Bureau to compile statistics; what was of value to Exodus was not only the commodities that had been shipped but the names of the exporters. And those names were in the bureau's microfiche collections.

On Saturday, April 30, 1983, Pat O'Brien drove from his home in New York to Washington to load up twelve boxes containing an estimated $30,000 of microfiche declarations. They had to be carried from the Exodus offices, where they had been delivered by the Census Bureau: "I remember sweating to death. We got one of those trolleys, wheeled the boxes to the elevator." Once O'Brien's large blue Chrysler was loaded, one of his agents drove the car back to New York. Meanwhile, O'Brien went to nearby Alexandria to get his personal yacht, which he sailed up the coast. It had been a good weekend's work. O'Brien says that senior Commerce officials never knew what he had got. But there was no index to the microfiches, which were arranged in chronological order. His agents were faced with the task of manually indexing all of the information.[51] Less than two months later, another operation to get information from Commerce, masterminded from New York, began to pay off.

The young and attractive woman had certainly been noticed by her colleagues. She was five feet ten, with dark hair and blue eyes. An enthusiastic, personable recruit, with a good sense of humor, she was liked at once by fellow agents in New York, and they missed her when, shortly after her arrival, she was sent on temporary duty to Washington. But that was an inspired decision. She was sent to the small, cramped liaison office in the Commerce Department, where she was to sit in a room with a Customs colleague. Also with them was a Commerce official who sat in front of an IBM 3270 display that accessed the Commerce Department computer.

Customs agents assigned to the office never found the atmosphere congenial. They were there only to ascertain the licensing status of equipment that had been seized at ports. Only Commerce had that information at hand — and some officials were loath to give more than they absolutely had to. So bad was the relationship between the two departments, there had been arguments even about the key to the liaison office door. Commerce refused to give a key to the Customs agents. Customs stole one, and Commerce officials found out. Eventually a compromise was reached: Customs was given a key, and Commerce officials installed a safe in the room for their papers.[52]

The new recruit was determined from the start. It was an unusual assignment, but she had been told in New York just how valuable the information in the computer was for her superiors. For days on end, she sat there in the room with the inquiry terminal. The Commerce official, also a woman, let the Customs agents read the printouts, looking for names. She would even let them copy down details. But she would not give them printouts of the data to examine on their own. Then the new agent came up with an idea. "When [the Commerce official] accessed the computer, she was only getting one copy out. She was using one-ply paper. She had access to all the denied licenses for every single Communist country. I knew what our analysts in New York could make of all that information." So the young Customs agent managed to persuade the Commerce official to use two-ply paper, which produced an extra green copy. Within days, the New York Intelligence unit was getting the information it wanted — on green computer paper.

"It was brilliant," a senior Customs official said later. "For two months we milked the computer." Eventually, the woman agent was accessing the computer herself. On the printout of each denied application were details of the exporter's name, the value of the equipment requested, the consignee's name, the American supplier, the end-user statement, and the Eastern bloc destination. "And they never knew we did it," said the New York agent who had helped to plan the raid. "It helped us enormously. We knew the Soviets were using multiple gathering techniques. They would try for a license first; if it was denied, they would try something else. What we found out this way was what they were after. We used the information to corroborate what else we knew."[53] Pat O'Brien was thrilled. "It was excellent," he said. "The information she got went right around the country. Washington agents wished they'd done something that good."[54]

Throughout 1983, Customs agents conducted what became known as "search and gather missions" at the Commerce Department. Although no one was quite as successful as the young woman agent, many did get results. One or two junior Commerce officials were sympathetic. Some information began to arrive in early 1983, in government-issue envelopes sent anonymously across 14th Street. "I was in headquarters one day," said an agent from New York, "and I saw printouts from the Commerce computer on a desk. I asked how the hell we had got them and was told there was someone in there who supported us." One result of the raids, he said, was that they managed to identify some of the manufacturers of the equipment that the proscribed countries were after. "And we began to target them with Exodus literature and visits. The information also helped with our undercover program. We have a special agent on the East Coast called Dr. Frankenstein, who creates legends — dummy companies — and the information we got helped him."

By the end of 1983 the pipeline from the Commerce Department closed down. New officials had taken over, and they were less sympathetic than their predecessors. Customs stopped getting the information it really wanted — the tip-offs received from industry with which Ted Wu was building up his own investigations. Customs agents never even found out where in the Commerce Department those files were kept.

But the rivalry between Customs and Commerce had an even more serious aspect. To everyone's embarrassment, it surfaced overseas, at a time when the government was trying to convince the Europeans that effective enforcement could not be undertaken without their help. Foreign inquiry by overseas enforcement agents had always been a most delicate and sensitive task, and close cooperation from the various host countries was vital.

The Commerce Department originally believed that it had jurisdiction to investigate export control cases abroad through foreign commercial service employees attached to embassies throughout the world. But these people were not trained in law enforcement. Senator Sam Nunn wanted the Customs Service to carry out investigations overseas. "Traditionally the U.S. Customs Service has had foreign investigative responsibility in smuggling and in export investigations. Assigning two agencies to the same mission is not good procedure. Jealousies, turf battles, and wasteful competition between the two ... have already developed and they are likely to continue," he told Congress.[55]

There was one task, unconnected to enforcement, that Commerce Department staff usually performed outside the United States. They determined whether dual-use products that came up for license were available in any other country. It was an important consideration in the granting of licenses; there was no point in depriving an industry of sales if the proscribed countries could get the technology from foreign suppliers. The matter required some delicacy, and the way that the Commerce Department handled it came in for severe criticism.

Richard Perle, of the Defense Department, who had developed the Pentagon's policy on technology transfer, said, "I have seldom seen a controversial license application in which the applicant did not argue that what he proposed to sell was a load of old rubbish available anywhere in the world." On closer examination, he added, it frequently turned out that the equipment was something the Soviets had sought year in and year out and had not been able to pick up anywhere. Foreign availability required close scrutiny, he told Congress. He had once carried out his own study while on vacation in France. He claimed he had been told by a senior executive of a French company that had been "fingered as a potential competitor," that there was "no way he could hope to offer what the American firm in question would be proposing to make available to the Soviet Union."[56]

Another traditional overseas task assigned to Commerce was known as postshipment verification, or PSV. The arrangement was first devised in 1969, and by 1983 was being described by hard-liners in Washington as worse than useless. Under a license clause for specific technologies there was a stipulated requirement for on-site visits once the equipment had been sold. This was to ensure that the technology was used solely for civilian applications, not military, and that the equipment had not been re-exported. Negotiations had always been sensitive, and the Soviet Union and the other Warsaw Pact countries had never been happy about the arrangement. It was said to be one of the reasons that some exporters did not apply for licenses, preferring to smuggle rather than to try to reach agreement with the Soviets on a troublesome PSV clause.

The idea that it would be possible to monitor the use of high-technology products once they had been shipped was first discussed by COCOM in 1969, when a British company wanted to sell a computer to a Russian nuclear research establishment. The possibility of visits was discussed at the U.S. National Security Council level. Under the contract, a right of access was one of the safeguards. Some of the postshipment visits were carried out by government officials in the U.S. embassy, organized by Commerce through the Department of State. Many foreign service officers, however, had difficulty in knowing what they were looking for — or at. A retired senior State Department official described the difficulties he encountered behind the Iron Curtain: "I had to conduct an on-site inspection in Czechoslovakia. It was the most frigid reception I have ever received in my life. They would not even let me in. It was, to me, the most graphic example of operating in the Soviet bloc."[57]

Congress heard criticism of the safeguards from Lawrence Brady in those hearings of May 1979: "We have file cabinets of safeguard reports ... and I don't think we have ever gotten one that had indicated any diversionary activity."[58] Commerce stood by the arrangement. The safeguards, along with the information from the Intelligence community, the intensive scrutiny given each license, and the possibility of revoking the purchaser's right to buy, were considered efficient. It was not, however, government officials who provided most safeguard information. The major source was the vendors. Asking business representatives, usually service engineers — technical experts who knew what they were looking for — to carry out on-site inspections saved the government money. There were many objections from industry: firms did not want their employees to behave as though they were spies in Communist countries. The arrangement also added to the cost of the sale; it was alleged that the price of one computer rose from $1 million to $2 million because of the extra cost of the personnel involved.[59]

One of the most complex aftersale arrangements was on the IBM 370/158, which was installed in the Kama River factory. Attached to the computer was a high-tech form of tachograph, which recorded what the computer was doing at any given time. The printout from this (usually called a "memory dump" by Washington officials) was to be collected every month and sent back to Washington to be "decoded." A Kama River representative was responsible for the monthly reports, which would be countersigned by an IBM employee and submitted to the United States embassy in Moscow. Although IBM objected initially, the company did agree to the arrangement in the end.[60] "I don't recall any startling analysis of these data," said Rauer Meyer, who was head of the Office of Export Administration at the Department of Commerce for thirteen years, until 1979. "At no time did we believe that the safeguards were an absolute insurance against diversion. To me, safeguards produced a mass of useless information."[61] And Richard Perle at the Pentagon said: "It's like the fox guarding the chicken coops. Devices like memory dumps are excuses for doing a deal. I think postshipment verification is a farce."[62]

When, as part of the sanctions imposed after martial law was declared in Poland, licenses were held up for the spare parts for computers already installed, the Soviets retaliated by refusing to allow verification or collection of memory dumps. Worried companies that had entered into such agreements wrote to Commerce to say that they could not fulfill their obligations. Secret negotiations took place in Washington between senior Commerce officials and economic attachés from the Soviet embassy. "The Soviets took a really hard line," said one of the negotiators.[63] The Commerce Department, however, was receiving intelligence reports that the computers in the Soviet bloc were continuing to function, in spite of the spare parts embargo. A senior official who had access to the reports joked that this should have attested to their reliability, but he added, "There was every indication that the Soviets were by-passing the sanctions and getting spare parts."[64]

It was the issue of the jurisdiction over investigations to be conducted abroad that caused the most serious disputes between Customs and Commerce. Each enforcement agency realized the importance to the techno-bandits of using companies based in COCOM and the neutral nations to transfer technology to the Eastern bloc. Commerce officials attached to embassies had traditionally determined the status of foreign companies that applied for licenses. But the real fight was over the investigation of ongoing cases. The dispute surfaced in 1982. One of the most delicate technology-transfer cases investigated by the Commerce Department concerned a major Spanish electronics manufacturer, the Piher Chain, which was also a military contractor. Commerce received information indicating that semiconductor-manufacturing equipment containing American components had been allegedly diverted from Barcelona to Cuba by one of the company's subsidiaries. Politically, the case was a minefield.

A Piher subsidiary, Piher Semiconductores SA, had a turnkey arrangement with Cuba, organized a decade earlier, for a factory to make color television sets. Commerce received a tip-off that some American technology was being shipped out to the factory under this same agreement. The commercial attaché in Barcelona was asked to investigate. After visiting the company outside the city, the attaché thought further inquiries should be made, and he contacted a U.S. Customs agent based in the Paris embassy. He also reported his suspicions to Washington. A series of meetings was set up so that Commerce and Customs officials could discuss the problem with Spanish officials. So serious did Commerce consider the Piher investigation, it was decided that an Assistant Secretary should attend to put "political pressure on the Spanish, to force them to take a tougher attitude."

Bo Denysyk, the Commerce officer responsible for the regulation of exports for national security and foreign policy, had served on the Reagan transition team for the Office of Personnel Management. But he was also a technical man; he had worked as an engineer with the Naval Surface Weapons Center and as a biophysicist/computer specialist with the Naval Medical Research Institute. A serious, considered man who measured his words, he would indeed be a tough negotiator. As one State Department man said of Denysyk, "He wasn't afraid to make decisions."

Customs was furious. The agency had claimed that it had information of its own on the Piher case. The fact that Denysyk was going to Spain was seen as a slap in Customs' face. And what infuriated the service even more was that it believed Denysyk had given the Spanish Government copies of Commerce Department documents that Customs had not been allowed to see.

Denysyk met with representatives from the Spanish Foreign Ministry and Department of Defense and with members of the Prime Minister's staff. He did not actually investigate the case; he was there to handle the political angle. Two Commerce officials who had visited the Piher Semiconductores plant said they had found a phony semiconductor manufacturing plant. "It was just a bunch of lights," one claimed.

Ten Piher companies were blacklisted on February 25, 1982; they were temporarily denied export privileges by the Department of Commerce, "pending the completion of an investigation of Piher Semiconductores' alleged role in the diversion of COCOM-embargoed semiconductor manufacturing and testing equipment to Cuba."[65] By April the department's hearing commissioner amended the order and excluded one company only: Piher Electronica SA. In June another company was exempted: Piher International Corporation. And another exemption was granted in August of the same year so that Piher International Corporation could make certain exports through September 1982. What had been discovered was that the Piher group was providing the video cameras to be used for the World Cup soccer matches during the summer of 1982. Much of the equipment was to come from America and the denial order would have ruined the contract. It would also have been seen as an acutely unpopular American move in soccer-mad Europe and South America. So the denial orders on the company were amended.[66]

Denysyk was later chastised in a report on Commerce enforcement. In June 1982 in the report of the Office of Export Administration Denysyk was reprimanded for failing to file a written report on the "sensitive" investigation of Piher and for having undertaken the task in place of experienced investigators from the department.[67] Denysyk justified his action by claiming the division's investigators were largely unqualified and were naïve regarding the political ramifications of their actions.[68] The matter also infuriated the Exodus agents. "It was a good case," said one mournfully. "We had information on it ourselves from our own source."[69]

There was a time when it seemed to those involved in the turf battle over technology transfer that there must be a way to resolve their differences. In August 1982, the principals came together one morning — in von Raab's mahogany row dining room — to have an early breakfast and discuss the problems. Senior people from both Customs and Commerce attended. Their differences had to end. Among those who attended were Lawrence Brady, Bo Denysyk, and Ted Wu from Commerce, and Commissioner von Raab and Pat O'Brien from the Customs Service. It all started amicably enough at seven-thirty. Pat O'Brien was getting along quite well with Ted Wu, explaining what his problems were as a law enforcement officer in the tracking of high-tech smugglers. Wu, as a successful prosecutor of techno-bandits, told him he understood where the pitfalls were. Denysyk was quietly diplomatic.

At some point, von Raab and Brady got into conversation about foreign jurisdiction. Von Raab told Brady he wanted Customs to have the responsibility for overseas investigations. Denysyk interjected that he would not mind if Customs did carry out that task. But Brady objected. At that point, von Raab said that the Commerce Department, instead of worrying about what was happening overseas, should put more of its resources into the licensing department. "Then it got ridiculous," one participant recalled. Another said, "They vented their spleen. They were emotional." The breakfast ended with Brady on his feet, reportedly shouting, "You can't tell Commerce what to do. It's our job. We're not going to ask Customs to do our job. We'll go down with guns blazing." Showing his frustration, Brady "left the room making gestures as though firing a gun. I think it was because, for years, Brady had been telling everyone about technology transfer. Finally, when he had a government on his side, he found that he was not in control." Von Raab, it was said, thought this was his chance to do a great job. "All he wanted was for the President to tell him he'd done well. I suppose that's all any of us wants."[70]

7

THE ALLIES

PRESIDENT REAGAN sat patiently behind his Oval Office desk and waited for the cue. It was Saturday, November 13, 1982, and the second hand on the clock ticked around to 12:06 P.M. precisely. The green light went on. The President had started the regular weekly radio broadcasts shortly after his inauguration, and he was particularly pleased with today's topic. At last he could announce the end of the most embarrassing foreign policy episode since he had come to office. A formula had been reached that would end the row with the Europeans over the Siberian gas pipeline.

For several days the announcement had been delayed, and U.S. negotiators, jaded after months of meetings, had been given a deadline: get something worked out in time for the next radio show on Saturday. The extra presidential pressure had worked. The dropping of the pipeline sanctions became headline news. The President said that "a substantial agreement to a plan of action" had been reached and that it would give "consideration to strategic issues when making decisions on trade with the USSR."[1]

As a result of the negotiations, the President announced, the allies had agreed not to engage in trade agreements that would contribute to the military or strategic advantage of the USSR or serve to aid preferentially the heavily militarized Soviet economy. "I believe," said the President, "this new agreement is a victory for all the allies."

Immediately after the broadcast, President Reagan held a press conference on the South Lawn of the White House. When asked whether he had caved in to the Europeans, he replied that the alliance was "probably in a better union and more united than it has ever been." And he added: "The agreement that we have reached is what we set out to get, and we only turned to the sanctions when we were unable to get it. But we have all come together on this. And it is so much more effective.... The sanctions have served their purpose."[2]

The sanctions had caused outrage at home as well as in Europe. In 1982, four days after the Reagan administration had announced that the foreign subsidiaries of American companies would be prohibited from supplying pipeline equipment to the Soviets, a meeting of foreign ministers of the Common Market countries declared that the United States had violated international law. The nub of the issue was that the export restrictions were being applied to situations where contracts had already been signed for the supply of the equipment in question. Europe reacted firmly. The French and British governments ordered companies affected by the embargo to defy the ban. This put the contractors between a rock and a number of hard places: they could be penalized financially by the U.S. Government; they could lose U.S. orders; they could find their supplies of American equipment cut off. On the other hand, they would be penalized financially if they did not go ahead with the contracts. The Italians moved in next with an announcement that their contracts with the USSR would be honored. In the summer of 1982, the EEC gave notice that all trade relations between the Western allies would be damaged "unquestionably and seriously" by the embargo.

The three-thousand-mile pipeline from Urengoy in Siberia would supply natural gas to France, West Germany, and Italy in one of the biggest-ever international energy deals. The United States had, from the very start, expressed its reservations; the pipeline would make the European allies far too dependent on the Soviet Union. The whole concept was politically and strategically unsound. But the countries involved ignored the advice from across the Atlantic and signed the treaties. Despite the growls from Washington, European companies, including the subsidiaries of a number of major U.S. corporations, planned to supply much of the equipment needed. The United States was frustrated in its efforts to stop the deal, but not for long. When martial law was declared in Poland in December 1981, the administration clamped down on the pipeline contractors as part of the wider embargoes. The controversy worsened in June 1982, when, disappointed by the lukewarm reception of the allies to the idea of restrictions on credits to the USSR put forward at the Versailles summit, President Reagan arbitrarily extended the controls to the overseas subsidiaries and licensees of U.S. firms.

Things were far from quiet on the home front; Washington felt the fury of businessmen faced with the loss of millions of dollars' worth of export trade. The House of Representatives was the first to bend under the pressure, and legislation was introduced to repeal the expanded oil and gas sanctions. There was further embarrassment when Edward H. Hewett, a senior economist with the Brookings Institute, said that the Soviet Union had enough technology to circumvent the embargo anyway. He told the Senate Subcommittee on International Economic Policy that denying the use of American-designed turbine motor blades needed for the massive compressors that would pump the gas through the pipeline would not hamper construction. The Soviets could use their own smaller turbines, perhaps in combination with some larger models that are designed by the United States but built by European firms.[3]

The Soviets began a campaign of defiance in July 1982. Grigory Sudobin, the Deputy Minister for Oil and Gas Industry Construction, said that the U.S. sanctions would affect only part of the work. Scheduled for completion in 1986, the pipeline was already growing at a rate of four and a half miles per day, and the nightly news on Moscow television was giving regular progress reports. The turbines were being tested at the Nevsky factory in Leningrad, and Soviet-made equipment was shown ploughing trenches through the Siberian soil.[4]

For more than a decade, controversy on an international scale had surrounded American export control policy. Since the signing of the U.S.–USSR trade agreement in 1972, the United States' "on-again, off-again" policies had caused many debates about whether trade should be used as an arm of foreign policy. Export licenses once approved were revoked, notably the suspensions after the Soviet invasion of Afghanistan. Exports for a major project approved by President Richard Nixon and Secretary of State Henry Kissinger were stopped.

President Jimmy Carter's grain embargo, imposed in December 1979, had been lifted by Reagan in 1981; that alone stimulated much debate. The Office of Technology Assessment, an independent congressional body, reported in May 1983 that "it is probably accurate to say that the costs borne by the American economy were at least as great as those which devolved on the USSR, and that the Soviet Union seemed to have succeeded in replacing the United States as its principal agricultural supplier."[5] As a result of the grain embargo, legislation had been enacted to prevent agricultural commodities from being singled out for use as a weapon of foreign policy. Grain contracts were guaranteed, much to the anger of other exporters.

Under the 1979 Export Administration Act, the U.S. Government may control the export of certain commodities for national security and foreign policy purposes. This export control program, as we have seen, is managed by the Office of Export Administration at the Department of Commerce. Meyer, former head of the office, recently said that the licensing of commodities fluctuated with the political climate: "When the Soviets invaded Czechoslovakia, there was a period of several weeks when somehow we just didn't manage to issue any licenses for the USSR. But there was never a public announcement of any restrictive policy." It was, he said, "an unfortunate fact of life" that action taken in a "warming period came back to haunt us in cold periods."[6]

The Siberian pipeline debacle created an even greater storm. Once again the wisdom of sanctions was questioned, and the lack of evidence that they work was manifest. Yet more seriously, the affair gave the Europeans a justification for refusing to endorse American views on East-West trade and led to accusations that the Reagan administration was conducting nothing less than economic warfare against the Soviet Union. There was no clearer indictment of the policy than that of the chairman of Congress's Joint Economic Committee. In his opening statement during the September 1982 hearings on the sanctions, Representative Henry S. Reuss of Wisconsin said:

The Administration ... has advanced its views against the united opposition of our European and Japanese allies. It has skirted, and some
would say crossed, the boundaries of international law in applying our
sanctions to firms operating in foreign jurisdiction ... It has pushed its
point to the extent of risking a deep rift in the unity of the Western alliance. The Administration has failed to state a single clear and com-
pelling rationale for the sanctions.[7]

The U.S. Government became determined to clear up the mess.
Media coverage at home and abroad had been unfavorable; the
pressure was on for a speedy, face-saving solution. It was against
this background that negotiations began between the allies and the
Americans over the differences on East-West trade.

But the hard bargaining of ensuing months was to no avail.
Within hours of the President's announcement of the release of European subsidiary companies from American controls, it became
evident just how hurried the negotiations had been. The French
broke ranks. President François Mitterand's government denied
that it was party to any agreement at all. Asked why the French
were disassociating themselves, White House press spokesman
Larry Speakes replied, "To assign motives to the French statement
would be beyond my capability."[8]

The negotiations, at various levels, had been spaced over a four-
month period. The controls were to have been lifted after the United
States got the allies to agree to a series of studies on East-West trade
policy. Five would be undertaken: one on economic trade flow, one
on financial aspects (mainly prepared by the Organization for Economic Cooperation and Development — the OECD), and two
others, on energy matters, that would be prepared jointly by the
United States and the allies. But the most significant concession
sought by Washington was an examination of ways in which existing controls on the transfer of high technology to the Eastern bloc
could be strengthened.

Perhaps by coincidence, the weekend of the presidential broadcast saw the publication of a Senate report which concluded that the
Soviet campaign to acquire Western technology was "massive, well
planned, and well managed." European individuals and companies
had been responsible for providing the Soviets with much of the
technology in question. It was, the Senate Permanent Subcommittee
on Investigations reported, "one of the most complex and urgent

issues facing the Free World today." It went further: "The Governments of Western Europe must be made to understand that the issue of high technology diversions to the USSR is not merely an American problem."[9] The ways in which the governments of Europe were to be "made to understand" the technology-transfer problem were, from the time of the presidential broadcast, kept out of the public arena. From then on, the bitter disputes, which were to give rise eventually to the most serious split ever seen in the alliance, were conducted behind closed doors. Secrecy was one matter all the governments could agree on.

The rue de la Boëtie in the heart of Paris is one of those quietly fashionable streets where smartly dressed women "of a certain age" pass the time of day in expensive cafés. Dating from the Haussmann era — when Baron Haussmann changed the face of the capital in the 1850s and sixties — it was once home to many middle-class families. Now, many of the large apartments, with filigree wrought-iron balconies, have been taken over by small companies. Halfway down the street, at 58B, is an annex of the United States embassy. Few people know it is there. The discreet entrance, between a small office of The Electricité de France and a beauty salon, is a dark archway just large enough for a diplomatic limousine. It leads to a typically Parisian cobbled courtyard, at the center of which is á lone sycamore tree.

   The only overt indication that 58B is a secure building is the small closed-circuit television camera on the outside wall. But the metal gates at the far end of the archway are opened silently by electric motors activated by a U.S. Marine guard from some hidden observation post. An American eagle crest perches over the large double doors of the entrance. On the third floor is located the headquarters of a joint organization that has for thirty years held secret talks here on the subject of the transfer of critical Western technology to Communist countries.

   The need for a coordinated embargo policy first brought the United States, France, and Britain together in January 1950 for the initial meeting of the Coordinating Committee for Multilateral Export Control, or COCOM. It is based on no treaties and has no charter, and it has always tried to live behind locked doors, for fear of domestic political pressure in its member countries. No details of COCOM decisions or debates are ever published. (A broad history of the committee will be found in Chapter 14.)

COCOM makes lists of products and technologies to be embargoed, and each nation takes its own list from the master catalogue. Theoretically, no country can license the shipment of sensitive material eastward without a COCOM okay. Even though the committee has its serious handicaps — its decisions must be unanimous, for example — it has more or less served its purpose as an overseer of technology shipment and as a forum in which the nations can agree or disagree on the governing policies.

In the 1980s, COCOM gained a sudden new prominence and notoriety when the Reagan administration decided to get tough about what it saw as a massive leakage of technology that, in the end, served mainly to build up the Red Army, Air Force, and Navy. The United States was determined to tighten the controls that had gone slack in the days of détente, to enlarge the list, and to ask for sanctions against countries that winked at violations.

This turned out to be as much of an international political nightmare as the Siberian pipeline affair. First, instead of accepting the usual discreet meeting on the third floor in the rue de la Boëtie and a gentleman's agreement, the United States pressed for a big meeting on the ministerial level (a level that had ceased to exist in the early fifties) in January 1982.

That was, of course, psychologically all wrong. The British and Europeans loved the wink and the handshake and the unspoken understanding. The Germans believed that anything more formal and public would never work. The French had always disliked the COCOM idea; many Frenchmen think that it is a relic of the cold war. In short, COCOM nations found it easier to do the unpopular business of embargo-setting in closed session — and that probably even worked to the advantage of the United States in getting agreement on controls.

Washington, though, had gone through a number of humiliating experiences in the past few years. In July 1978, the Soviet news agency TASS, getting ready for coverage of the 1980 Olympics in Moscow, ordered a $6.8 million computer system from Sperry. The deal was set, but President Carter disapproved the license. And, furthermore, the administration requested other computer-exporting nations to withhold their items, too. Here, then, was a vacuum crying to be filled.

The French were immediately eager to be of service. "It is not the habit in France to subordinate, for political considerations, the sales abroad of material for civilian uses. Where would we sell if that were the practice?"[10]

The Carter administration scrambled to salvage the affair and decided, in April 1979, to license a modified version of the Sperry system and to get a COCOM exception. But it was too late. The French company CII-Honeywell (in which Honeywell has a heavy investment) got the order, built an even larger computer than originally specified, and thumbed its nose at COCOM.[11]

And there were other galling examples. An important American manufacturer of machine tools, testifying before a congressional committee, said that the Japanese had sold "a very sophisticated, extremely accurate, five-axis machining center to the Hungarians and the Rumanians." He added, "We [aren't permitted] to sell them even a three-axis machine."[12]

One of the most experienced veterans of the controls wars is Theodore L. Thau, formerly executive secretary of the Export Control Administration Review Board. He believes that "COCOM has always been a servant of business interests [which are] always much more predominant than the security agencies."[13]

The grand, ministerial-level meeting convened at the Avenue Kléber conference center, where the Vietnam peace talks had taken place, in January 1982. The mood around the big, rectangular table seemed optimistic at the start and there was talk of "the first broad reconsideration of our technology control system in nearly thirty years."[14] The bonhomie lasted just two days.

The Americans effectively banished it by submitting that COCOM should have a new committee made up of military representatives. The allies had no objections to getting some military information, but they immediately feared a military takeover of COCOM. "They [the Americans] began to get themselves into diplomatic messes. Then they began to look to the British to get them out of the corners," said one senior British diplomat.[15]

It was hardly an auspicious start in the effort to bring COCOM around to seeing controls the American way, but Under Secretary of State James L. Buckley, who led the U.S. delegation, tried to keep up a brave smile. At the end, he issued one of those determinedly cheerful statements which are often made after disastrous meetings: "There was a concrete consensus that the member governments should increase their efforts to improve COCOM's effectiveness. We have been encouraged by what appears to be the attitude of other COCOM governments and we feel that this meeting forms a basis for a revitalization of the COCOM system."[16] America still had hopes of getting its allies to understand.

If it was a bright spring day in Paris, none of the delegates knew it. What little light that came through the net curtains in the third-story room was diffused in the haze of cigarette smoke. The working group that crowded around the table was trying to get agreement on the regular three-year review of the computer embargo list. The item being considered was the kind of software that can be used to produce other software — applications generators. The discussion was calm and considered as the delegates struggled for a clear definition. The British delegation had just begun a series of questions when the door opened and a visitor walked in. William Root, the head of the U.S. delegation, stood to greet Richard Perle, the powerful Assistant Secretary for International Security Policy and one of the most determined advocates of anti-Soviet policy in the Pentagon. There was no love lost between Bill Root and Richard Perle. Two different personalities; two different styles. Once the introductions were made, Perle sat and listened. His visit lasted a mere fifteen minutes. Hiding his irritation, he stood and left the room; he had heard enough to confirm all his worst fears about the institution. "It was a pretty desultory discussion," he said in an interview later that year. "I learned more about the organization than I did about the subject they were discussing. Philips from Holland had a representative at the meeting. The British delegation also had private industry people with them, ICL and others. This is a regulatory institution with the regulees present.... The potential for self-deception is very large."[17]

Richard Perle's opinion of COCOM, shared by many in the Department of Defense, was not new. In March, during hearings held by the House Committee on Foreign Affairs (Subcommittee on International Economic Policy and Trade), he had said that the body had been allowed to decline. "It occupies a couple of borrowed offices in Annex B of the American embassy in Paris. . . . Even though two languages are the official COCOM languages, French and English, there is no simultaneous translator because they cannot afford it. It is a disgrace." But what really angered William Root was the subsequent discovery that Perle, after his brief visit, had flown on to London and made his views on COCOM quite clear to the British. British officials in Washington were later to tell Root how upset they were about Perle's remarks.

Since 1976, William Root had held the key job of director of the State Department's Office of East-West Trade. A brilliant career diplomat, this Bostonian had spent a large part of his service in the State Department's budget bureau. He had been appointed to Bonn in West Germany and Copenhagen in Denmark, was an economic officer in Vietnam, and then went to Berlin, before returning to Washington in 1974 as director of the Office of Soviet and East European Scientific and Technical Affairs. As immune as he was to Washington's political infighting, he could not get used to what he considered the abrasive manner of the Reagan administration's more ambitious proconsuls. He considered them both undiplomatic and inexperienced as policymakers.

Richard Perle is the type who attracts labels: "brilliant," "smart," "an evil genius," and even "the Prince of Darkness." In his early forties, and a son of Russian immigrants, Perle bears a resemblance to film star Rod Steiger; he looks permanently tired, with dark circles under deep-set, dark brown eyes.

He is, by his own account, a bon vivant, and on official trips to foreign capitals he will always find the superlative restaurants. In October 1980 Perle was known well enough to be the subject of a full-page feature article in the *Washington Post*. It concentrated mainly on the renovation of his newly acquired home in exclusive Chevy Chase, and the kitchen was difficult to ignore. His love of cooking was evident: ". . . two sinks, two dishwashers, 55 linear feet of butcher block . . . counter, handmade oak cabinets, a restaurant gas oven . . . four ovens, a huge gas grill with its own flue, enough copper pots and pans to cause a penny shortage ... not only a Cuisinart but also an electric cheese grater and electric pasta maker ... Kitchenaid mixer ... octagonal Mexican tile floor. ... The rest of the house seemed to be an anteroom."[18] Richard Perle is a soufflé fanatic. He claims to have designed his own soufflé oven and talks at length about how eggs should be folded. He is particularly proud of his own creation — a Tia Maria soufflé, and he claims to have found the reasons why some soufflés tend to collapse. "You analyze the vulnerabilities," he says, "rather like finding weaknesses in the Russian Navy."[19]

Perle's high political profile on Capitol Hill, even before he reached his elevated position at the Pentagon, was testimony to a determined plan to gain power and prominence. His title was modest: professional staff member of the Senate Committee on Governmental Affairs. The title almost disguised his key role as national security adviser to the late Senator Henry M. Jackson. The "Perle imprint" can be seen on many of Jackson's legislative and political successes. An early example was the famous Jackson amendment to the 1974 trade bill; it withheld most favored nation status from Socialist countries that restricted the right of citizens to emigrate. After its adoption, the USSR abrogated the 1972 trade agreement with the United States — and actually reduced the number of Soviet Jews allowed to leave the country. It was said by some that the amendment altered the course of détente. Perle's work for Jackson was described as "a détente-wrecking operation,"[20] or, as others put it, "Richard Perle had a substantial role in the defeat of détente."[21] His own way of putting it is that he participated in "innumerable little operations to affect the way things turned out."[22]

Richard Perle began reading about strategic matters at Beverly Hills High School in California. He was at one time politically sympathetic with the Committee for a Sane Nuclear Policy but that was all changed by someone he met at the home of the right-wing philosopher Albert Wohlstetter.[23] After graduating from the University of California, he went to the London School of Economics but returned to the United States with his doctoral thesis incomplete. Back in California, he was asked by Wohlstetter to help with the campaign in favor of the antiballistic missile. It was during that time he met Senator Jackson.

In Washington, D.C., he began to establish an impressive network of contacts. Officials in the Carter administration said that he knew more about the status of the SALT talks than many high-ranking State Department people, and, indeed, during the hearings on SALT, Senator Jackson established his reputation for finding weak spots, loopholes, and hazy wordings in the agreement with the Soviets. In spite of those successes, it was said that Jackson and Perle could not have frustrated Kissinger on SALT without enormous help from Rumsfeld and Reagan. According to the columnist Mary McGrory, Perle invented the term "Protestant angst" to explain the European peace movement.[24]

At the time of Andropov's elevation to supreme leadership of the USSR, Perle was quoted as saying that "between contemporary Soviet history and Catherine the Great is a continuum, and I don't see any evidence that [Andropov's] succession will mean an abrupt change."[25]

In early 1983 the COCOM nations agreed that the computer embargo list should be updated, and by April a working group had drafted an agreement on the revision. It highlighted areas where existing COCOM doctrine was unclear: signal processing, image enhancement, automatic telephone exchanges, and, most difficult of all, software. At the time the list forbade the export of computers with a potential memory capacity greater than two thousand bits — effectively barring all machines more powerful than the abacus. It was decided that each government would draw up a paper setting out its particular positions. All these national studies were to be distributed to COCOM members no later than September 15.

William Root claims that the Pentagon stalled. The Department of State was charged with writing the U.S. position paper, with help from the Department of Defense. The very day before the paper was to be delivered to COCOM, the Pentagon told State that it believed the committee was inadequate for controlling high-tech exports. In any case, Root was told, the Pentagon not State, ought to be responsible for drafting the position paper and should take the lead in future meetings in Paris. "They said we were not taking adequate steps for preparation," Root remarked later.[26]

Five days later William Root resigned. Like many State Department officials involved in the affair, he was tired of being blamed for what the Pentagon repeatedly called the "hemorrhaging" of American technology during the last two administrations. Worse than that, however, Root felt under threat from the Department of Defense. Toward the end, his role became untenable, he believed, because the Pentagon was "making a power grab." In Root's view, Secretary of Defense Caspar Weinberger seemed to have the President's ear, and his views were beginning to prevail over those of other departments. Everyone recognized that the Department of Defense, under the 1979 Export Administrations Act, had a veto over critical military technologies. What the State Department staff objected to was the Pentagon's encroachment into other areas of technology.

Root was much respected by his colleagues at State for his quiet intelligence, and his departure was a severe blow. Fred Asselin, of the Senate Permanent Subcommittee on Investigations, who had spent eighteen months investigating high-tech transfer, went so far as to say that "when William Root resigned, it meant an effective brake on United States government operations at COCOM."[27] Root was uncharacteristically blunt to the press about his views: "Effective controls depend on negotiations. The United States is not the unique supplier of the most strategic equipment."[28] In an open letter to President Reagan, dated September 25, 1983, he stated that the United States had·been redoubling its efforts to "convey to our allies that their views do not count, that we know best, and that they had better shape up." What was clear was that Root, the loyal diplomat, was ashamed of the behavior of the United States toward its allies.

Increasingly impatient with lengthy negotiations through COCOM, Washington decided to accelerate the process by using exactly the same approach it had adopted in the Siberian gas pipeline affair. This method was only once hinted at publicly. An Office of Technology Assessment Report of 1983 stated: "The Reagan administration has linked progress in COCOM to changes in controls on U.S. trade with COCOM countries."[29] This strong hint about a withdrawal of U.S. technology supplies was a particularly effective threat to the European computer industry, which depends heavily on the United States.

A disgruntled former COCOM official said, "I just didn't see the long-term benefits. It soured relationships and did serious damage in COCOM. We can't ram things down people's throats."[30]

It was a genteel, informal luncheon, the sort of diplomatic function that takes place somewhere in Washington every working day. It was held in a mansion in an exclusive area of the capital, just off Embassy Row. The official residence of General Thomas Anthony Boam, Defence attaché at the British embassy, was neither ostentatious nor particularly modern. Comfortable, plain, but expensive was the best way to describe it.

"Tony" Boam himself is an Englishman of the stiff-upper-lip mold, and he knew exactly how to conduct this sort of function. He wore his dress uniform and had uniformed army stewards in attendance, serving the food and drink. The reason for the display of British hospitality on Tuesday, February 22, 1983, was the arrival in Washington of Deputy Defence Minister Geoffrey Pattie. Like Boam, he was a typical British gentleman, old-fashioned, well mannered, and avuncular, and his social skills were remarkable. Pattie was in charge of weapons purchasing, and he was visiting Washington with the particular purpose, it seemed, of lodging a complaint that British defense industries were being kept out of the lucrative American marketplace. This was what he wanted to discuss with the Washington correspondents assigned to cover the Defense Department. Each had received an engraved invitation.

As they worked their way through the leek and potato soup and the chateaubriand, the journalists were surprised at the Minister's awareness of what they'd written in recent stories and at his ability to swap gossip about their newspapers. Once the writers began to relax, they were ushered into another room and invited to make themselves comfortable in deep easy chairs. Pattie was quite frank. He had come to Washington to make sure the United States did not retreat into "protectionism." He remarked that there had been congressional efforts to stop British companies from getting contracts for aircraft ejector seats. Attempts had been made to block the supply of engines made with special metals.

Suddenly, he changed tack. He told the journalists that the United States had been stalling on the signing of a technology-transfer agreement with Britain, Germany, France, and Italy for the multiple launch rocket system — an advanced system that the NATO allies were supposed to be developing jointly with the Americans. A memo of understanding should have been signed, but there was now a delay. One of Pattie's missions in Washington was to persuade the Americans to share what they had agreed to share. Another British official then entered the discussion. Dr. Stanley Orman, then deputy head of the British Defence staff at the British embassy, asserted that the United States was also being difficult about giving the United Kingdom access to top American technology secrets, such as VHSIC (very high-speed integrated circuits) and Stealth, the "invisible bomber."

"Are they holding back because of the British spy scandals?" one of the correspondents asked. "No, this is not the case," replied Pattie. "I am sure they will eventually come across."

Despite all the effort, the event was hardly a great success; only two small stories were published about the British complaints. Nearly a year later, senior Pentagon staff were saying, quite along the lines of Pattie's remarks, that the U.K. would have a long wait if they were expecting to receive details of VHSIC and Stealth technologies.[31]

Back in Washington, Perle described the approach as "pushing the system awfully hard." "How good our relationships are with a country, colors licensing decisions," he said. "We made it clear that the extent to which we are prepared to share our technology will relate to the extent to which they are willing to protect it."[32] In June of that year Perle caused another stir on the international scene when he released to the Armed Services Committee Technology Transfer Panel a list of seized embargoed technology and products, which "included diversions from COCOM countries." The U.K. was at the top of the list, with 145 shipments seized in the previous eighteen months on the grounds that these might get diverted to the Eastern bloc.

By that time, the Department of Defense — whose technology-transfer policy was masterminded by Perle — was trying to have a say in the licensing of goods being exported from America to other Western countries. Under the provisions of the Export Administration Act of 1979, the Pentagon had the right to monitor the sale of dual-use technology destined for Communist nations. But it was the

Department of Commerce, consulting with the Pentagon, that was charged with controlling the export of dual-use technologies to the allies. It was not an easy task. "I believe," Perle said, "that the Export Administration Act gives us authority to review West-West cases. The Commerce Department has said no. This is a very sore subject between us."[33] The Commerce Department was certainly not pleased at the Pentagon's further attempts to move onto its turf, and the only concession was described by Under Secretary Lionel Olmer as a "limited right to review" that involved just eight countries and did not include the power of veto.[34]

Commerce, in any case, was taking an increased interest in West-West exports. Some licenses for shipments to COCOM and neutral nations were already being held up. "Exporters would call and then governments would call. We would just say there were problems," a former senior Commerce staffer said. "There were very large computers we did not approve. Also military jet engines. What we were looking for were assurances. We wanted an overhaul of the security apparatus. Only when certain assurances were given were deals made." Eventually he, like William Root, became disillusioned: "It was blackmail. Sometimes it was implicit . . . sometimes it was open blackmail."[35]

In the spring of 1983, British industry pleaded with the Americans to abandon export controls as an expression of its foreign policy. "We believe that the [Export Administration] Act will continue to do serious harm to economic and political relations across the Atlantic," wrote the Confederation of British Industry, a group of the top twelve thousand U.K. companies. In a submission to Congress, the CBI claimed:

> The recent dispute over the supply of equipment for the West Siberian gas pipeline did, however . . . highlight not only the shortcomings of the Act . . . but caused severe disruption to international commerce and long-established relationships. . . . British business, as a major partner of the USA in the exchange of goods, technology, and industrial investment . . . has an interest in the future shape of the Act.

The CBI went on to tell the Americans that the use of controls had a negligible effect on Soviet policies and the main result of embargoes had been to alienate trading partners and allies. Although there was a need to control shipment of goods likely to aid the military effort of an enemy, the use of embargoes on external trade was likely to be a "two-edged weapon."

There was some further advice. The United States was invited to consider whether future attempts to exercise these powers would really arrive at the stated objectives. There was little likelihood that the measures could be operated in such a way as to "regulate the conduct of European companies." Then came a warning. The powers of the act might be effective only in cases where other sources of supply were not available. These would be few in number, given that "much of the most advanced technology is now indigenous to Western Europe and Japan."[36]

The fact remains, however, that the United Kingdom relies on America for 80 percent of her computers, peripherals, and components. Any threat to curtail this source would mean potential disaster for the "sunrise industries" in the harassed British economy. In June, a British Sunday newspaper reported that threats to cut these supplies had been made by U.S. officials in an attempt to force the British Government to increase its efforts to stamp out the smuggling of high technology to the Soviets and their COMECON partners. Richard Perle's statistical "proof" that Britain was the worst offender was also published.[37] The Department of Defense confirmed that two major investigations of leakages from Britain were under way. One concerned computer equipment worth more than $2 million that had ended up behind the Iron Curtain. The other related to semiconductor-manufacturing equipment that had gone to Poland, Rumania, and Bulgaria.

Traditional Whitehall reserve inhibits British civil servants from expressing their views in public. But the anger felt in the Foreign Office and the Department of Trade rivaled earlier feelings over the pipeline embargo. "COCOM meetings," said one official, "have become nothing more than a series of demands from the Americans." By the late autumn of 1983, when the subject of extraterritoriality was being discussed, the meetings had become fractious affairs. "The U.S. delegation has no diplomatic skill at all," one British participant complained. "If they don't get total commitment, they are lost. In true diplomacy there is always a middle ground. They just cannot learn to live with compromise."[38] The communication gulf had deepened when the delegates lost the skills of Bill Root.

Meanwhile, Prime Minister Margaret Thatcher decided that Britain should have an equivalent to Operation Exodus, and a group of senior civil servants was convened to set up a system for stemming the flow of illicit technology from Britain. The new committee held its first meeting on October 20 at 1 Victoria Street, a drab Department of Trade building near the railway station. Present were members of Britain's spy agencies, MI5 and MI6, officials from the Department of Trade, the Foreign Office, Ministry of Defence, and Customs agents. Customs had been pressing for greater backing; it had a team of only nine full-time agents working on high-tech cases but was already claiming possible successes with eleven ongoing investigations.

The chairman of the group was David Hall, a graying, soberly dressed Assistant Secretary from the Department of Trade. Hall, like many other British civil servants, believed that the control of technology transfer was a purely interdepartmental affair and that the British already had strict, clearly defined guidelines for licensing and enforcement. He also believed, along with others who had made careers in the trade control area, that the role of the civil service had always been adequate. They did not take kindly to American criticism of their efforts.

Throughout the year, the British civil service establishment had looked on the battles between the Department of Commerce and the Pentagon with smug amusement, claiming that such infighting was uniquely American. "The United States became a joke in Paris," remarked one British COCOM delegate. "Our own institutions had worked together for years on this. We did not have their problems. And we had always involved our Defence people." However, this "whiter than white" image was not entirely without blemish. One of the difficulties of British Customs was the reluctance of the Security Service to share essential information. One agent who had worked on technology-transfer cases said, "If they ever do cooperate, it will be like opening Pandora's box for us."[39]

This very reticence led to an embarrassing episode. At the end of September 1983, a shipment of spare parts was en route from the United States to Switzerland. On its way through London's Heathrow Airport, it was seized by Customs. As it happens, the shipment was being monitored by the FBI, which believed it was going on to the Eastern bloc. Some critical components had been removed, making the goods worthless. It was an important case for the FBI. Because of a possible espionage factor, the FBI had informed MI6, which, unfortunately, failed to inform Customs. It took several hours of secret negotiations before Customs would release the shipment.[40]

Despite this, within days of the Victoria Street meeting, things began to happen. The first person to feel the effects of this new effort was an English-born fugitive from American justice, Brian Moller-Butcher. After an eight-month investigation by the U.S. Exodus, Moller-Butcher had been indicted in February 1982 by a federal grand jury in Boston for illegally selling semiconductor-manufacturing equipment to Poland, Rumania, and Bulgaria. He was charged with thirty offenses in relation to shipping controlled goods worth $500,000. The case had been the first Operation Exodus indictment. Within a week of the establishment of Project Arrow, the British equivalent, he was summoned to a British court for thirteen alleged offenses involving shipments to Poland and Czechoslovakia.

By the end of 1983, the Americans were pleased with the progress the "cousins" had made. Richard Perle said: "Initially they had not been prepared to go very far. But the British have taken some positive steps in the areas of enforcement and intelligence. Britain is pulling together a much better institutional arrangement. Some of the best cooperation we have had has been British."[41] A former official of the Commerce Department agreed: "Some of the best intelligence we get comes from the British. They now have the best Soviet analysts."[42]

But the initial success of the joint U.K.-U.S. enforcement operation could not totally disguise the fundamental political and diplomatic differences between the two over the issue of technology transfer. As a result of attempts to tighten controls on technology, the Americans were, by the end of 1983, being accused of economic imperialism.

In December the Americans told the British that every U.K. user of advanced American computers would have to apply for a U.S. license if it decided to move the machines from one facility to another. IBM initially broke the news in a letter to thirty British leasing companies, telling them that any change of use or movement of advanced computers within the U.K. would have to be approved by the Commerce Department. At the same time the Pentagon threatened that any country not complying with the regulations would be faced with a total embargo of technology.[43]

The British Government found itself in an extraordinary position. Many advanced computers — nine out of ten in use in the U.K. — in the stock exchange, major banks, and government ministries used American components or were American-made. The British Defence Department and the intelligence-gathering Government Communications Headquarters (GCHQ) — the British equivalent and partner of the National Security Agency — relied heavily on American machines. Fears were expressed at the highest level of government about the threat posed to the working of the computers. Only six weeks' supply of spare parts was thought to be in stock.

Much to the government's consternation, the row surfaced briefly at the House of Commons. For the first time in many years the name COCOM was heard at Westminster. Liberal Party spokesman on technology, Paddy Ashdown, attacked both the committee and the Americans, listing the absurd instances that had resulted. COCOM, he said, was so much in the hands of the American administration "that it is being used as an instrument by which the Americans regulate trade to their own advantage." The embargo list being put forward in Paris by the United States, Ashdown declared, was nothing more than the entire American technological warehouse. To agree to it would be technological suicide. Technology items already embargoed by the committee were indicative of how ridiculous the system had become. He told the House of Commons that anyone leaving Heathrow Airport with a digital watch on his wrist was breaching the little-known committee's regulations. The chips inside such watches were embargoed. The same applied to a certain brand of heart pacemaker. And Ashdown revealed that the Pentagon had recently persuaded British Customs to raid a store in the departure lounge at Heathrow and seize what he described as "toy" microcomputers. What he referred to was the highly successful home computer, the Sinclair ZX80, available throughout the U.K. A returning U.S. Defense Department official had noticed them on sale, and his department had told the British that it was ridiculous to sell, on the duty-free side of the barrier, a computer that required an export license.

Ashdown told his fellow M.P.s that the U.K. was largely dependent on U.S. technology, but it was unacceptable for the Department of Trade to lie down in front of the U.S. high-tech industry. It was becoming a deeply dangerous situation. Britain had been maneuvered into technological subservience to the United States and had assumed the status of a technological satellite.[44]

Secretary of State for Trade and Industry Norman Tebbitt was forced to answer criticisms that his department had caved in to American pressure. The IBM letter, he said, was quite clearly an attempt by the U.S. Government to impose its laws within the U.K. And that, of course, was contrary to international law. It was, he said, a "very great problem" for the British Government.[45]

It was to be one of the rare government statements about the controversy. Prime Minister Thatcher and her ministers were intent on keeping the Anglo-American problems under wraps. The government deflected calls for a parliamentary debate, and Thatcher refused to answer questions on the grounds that they involved security and intelligence. The issue was threatening the internal working of the alliance, but neither the U.K. nor the U.S. wanted the kind of public exposure there had been in the debate over the pipeline.

There were also rumblings of discontent in the British high-tech industry about American behavior over export controls. Complaints centered on the U.S. decision to relax trade restrictions with China. The Americans were accused of trying to sell the Chinese equipment that was subject to COCOM controls. Plasma Technology, a small British company, one of the few in Europe producing microchips, told the Minister for Trade that President Reagan's intention to visit a trade exhibition in Beijing in 1984 was an indication that the U.S. had stage-managed the event. U.S. manufacturers of high-tech equipment would get immediate entrée into a market from which British and European companies were barred by export controls. Plasma Technology had been negotiating with the Chinese for a contract worth £1.5 million (about $2.2 million) but could not get license approval. "Until now," wrote Plasma director David Carr, "I have always understood that uniform export control practices have been applied by all COCOM nations. . . . Now we appear to have a situation where the U.S. has (for the first time ever) enacted unilateral legislation to ease restrictions on its own manufacturers without reference to COCOM." He said his agents in Hong Kong had discovered that U.S. competitors were offering much more sophisticated technology than he was allowed to sell and certainly more advanced than anything permitted by U.S. regulations. Carr was told by the Industry Department, "We shall take every possible step to avoid the danger of the rules being manipulated to give unfair advantages to any one COCOM member." It was hardly sufficient assurance to the company.[46]

The British high-tech industry began bombarding the Ministry of Trade and Industry with complaints. The Americans were accused of prohibiting export of technology that was already in the hands of the Russians. Industrialists could not understand why some Digital PDP 11s — part of a shipment seized at the Dover docks in May — were the subject of enforcement activity. The U.S. had been selling them openly to Yugoslavia. And although the United States heralded the 1983 seizure of the VAX 11/82s in Sweden as a major blow against the technology smugglers, British computer programmers were working on identical VAX machines in Moscow hospitals (and earning $1400 a week).[47]

The British company ICL, second only to IBM in the U.K., with a turnover of £711 million ($1 billion), produced an internal memorandum at the end of 1983, revealing that the Americans were insisting on the licensing of scientists and engineers.[48] When the company employed an American scientist or engineer to write a report, his work was subject to U.S. law. "ICL has in fact had to obtain U.S. export licenses to cover knowledge carried in the heads of American engineers." This particular regulation had caused considerable dissent at COCOM meetings. West Germany did have legislation covering "invisible technology." But Britain did not.

The ICL report, which was not made public, stated: "The U.S. appears intent on controlling trade in high technology worldwide.... The picture is one of growing technological imperialism by the United States ... it is free trade along a one-way street." Britain must not, the report concluded, be dependent on another nation for technology critical to her defense.

The conclusion touched on the most serious and most secret division between the United States and Great Britain. It had been raised by Geoffrey Pattie at the Washington luncheon in the spring of

1983, when he said the United States had been stalling on the signing of a technology-transfer agreement for the multiple launch rocket system. By the end of the year he was even less optimistic about cooperation. The U.K., he said, needed to turn more to European partners.[49]

By that time, it had become evident that British officials and scientists were not only being denied VHSIC and Stealth bomber technology; they were also being denied access to the secrets of the new "killer" satellites, designed to patrol high frontiers in space. "We will share 97.3 percent," said a senior Pentagon official, just after the British had been told that they could not attend a top secret conference. "The British still get a better deal than the rest of the allies, but there are some technologies we won't share."[50]

8

AUSTRIA

OF ALL THE COUNTRIES subjected to Reagan administration pressure, by far the most sensitive is Austria. After Austria concluded a special treaty of neutrality and the Soviet occupation forces pulled back in 1954, she began to walk a tightrope between East and West. In the fifties, Vienna gained a sinister reputation as the European center for intrigue and espionage — based partly on films like *The Third Man* and partly on such stranger-than-fiction events as the defection of Major Peter Deryabin of the KGB. This reputation overlaid the old image of Strauss waltzes, dashing cavalry officers, and Sachertorte. Then, starting in the mid-1960s, the city became a business and diplomatic city, attracting many multinational companies and financial organizations.

Few Austrians have fond memories of the Russians, but the Hapsburg-era closeness with Czechoslovakia, Hungary, and Yugoslavia remains strong. Budapest is a popular day trip by car, and the only thing that might hold up a traveler at the border is the mistake of bringing too many Hungarian forints back into Austria. Less than a hundred kilometers across the Czech border is the old city of Brno (still called Brünn by German-speakers), where the beer is quite special. Over the mountains to the south in Yugoslavia is the old imperial province of Slovenia, where many people still speak German and where holidays are agreeable. The Austrians have never taken the Iron Curtain idea as seriously as the rest of the world has.

All in all, Austria suffers many of the ills and many of the advantages of being a buffer country and a broker country. The gray Danube (it has lost its blue) still snakes through Vienna. The Austrians have one of the highest standards of living in the world, yet they are the one people in the world with a higher suicide rate than the Swedes. For businessmen, the advantages of neutrality are obvious, and year after year Socialist governments get a substantial support from the capitalist rich. It is hardly surprising, then, that this comfortably mixed nation on the border between East and West has become a conduit for the flow of Western high technology to the Eastern bloc.

When Socialist Chancellor Bruno Kreisky visited Washington in early 1983, he could hardly have been surprised to find himself under pressure on this issue. There were already rumors that President Reagan planned to install, as his new ambassador to Vienna, Helene von Damm. She had been his executive secretary in Sacramento and later his executive assistant from 1975 to 1979. Von Damm, born in Austria in 1938, had emigrated in 1959. She was known for her anti-Communist views, and some observers felt that her appointment did not bode well for future U.S.–Austrian relations. But at least she spoke the language.

What Chancellor Kreisky could not be quite certain about was exactly how the Americans would apply the pressure. The delays in granting export licenses had increased, but that had happened before. Washington had, it was said, managed to stop many of the leaks in Sweden, Finland, India, and Hong Kong, and there was no question but that Austria was quite as dependent on U.S. technology as they were. Any embargo against the small country was bound to have an adverse effect on the international trade so important to it.

As things turned out, Austria's desire to minimize its dependency on the United States was what persuaded her to give in to the pressure. The huge West German conglomerate Siemens had already committed itself to establish a plant for manufacturing semiconductors in Austria, and the first factory to build 64K-bit memory chips was under construction. As part of the same program of development toward greater independence, the Austrian Government had brought about an arrangement between the Silicon Valley company American Microsystems, Inc., and Austria's largest steel manufacturer, Voest-Alpine. They would jointly fund a facility in Austria to manufacture memory chips for distribution throughout the breadth of Europe. The whole project would cost $46 million, and the American firm, AMI, would hold 51 percent of the stock. The AMI deal was considered to be a major step forward in making Austria a high-technology center for Europe.

By the time of Chancellor Kreisky's visit to Washington, AMI was beginning to suspect that something was going wrong with the deal. It had already submitted applications for the appropriate export licenses before beginning construction of the manufacturing facility that was to form the first part of the project. The U.S. Department of Commerce's approval procedure was not completed in the usual period of thirty to sixty days, and the months dragged on. In the interim, the U.S. Government had made approaches to the Austrians. Vienna was asked for an assurance that it would protect any critical technology sent from the United States.

In January 1983, a few months before Kreisky's visit, a team of government negotiators flew from Vienna to Washington. They were led by Ferdinand Lacina, foreign affairs specialist of the Bundeskanzleramt. In an interview with *Business Week,* he talked about the meetings: "We made it clear that we had no interest in Austria becoming an illegal transfer point of technology to Eastern European countries." It was agreed that the discussions had been successful. One Commerce Department official admitted, "We didn't get everything we wanted but we got a lot." Within days, the licenses were granted.

The rules of diplomacy dictated that neither government claim a victory. However, AMI had something to say about the affair. From his corporate headquarters in California, AMI's chief executive, Glenn E. Penisten, voiced a complaint: "We feel a little used. There has definitely been a delay, and a fairly painful one at that." He went on to say that the plant included in the contract was "hardly state-of-the-art" and suggested that the Soviet Union could have bought the same kind of manufacturing system some time ago from the Japanese or the West Germans. When Chancellor Kreisky was asked by journalists how the flow of technology to the Eastern bloc through Austria would be stemmed, he said, "We will use the same procedures the Swiss use to protect American technology."[1]

"I have lost count of how many bad grades I got on graduating from high school. . . . One thing I was successful at was pinching groceries from the Americans."[2] So says Udo Proksch, one of the most colorful characters on the Viennese scene and a close supporter and confidant of Bruno Kreisky's. "Goldfinger," "gambler," "opportunist," "gun-runner," *"pistolen-mann,"* and "enfant terrible of the social scene" are just a few of the expressions used by the Austrian press to describe this Socialist millionaire playboy.

Born in 1933 in Rostock, in what is now part of East Germany, Proksch moved to Berlin and Munich with his parents before arriving in the Salzburg area of western Austria at the end of the Second World War. His father settled there and eventually rose to become a senior civil servant in the local trade department. In spite of his poor school record, Udo managed to get a place at the Senior Agricultural College at nearby Seefeld; he lasted just two and a half years: "They kicked me out in 1952 — they did not like my style."[3]

For most of the 1950s, Proksch studied art and design. Starting at the Graphics Art School in Salzburg, he eventually moved to Vienna and attended design school there on a part-time basis. Now well into his twenties, Udo still had problems with educational institutions; after being thrown out a number of times, he left for good in 1960.[4]

In fact, in 1960 he left Europe altogether and traveled to the United States and the Far East. He was reported to have been in Vietnam and the Philippines but refused to say much about his four years in Southeast Asia. Back in Vienna, he met up with an old friend, Rudi Wein. They had first met by chance in Moscow during the 1957 Youth Games festival. Wein was a professed Communist but had left the Austrian Communist Party because of the invasion of Hungary. Proksch had managed to put his design qualifications to practical use when he worked for a company called Anger Plastic Processing Machines; his specialty was the design of spectacle frames.[5]

Reunited, Proksch and Wein pooled their resources in the establishment of a new company. The firm was to be involved in general trading, building construction, and the development of inventions and industrial processes, as well as the encouragement of new business ventures. They needed a name, and Wein, a Jew, suggested "kibbutz." To counter this, Proksch suggested "Napola," the name of the World War II school for the children of the Nazi elite. They compromised. The firm, Kibolac, started business in April 1966 and was soon flourishing — especially in its trade with East Germany.[6]

One of their earliest recruits was an electrical engineer named Karl-Heinz Pfneudl, whom they signed up straight from the university. Then came his fellow student, Rudolf Sacher, with a doctorate in physics. Both of the young employees were so successful that in 1969 they set up their own company, with the financial help of their mothers. That company, first called Rudolf Sacher GmbH, was described on the plaque beside the door of its offices in Vienna as a "Laboratory for Technical Development."

In the meantime, Kibolac continued to perform well enough for Wein and Proksch to expand their interests. Rudi Wein bought the Club Gutruf café, which became a favorite watering hole for the city's intellectuals; writers, actors, and musicians all gathered there. But Udo Proksch was to go him one better.

In the spring of 1972 much publicity in the gossip columns was given to the proposed takeover of Vienna's most genteel coffee house. Demel's House was renowned for its huge range of elaborate confectionery, and its paneled, mirrored rooms, lighted by chandeliers, were frequented by the city's rich and aristocratic elite. Shortly after the establishment of Demel's House in 1857, it received the distinction of official patronage from the family of Emperor Franz Josef. Indeed, even in today's Republic of Austria, the name of the Demel is often prefixed by the letters "k.k.," for Kaiserliche und Königliche Zuckerbäckerei, or Imperial and Royal Confectionery. The owner in 1972 was an Italian-Austrian count who had married Anna Demel, a survivor of the founding family. The count decided that he preferred to run his art studio in Manhattan rather than deal with the day-to-day problems of overseeing more than a thousand recipes. Demel's House was put on the market, and the buyer most likely to succeed in the purchase turned out to be a stocky, slightly balding, thirty-nine-year-old named Serge Kirchhofer.

His partner in the $750,000 deal was a company called Hermine Ettrich GmbH. Subsequent investigations showed that the firm was owned by an Austrian woman of the same name and a Swiss company called Lylac AG. Lylac, in turn, had been set up in the Swiss town of Zug by Max Peterhans and Grete Fischer. Kirchhofer was to buy 10 percent of Demel's, and the Lylac group the rest. The deal in general and Serge Kirchhofer in particular attracted much press attention during the negotiations. But the astute Vienna newspapers were not fooled; they quickly identified Kirchhofer as none other than Udo Proksch. He had upstaged his friend Rudi Wein very effectively.[7]

But why all the fuss? Vital to the issue was that Proksch was a self-professed left-winger, an ardent supporter of the Socialist government of Kreisky, and a trader with the Eastern bloc. He had bought the commissary of the one-time ruling class. Perhaps suspicion had been aroused because the lawyer who negotiated the deal was Jakob Zanger, who operated from the same prestigious address as Hermine Ettrich: 1010 Vienna, Neuer Markt 1. Zanger was known to hold a senior position in the Austria–East Germany Friendship Society and was a member of the Communist-dominated Austrian Peace Council.[8] He was also involved in the International Union of Democratic Lawyers. The worst fears of the conservative press were confirmed when a huge new cake appeared in the window of Demel's: across it was emblazoned the emblem of the Georgian Soviet Socialist Republic. Another photograph showed "Kirchhofer" holding a cake in the form of a Russian satellite. In reality, all Proksch was doing was continuing a great tradition of Demel's House by preparing a new cake each week for the display window in honor of a trade show, conference, or visiting foreign delegation. That was just good business.[9]

But why the change of name? Was there something sinister in that? Probably not; Proksch had used the name before when he had worked for Anger as a designer. The surname Kirchhofer would suggest (to German ears) family origins in the landed gentry or even the old Austrian imperial nobility. Plain Proksch does not have such classy connotations. And Serge, he once explained, had romantic Eastern connections; it is the French version of the Russian Sergey.[10] In spite of their opposition, the press got much mileage from the voluble Udo. He had been married four times, once to one of

Austria's most famous actresses and another time to Daphne Wagner, a great-granddaughter of the German composer. He even appeared on television, propounding the "thoughts of Udo Proksch." About women, he said: "I'd like to have a special effect on women, because I get a kick out of it. But I only have the same effect as any other man." About marriage, he said: "I've had it with marriage. The only benefit goes to industry — you need two of everything: iceboxes, bathtubs, automobiles."[11]

Soon the dust settled, and Udo Proksch disappeared from the gossip columns. But he reappeared later, in the early 1980s, when he was accused of being a gun-runner to European terrorists and a Soviet spy.[12] He was seen in full-page advertisements in support of the re-election of Bruno Kreisky and in a minor acting role in an Austrian movie.[13]

The 1970s were a period of expansion for Sacher Technik Wien (Sacher Technology, Vienna). The potent combination of the theoretician, Dr. Rudolf Sacher, and the skilled technician, Karl-Heinz Pfneudl, was to prove very effective. Pfneudl offered both style and the experience of having studied electronics in the United States. For some years, he was the company's link with the advancements in U.S. integrated-circuit technology. During the late 1970s, his salary, $800 per month, was low by Silicon Valley standards, but he was able to draw as much as $1000 per month in business expenses. His style was exemplified by the personal car he kept in the United States. It was a Lincoln Continental Mark IV — the closest America can get to the Rolls-Royce. But it was not a regular model, and Pfneudl explained why he had bought it: "The salesman was cute enough not to dwell on trifles like gas consumption and speed, but stressed instead that it had a Cartier quartz clock mounted on the dash and silver trim by Tiffany round the rear windows."[14]

In interviews with the press, Pfneudl made no secret of the firm's trade with the Eastern bloc and explained at length the problem of dealing with East Germany:

To be able to offer them something useful, you obviously have to know at which points they've got problems. That's obviously extremely difficult, because they're very unwilling to give away the technological level they've reached. In special areas, they're often a long way behind, but the DDR has made huge efforts on a broad front. Many owners of radios and cassette recorders here don't realize they've got an East German product.

He described his early impression of his East German customers: "At this point the East German whiz kids couldn't even tell an ion gun from a steam engine."[15] The significance of this observation would become clear only later.

It was while he was in New York that Karl-Heinz Pfneudl initiated the next stage of development in Sacher Technik Wien. He and Rudi had agreed that to succeed against the massive resources of Silicon Valley, they had to specialize in an advanced area that seemed to be ignored by the giants of the south Bay Area. But Pfneudl had to go back to Austria, so it was essential that he establish a permanent link in the Valley. The opportunity came one day when the young Austrian read an advertisement in the *Wall Street Journal*. It had been placed by Peter Gopal, who was looking for additional funding to expand his business. He had been employed originally by Texas Instruments in Dallas and now ran his own consulting firm in Sunnyvale, specializing in "reverse engineering." Gopal would buy a chip on the open market and then, through the use of a microscope and a camera, backtrack to the original design masks. This would make it possible for him — or a customer — to move directly into manufacturing, by-passing the lengthy and expensive design process.[16]

The technique was not original with Gopal, but neither Pfneudl nor Sacher had yet encountered it, and when Sacher heard about it from his partner, he was sufficiently impressed to buy a 50 percent share of Gopal's company, Semiconductor Systems International, Inc. (SSII). It was 1973, and for Gopal, born in Singapore and educated at college level in London, it boded well for his future in the United States. The relationship with the Austrians worked well, and the engineer prospered. From time to time, Gopal would sell Sacher the result of the reverse engineering work he performed on state-of-the-art microchips. But more often, he would fill Rudi's order for the high-tech semiconductor development and test systems that Sacher needed to keep pace with the development work he was performing for the East Germans.

Just one example was invoiced on December 20, 1977. It was a Megatest Q8000 Test System with a power-supply modification enabling it to run on European 240-volt power supplies. The invoice specified that the amount had to be paid in advance and that the freight charges would be paid, collect, in the SSII checking account number 0570–02300 at the International Science Center Branch of the Bank of America, Sunnyvale. The amount was paid in full on January 31, 1978, and the shipment went ahead as planned.[17] There were even opportunities for Gopal to do some direct business on his own account with the Eastern bloc. In particular, Sacher was to take Gopal on his first trip to the Soviet Union to start negotiations for the sale of light-emitting diodes (LEDS), which at that time were used to display the numbers on pocket calculators. In the end, he did not get the lucrative contract, but it was not for want of trying.

When visiting Vienna, Gopal often met East European businessmen in the Apollogasse 6 office of Rudi Sacher. One was a senior Polish official, Zdzislaw Przychodzien, who was introduced as the Deputy Director of the Ministry of Machine Industry in Warsaw, Poland. Further meetings with Przychodzien took place later.[18] The money continued to flow in for the next five years. During the first six months of 1978, SSII received from companies associated with Rudi Sacher payments of $48,500, $28,400, $65,000, $125,000, $45,000, $50,000, $270,000 and $20,000.[19] In fact, business was so good that Gopal and Sacher were able to dabble in the California real estate market. And the amounts involved were substantial. In a telex to Gopal, dated June 6, 1978, Sacher said:

DEAR PETER, DO YOU HAVE SOME NEWS? HOW ARE YOU? IT SEEMS TO ME THAT I HAVE FOUND A SOLUTION FOR ITEM 1. (I WILL WRITE YOU A LETTER WITH SOME MORE DETAILS IN THE NEXT DAYS.) ARE YOU IN A POSITION TO MAKE AN OFFER FOR 8702 (1702A), PACKAGE SIMILAR TO OUR DISCUSSION IN MILANO? SCHIELERS FRIEND SOUNDS POSITIVE: HE BELIEVES THAT DECISION WILL NOT BE MADE UNTIL THE END OF THE MONTH. ASK DAN IF HE IS INTERESTED IN AN INVESTMENT OF 400 KDLRS. COULD YOU GIVE ME SOON HIS STATEMENT ABOUT CONDITIONS? (MAIN QUESTION: HOW MANY % OF THE SHARES?) PLEASE GO AHEAD WITH ROM PROGRAM YOU SELECT. BEST REGARDS, RUDI.

The 8702 referred to is a Texas Instruments microchip; 400 KDLRS is $400,000. By the summer of 1978, SSII had $471,056 in its savings account.[20]

Suddenly, the heady relationship went wrong. On September 28,

1978, Peter Gopal was arrested by the Sheriff's Department of Santa Clara County. His home and office were searched, with the active participation of technical staff from both the Intel Corporation and National Semiconductor. Many documents, computer tapes, and chip design materials were seized. Peter Gopal was charged with stealing the trade secrets of Intel and National Semiconductor.[21] As soon as he was released on bail, one of the first people Gopal called was Rudi Sacher. Sacher visited Gopal in January 1979, and gave him substantial moral and financial support in the following years.[22]

Gopal's case did not come to trial in Santa Clara County Court until November 1980. The searches had uncovered the business cards of many Russian and Austrian businessmen, including the cards or addresses of Rudi Sacher, Udo Proksch, and his brother Roderich Proksch, as well as other firms believed to be involved in trade with the Eastern bloc. Invoices suggested that Gopal had sold the designs for a variety of memory chips to intermediary companies, which may then have shipped them on to East Germany, Poland, and the Soviet Union.[23] It is believed that both the FBI and the CIA were involved in the investigation of the Gopal case.

Even before the trial of the Texas Instruments–trained reverse engineer, another bombshell was dropped. Early in 1979 a senior officer of the Staatssicherheitsdienst (SSD), the East German Security Service, defected to West Germany. He was Oberstleutnant (Lieutenant Colonel) Werner Stiller, and he brought with him many documents and papers that took the German authorities months to analyze. Of particular interest was a list of names and other information identifying a number of people in the West as agents or contacts of the SSD. Most of them were in West Germany, and a series of raids and arrests there soon followed. Another part of the list could not be acted on by the Germans; it was a list of Austrian names and was passed to the security service in Vienna.

That list caused a sensation. The names on it were said to include those of Dr. Rudolf Sacher and Karl-Heinz Pfneudl. Also described as an agent for the Soviet Union was the unnamed owner of a prominent café who was well connected in Austrian Socialist Party circles. This last was enough for the Viennese press; within days, the headlines began to appear: HERR PROKSCH, ARE YOU A SPY?[24] All three men were questioned closely by the Austrian security service, but unlike events in West Germany, no arrests were made. None of them denied his connections with the Eastern bloc, but all denied vehemently being involved in any form of espionage. Rudolf Sacher commented in a press interview: "They say I am an East German spy because I do business with East Germany. Does that mean that *anyone* who does business with East Germany is automatically a spy?"[25] Peter Gopal must have been horrified. Stealing trade secrets was a bad enough charge, but did the latest developments mean that he could be accused of espionage?

Udo Proksch responded to the questioning with characteristic panache: "Everything that's been written about me recently is a textbook case of how to frame someone as a spy. Unfortunately, I'm not a spy ... but there are times when I might have enjoyed being one." He went on to imply that the Austrian security service was using him to blacken the name of Chancellor Kreisky during an election year. "The Stiller memorandum and others like it are complete humbug. When someone changes sides he has to 'sell himself' somehow and make himself interesting," Proksch declared.[26]

In spite of the denials, some important issues were left unresolved. Although the U.S. Department of Commerce did carry out a post-shipment verification on the licensed equipment that Gopal had purchased for Sacher Technik Wien, there was little they could do to locate the whereabouts of the hardware sent from Semiconductor Systems International to two Swiss companies, Optron AG and Implama AG.[27] In the period between Gopal's meeting with Zdzislaw Przychodzien in late 1977 and his arrest the following fall, there were at least four shipments to these two companies of goods with a total value of $460,000. Payments were received promptly from accounts with the Union Bank of Switzerland.[28] But was there a connection with the "Vienna Ring"? And were the goods being diverted to Poland?

The addresses of Optron and Implama were the same: Postfach 1157, CH-6300 Zug, Switzerland. (*Postfach* is a post office box.) Postfach 1157 was also the address for the offices of Max Peterhans in Artherstrasse 12 in Zug.[29] Peterhans was one of those involved with Udo Proksch and Hermine Ettrich in the 1972 takeover of Demel's House in Vienna. Even more significant, Implama's company records named Karl-Heinz Pfneudl, Sacher's partner, as "responsible director."[30] Max Peterhans appeared to operate as the administrator of Swiss companies on behalf of a variety of other people. Nearly fifty such firms were said to be registered at his office in Zug, which is in a cantonment to the south of Zürich whose laws particularly favor corporate privacy. Peterhans was known to have an interest in other Proksch companies and was also an associate of Rudi Wein. Peterhans's name and address were in Peter Gopal's contact book. But did Optron and Implama ship the goods from Semiconductor Systems International on to Poland? The only evidence for this that is not circumstantial was cited by the Santa Clara County prosecuting attorney, Douglas Southard, to a Senate hearing in May 1982:

> The investigation continued after Gopal's arrest, however, and a business associate was located who told authorities that Gopal bragged of having purchased certain integrated circuit testing equipment and selling to Poland via one of his Swiss intermediaries. Gopal bragged to him that he had received three times the fair market value of the equipment in cash, and had successfully smuggled the cash back into the United States without interdiction by Customs or Commerce officials.

Southard confirmed that Gopal had indeed purchased the test equipment, but its "ultimate" purchaser could not be identified.[31] The implication was that Gopal made a clear profit, on the deals with the Pole, of more than $1 million in cash over a period of not much more than seven months.

The Commerce Department investigation into the affair concluded that probably nothing more than misdemeanors could be proved under the Export Administration Act and that the penalty would be no more severe than blacklisting through a denial order. Nor were espionage charges brought by the FBI, and the Santa Clara County District Attorney's Office was left to its own devices. Gopal was found guilty in 1981 on six counts of receiving and possessing stolen trade secrets, bribery, and conspiracy. He was sentenced to a prison term of two years and eight months, but was freed on bail pending an appeal. At the end of 1983, the appeal had still not been scheduled. In spite of massive legal expenses, Peter Gopal lives well by most standards. Although he has been unable to continue to run Semiconductor Systems International because the court holds all the company records, he does have income from real estate investments.[32] When he arrives at the Peppermill, his favorite bar, just off U.S. 101 in Silicon Valley, he now drives a Honda Accord rather than his Porsche 928.

When asked why he did not plea-bargain, he said: "Because I was not guilty of the charges. I did not steal those materials and did not know they were in my office." Asked about his plans for the future, he replied: "I will get back into reverse engineering. That is what the semiconductor industry trained me to do and it is definitely not illegal."[33]

The reverse engineering of integrated circuits is by no means a Soviet threat against the American electronics industry. The technique of buying new, competitive chips on the open market and then using microphotographic techniques to derive the original design schemata was a procedure developed in the West by the industry itself. The purpose of this is not necessarily sinister. When Peter Gopal worked for Texas Instruments, he was specifically employed to do this task and then to write a report for other designers on the quality of the chip, new layout concepts, and so forth.[34] Although most semiconductor manufacturers use the technique in this perfectly legitimate manner, others have been known to use it as the same sort of short cut that the Eastern bloc has been accused of taking. Shortly before Gopal's trial, the television program "NBC Magazine" commissioned a circuit designer named Bert Tunsy to reverse-engineer a chip. For "a few thousand dollars" he returned them the masks that could be used to start the manufacture of chips identical in all respects with the original.[35]

Peter Gopal admits to selling reverse-engineered chip designs to the dummy Swiss companies, but there is no real evidence of the designs having been resold to any Eastern bloc companies.[36] Peter Stoll, a designer employed by the industry giant Intel Corporation, claims that the Russian memory chip design he saw reproduced in a Soviet trade magazine was identical with one of his own company's products.

That Russian chip is simply this American chip copied. . . . Ordinarily, an engineer is too proud to copy this fine level of detail that is clearly not related to the proper functioning of the device. This chap was either so frightened by his boss, who told him it better be exactly the same or I'll want to know the reason why, that he was unwilling to make any new engineering changes. He only removed such trivial details as the initials of the designer. . . . Or he was working from a stolen copy and was only making such changes as removing our copyright.[37]

Does that mean that one of Peter Gopal's reverse-engineering designs did find its way to the Soviet Union? Or did Soviet engineers do the job themselves? According to Gopal, the process is not that complicated.

If American federal agents found it difficult to investigate the Austro-Swiss dimension of the Gopal affair, it is hardly surprising. The network of more than twenty-five people and companies has a complexity bordering on the labyrinthine. But it does provide an interesting insight into Austrian society, which has a more complex structure than a microchip. In addition to Proksch's involvement in Demel's House with Hermine Ettrich, he also owns the Studio für Werbegestaltung, the chief designer for which is Hermine's husband, Emile. With Rudolf Sacher and Peter Daimler, Proksch was part owner of the now-defunct Optico AG; now Sacher and Proksch are in partnership with Richard Drasche-Wartinberg in Serge Kirchhofer GmbH. Peter Daimler used to be the co-owner of another fashionable coffee house called Das Café in Salzburg; he is now involved in Sacher Technik Wien.

In addition to Sacher Technik Wien and his 50 percent stock holding in Peter Gopal's Semiconductor Systems International, Rudi Sacher had two other companies, Transfina and Italcar, and an interest in a third, Wiener Nevosad. Max Peterhans, Grete Fischer, and Karl-Heinz Pfneudl were all involved in the Swiss company Optron AG, which no longer trades but which was one of Semiconductor Systems International's major customers. Peter Gopal may also have had an interest in Optron; he has described it as "my Swiss company."[38] Karl-Heinz Pfneudl has a company called Karl-Heinz Pfneudl GmbH, in which Rudolf Sacher has an interest. All this started when Udo Proksch set up Kobilac with café-owner Rudi Wein, a friend of Max Peterhans.[39]

The early decision by Sacher and Pfneudl to specialize as a small expert team concentrating on an area of technology not yet fully exploited by the big names of Silicon Valley seems to have paid off. Sacher's group of more than thirty highly qualified technicians eventually won solid funding through a development contract from the East German foreign trade organization Industrie Anlagen Import (IAI). In fact, Sacher's initial contact with the German organization caused him some difficulty at a later date. The East German defector Stiller alleged that Sacher had written a secret seventy-four-page report on the state-of-the-art in semiconductor manufacture. Sacher explained in reply to this charge that all he had done was give a professional assessment of Western chip-making drawn entirely from public sources. He had sent four copies to East Germany, as requested. In the course of things, one copy apparently made its way to the Staatssicherheitsdienst, where Stiller had access to it. There was nothing in the least sinister about the report, Sacher insisted.[40]

The research that IAI commissioned from Sacher involved new techniques to produce microchips. The regular photograph-plus-chemical-baking approach employed short-wave ultraviolet light. The method researched by Sacher was based on implanting the miniature circuits directly onto silicon wafers with a superfine beam of ions, very accurately controlled by a computer. The computer is programmed with a database that specifies very precisely the layout of the circuit. The computer then directs the beam in the right pattern to implant the circuit onto the pure silicon.

The benefits of the process are many. The number of chips to pass the quality testing is very high compared with current techniques. (Peter Gopal claimed that toward the end of his research Sacher was achieving 100 percent success rates.) The quality of the implanted circuit, with its very low signal-to-noise ratio, combined with the compactness of the chips produced by this method, makes it possible for the circuits to run at very high speeds. The density of ion-beam chips puts them in the VLSI category — hundreds of thousands of components per chip. By the early 1980s, the new ion-beam implantation production techniques were still relatively slow and the end product expensive, but development technicians are confident that there will be marked improvements in the production process to compensate for this.

Most major American semiconductor companies are known to be making large investments in the field of ion-beam implantation. Technical representatives of IBM visited Rudi Sacher in 1978 to discuss the state of his research. It is not known whether the East

Germans are in advance of IBM, Texas Instruments, or any of the other American companies in state-of-the-art technology, but Peter Gopal has confirmed that Rudi Sacher completed the East German order for ion-beam equipment during 1983.[41]

Other Austrian and Swiss firms have run afoul of the U.S. Department of Commerce from time to time and have been formally denied export privileges. However, despite the barrage of accusations directed at the Austro-Swiss group with which Sacher and his associates were involved, not a single one of them has been charged with spying, smuggling, fraud, conspiracy, stealing trade secrets, or any other form of wrongdoing, in the United States or anywhere else.

9

SOME BANDITS

IN DECEMBER 1981, the first major clandestine supply network from the United States to the Soviet Union had just been broken. Everything about the event seemed to set records. The network appeared to have been the most successful collection effort ever launched by the Russians, and, correspondingly, the American investigation had the hallmarks of the best of its kind to that date. The Customs and Commerce agents involved were congratulating themselves on the number of convictions they had obtained. One West German involved had made his fortune as a dollar millionaire. The Russians had managed for the first time to get all the complex systems needed to equip a new semiconductor-manufacturing plant. Practically everybody had come out ahead.

The American investigation began in March 1980, and it determined that for the past three years the underground network had used dummy corporations in Los Angeles and West Germany to export state-of-the-art technology worth over $8 million. The Soviets, of course, had paid three times that much, and the operators had netted more than $4 million — but the Soviets, with their new plant, were the most satisfied of customers.

Very early on, the case looked so complex and important that the investigators called in one of the country's foremost experts on Soviet computing and technology, Dr. Lara H. Baker, of the University of California's International Technology Office. Dr. Baker's expertise is impressive. He has been an adviser to U.S. Intelligence agencies and was the chairman of the technical task group that rewrote the computer embargo lists for presentation to COCOM.

Dr. Baker began to read waybills. During the investigation, he read, with an educated eye, over four hundred waybills and other shipping documents that had been seized in California or Europe. Putting all the pieces together, he was able to reach the conclusion that during the previous three years the exporters had sold at least one complete integrated-circuit production plant to the Soviets. From the evidence of the papers, he could see that the Soviets were very logical shoppers. "They know exactly what they want, down to the model numbers," he told a Senate committee in May 1982. "High-quality integrated circuits are the basis of modern military electronics . . . [and] form the basis of modern weapons systems, which are more flexible, more capable, and more reliable."[1]

To connoisseurs of smuggling, this was a classic case. Misdirection had been perfected. One company purchased equipment and another exported it. The unwitting original manufacturer-suppliers had been fed elaborate cover stories. Shipments had been wrongly described and undervalued on the export declarations. At least one of the clandestine shippers had requested the innocent manufacturers not to send salesmen or repairmen around — because the work involved was classified!

The underground channels to the East were equally ingenious. The California company would forward the equipment to a false-front company in West Germany. Then the German collaborators would transship through a neutral like Austria or Switzerland. Another favored route was from Germany to Schiphol Airport, Amsterdam, where Soviet Aeroflot jets picked up the illicit cargo.

As the investigation progressed, one interesting question that arose was this: Just who in Moscow was the mastermind behind this very astute operation? During one raid on a company in Düsseldorf, agents uncovered a purchase order dated March 9, 1978. It was from the foreign trade organization Elektronorgtekhnika (Elorg), Ministry of Foreign Trade Building, 32/34 Smolenskaya Square, Moscow. That was the first clue.

According to the purchase order, Elorg was to pay $263,000 for twenty-three pieces of equipment that made up a complete Data General Eclipse S-230 scientific minicomputer system. This included a display console, disc storage drive, magnetic tape unit, paper tape reader and punch, and a card reader. But the curious thing about the order was that it also requested a 4206 Multiprocessor Communications Adapter — equipment used to link together two Eclipse machines. Apparently, the Soviets already had one and wanted a pair.[2]

What was even more fascinating about the purchase order was that it furnished the final clue as to the Moscow mastermind. In a perfectly regular and ordinary way, his signature was affixed to the order. He worked in Office Number 8 of Elorg, and his name was Viktor Nikolayevich Kedrov.

Kedrov was no faceless bureaucrat in the foreign trade *apparat*. In 1974, when the Danes expelled him from Denmark for high-tech espionage, he was believed to be an officer in Soviet General Staff Intelligence Division, the GRU. Before that, he had served four years, from 1964 to 1968, as a member of the Soviet trade delegation in London. Back in Moscow in 1979, Kedrov profited from a reorganization of Elorg when he was promoted to the board of deputy directors, the six men who manage the whole Elorg enterprise. Although the other five are written about in Soviet publications, no biographical information on Kedrov appears.[3]

Then, among other papers taken in the Düsseldorf raid, another, later purchase order turned up, also signed by Kedrov. It was dated November 1979, and it was for $160,000 worth of equipment. It was apparent that the Soviet end-user had taken delivery of his Eclipse, had linked it with the other, and was preparing for full operation. Elorg now wanted an additional power supply, three spare kits, operation and service manuals, a package of service equipment, and a printer-plotter.

One interesting sidelight in the five-page contract was the specification that any dispute that might arise between Elorg and the supplier would be settled by the arbitration commission in Stockholm.

At the end of the document was a handwritten note in English, stating that the 12 percent discount on the $26,000 purchase was to be used to buy a larger memory for the CPU (central processing unit) — 256K bytes instead of 196K bytes.[4]

The case came to be known as the Bruchhausen case, after Werner Bruchhausen, the West German millionaire who was the architect of the clandestine supply network. In December 1981, when the case was closed, Commerce and Customs investigators thought they had good reason for celebration. The investigation had been large and the cooperation had been good. Fifteen U.S. Customs agents and their West German counterparts had participated, as well as Commerce Department officials and two experienced Internal Revenue Service special agents. The documents had been splendid evidence, and one of the best Soviet supply lines had been cut.

In reality, the Bruchhausen case is far from a success story. The government acted neither very quickly nor very efficiently in the matter. The very first signal was an anonymous letter to the American consulate in Düsseldorf, where one of the main Bruchhausen companies was located. The letter accused Bruchhausen of violating U.S. export controls and said that his export documents had been falsified. It noted Bruchhausen companies in West Germany and California and went on to say that the exporter was "in cooperation with Intra-Engineering, working on a complete installation for the production of semiconductors for an embargo country." The letter was signed "Former employees."[5]

Less than nine months later, the "Former employees" wrote again, this time with more details. Bruchhausen was now accused of writing false descriptions of equipment destined for delivery in countries on the embargo list. Pan Alpina in Switzerland was specified as a freight forwarder involved. Enclosed were copies of documents proving that Bruchhausen had supplied a company on Commerce's blacklist. It continued, "Mr. Bruchhausen's high profitability from such dealings is evident from the fact that he was in a position to furnish a surety bond amounting to DM 1.5 million at the American Express Bank in Düsseldorf for the construction of a semiconductor manufacturing plant. Mr. Bruchhausen will construct such a plant with Intra-Engineering GmbH and furnish it with American equipment."[6]

The consulate translated the letters and sent them on to the Compliance Division of Commerce, which did nothing about them.

There were other people — in Silicon Valley and elsewhere — who were beginning to get a bit suspicious of Bruchhausen by this time. Robert Markin of the Perkin-Elmer Company in Wilton, Connecticut, investigated an order he'd received from the Bruchhausen-owned California Technology Corporation (CTC) and reported to Commerce that he thought CTC must be a front.[7] At this point, the Compliance Division — a year and nine months after the first anonymous tip — took some action. It sent an agent to interview Anatoli T. M. Maluta, Bruchhausen's chief associate in Silicon Valley.

Maluta was born in Kharkov, former capital of the Ukraine, in 1920, and was now a naturalized American. He headed CTC on Hawthorne Boulevard in Torrance, California, whose export business, he said, was quite small. Mainly, he acted as a broker for foreign companies.

The agent then asked him about a piece of equipment he had ordered from Perkin-Elmer on July 7, 1978. It was a powerful semiconductor-testing system known as Micralign, valued at $150,000. It required an export license to be shipped abroad, but it was definitely embargoed for Soviet bloc shipment. Maluta replied that he knew little about export regulations. The agent asked to see the license-application documents. At that, Maluta offered to cancel the order — and he later did.

Eight months later, the export administration manager at the Fairchild System Group of San Jose became concerned about Mr. Maluta. After receiving an order from him, Fairchild did a background investigation while holding up the order. The Fairchild manager then queried Commerce, the Office of Defense Intelligence in Washington, and the FBI. To Commerce, he wrote that Maluta wanted to buy several semiconductor memory test systems valued at $740,000.

The Fairchild investigation had turned up the facts that Maluta was "a naturalized citizen who had served with the United States Air Force in Berlin, Frankfurt, and Munich and at Edwards Air Force Base. He held a top secret clearance in the military."

Neither the FBI nor the Office of Defense Intelligence saw any reason that Fairchild should not make the sale. Maluta himself, they had been informed, had signed a declaration that if the systems were ever resold, all rules and regulations of the Department of Commerce would be observed.

A month later, Commerce had another suspicious query about

Bruchhausen. The security manager of the Watkins-Johnson Company in Palo Alto, which had been doing business with Bruchhausen companies, wrote, "Since they have changed names frequently, we are concerned that there may be a reason. Could you please check on their current name and past identities and advise me by telephone." He also quoted from a Dun and Bradstreet report that described Maluta's firm as manufacturing surveillance equipment for "area protection" for the Air Force, Navy, and Atomic Energy Commission.

Special Agent Robert Rice of the Compliance Division arrived at Watkins-Johnson and learned that Maluta had four pending orders, totaling $983,663. The largest was for a Model WJ 1240 microwave receiving and antenna system. There was another for a WJ 940 model, which Maluta had said would be used in an "intrusion detection system" at the Fort Huachuca, Arizona, site of the Army's Communications Command and an Army Intelligence School. Rice called at Fort Huachuca. Headquarters there had never ordered anything from a Maluta company.

Back at Fairchild, Rice found out that Maluta companies had bought several of these security systems between 1977 and 1979 and, interestingly, had never allowed a Fairchild representative onto Maluta premises for installation or repair work. Rice presented his evidence to the office of the U.S. attorney in Los Angeles, and the Bruchhausen investigation finally began.

The assistant U.S. attorney who received Rice's evidence was Theodore Wai Lu. Listening to the agent, he got his first inkling of what he later called "the largest illegal strategic export venture in scope and most deliberate in planning and execution." This was, he thought, a conspiracy that had been "virtually impossible to detect on its own."

But Wu had a problem. Compliance Division agents are not law enforcement officers with the power to search, seize, or arrest, and Commerce had neither the manpower nor the authority to pursue the Bruchhausen case. Wu called on Customs; fifteen Customs agents were immediately deployed in California, Texas, and Western Europe.

Investigators quickly determined that Maluta was now in the process of buying two sophisticated Hi-Pox high-pressure furnaces, valued at $300,000, from Gasonics, Inc., of Sunnyvale. These are used in the manufacture of integrated circuits. Wu wanted very much to find out the eventual destination for this equipment, so he decided to play a traditional trick.

The Hi-Pox furnaces were taken out of their packing cases and replaced by sand. (This operation cost $10,000, and the Compliance Division back in Washington, worried about the taxpayers' money, refused to foot the bill. Customs paid.) The consignment was to follow an evasive course from California, to Munich, to Vienna, and finally to Schiphol and the June 7, 1980, departure of Aeroflot flight 702. It never made it. Things began to go wrong on June 3.

Dietmar Ulrichshofer, Bruchhausen's partner in Vienna, went to the warehouse where the crated furnaces were stored; he intended to insert an operating manual into one of the boxes. When he discovered the $10,000 worth of sand, he cancelled the shipment.

Ulrichshofer's first thought was that he had been cheated by Bruchhausen, "because I make him a down payment for these machines for $400,000 and this money is away from me now. I never get it back."[8]

On August 19, 1980, agents closed in on Maluta and arrested him and his German lover, Sabina Dorn Tittel, in a parking lot in Palm Desert, California. They found three handguns in the back of his car.

The same day, a federal grand jury in Los Angeles handed down a sixty-count indictment against Bruchhausen, Ulrichshofer, Maluta, and Tittel. The charges were that they had conspired to export more than $8 million worth of high-technology products to the Soviet Union. Maluta and Tittel were also charged with tax evasion. Bruchhausen and Ulrichshofer remained prudently in Europe, not subject to extradition.[9]

In December 1981, U.S. District Court Judge William Matthew Byrne, Jr., sentenced Maluta to five years' imprisonment and fined him $60,000. Tittel got two years and a $25,000 fine.

Bruchhausen, in July 1983, gave an interview to the BBC program "Panorama." He explained: "It was not against the law to ship material from the States to Germany. And it was not against the law to ship it from Germany to Switzerland. And it is not against the law to ship it from Switzerland to the Soviet Union." He did concede that it was "a slight infringement of the rules." Asked whether he was still making money in 1983, he replied, "Yes. It was a good trade and we made some extra money on that and that's why I took the chance."

Theodore Wu said that the positive outcome of the case lay in the fact that the investigation had stopped the conspirators from selling the Soviets additional equipment on order. It included $1.3 million worth of semiconductor-test equipment and a $700,000 microwave surveillance system capable of missile tracking.[10]

Dr. Lara Baker also found a silver lining. "What is lost is lost. . . . But there is a positive side to this case: it is what we can learn from it. There is a wealth of intelligence to be learned from the Bruchhausen case."[11]

In May 1982 Dr. Baker, at a congressional hearing, was asked whether he had ever been questioned about the case by anyone from a government Intelligence agency.

"No, sir," he replied.

A senator pursued the line of questioning. "Do you know anyone who has? Do you know whether they have ever studied the case?"

"No, sir," Dr. Baker repeated. "If they have, I don't know about it."[12]

It was to Santa Clara County that the entrepreneurs of the information age came to find their fortunes. Silicon Valley was, for many, a place of fabulous wealth. In the years from 1962, sales revenues in the south San Francisco Bay Area rocketed from $40 million to an incredible $4.5 billion.

But in the wake of such rapid growth came life styles and attitudes that many despaired of. One businessman described the effect the place had on his life: "The fast pace, the drugs, the alcohol . . . no company loyalties. . . . You have an industry that's so ripe with contradictions, no one knows what is right or wrong."[13] Talking about microchips, another commented, "All of a sudden the whole world said, 'Goddamn revolution is here, baby, these things are priceless.'"[14]

Crime grew in the Valley as rapidly as the wealth. Among those who felt depressed by what was happening to Santa Clara County were the law enforcement officers. In 1980 an estimated $20 million of the new gold nuggets — microchips — were stolen. "Not since the narcotics traffic became streamlined and organized has law enforcement been faced with such a monumental problem," stated a memorandum from the District Attorney's Office that year.[15] And in 1983, the local newspaper, the *San Jose Mercury,* editorialized: "Every electrical engineer with a bright idea ... can start his own company, technological development is rapid — and uncontrollable.... Everybody's making [chips], selling them and stealing them.... It's far too late to put the electronics industry back under Department of Defense control."[16]

Douglas Southard is an experienced deputy district attorney for Santa Clara. He is a graduate of Stanford University with a degree in philosophy and has a J.D. from Hastings College of Law, University of California. For him, the Valley is a prime example of capitalism on the rampage: "Everyone wants to become an overnight millionaire, and money flows like water, tempting the otherwise honest citizen to scramble fast to get his share of the pie."[17] When, in 1982, he was called to testify to Congress, he said: "In the last five years I would estimate that in excess of a hundred million dollars of technology and products have been stolen, illegally copied, or counterfeited from Silicon Valley firms."[18]

Southard described one of his high-technology cases to Congress. It was, he said, littered with dead bodies, assaults, sophisticated thefts, and drug sales. "Scores of criminal conspirators appear to be involved. It represents the largest case of consistent, habitual, organized criminal activity aimed at Silicon Valley." It was a despairing Southard who testified. In the case he was talking about, over eleven thousand integrated circuits valued at more than $100,000 had been stolen. The middleman in the conspiracy had been murdered and a key witness severely beaten.[19] Greed, he said, had spawned the gray market, where technology thieves got rid of their bounty. The electronics industry had created an anything-goes marketplace. "It is really no different from pork belly futures," he said and went on to explain the industry's hierarchy.[20]

Placed between manufacturers (like Intel, National Semiconductor, and Texas Instruments) and the customers (like IBM, Burroughs, General Electric, and the numerous Defense contractors) were the franchised distributors. Although major companies dealt directly with the original manufacturers, the distributors took up production slack and connected supply to demand. But there were also independent distributors who obtained electronic components from other dealers as well as from the manufacturers. They also bought up surplus stock, scrap products, and used parts salvaged from obsolete machines. Southard said that a shortage of parts between 1977 and 1980 had made a lot of people a lot of money.[21] Many rejected chips were not destroyed because their intact value was worth more than the scrap value. Unmarked parts were easy targets and were often stored for months. But the main problem with this scrap technology was not national security, but safety. If these chips were to be installed in medical equipment, airplanes, and microwave devices, critical systems could start failing. "People are going to get hurt," Southard has warned.[22]

Fly-by-night independent distributors sold high technology from low-rent office suites, their homes, or from the trunks of cars. Their suppliers were mostly corrupt Silicon Valley employees. Southard told Congress that the chips, no bigger than contact lenses, could be stolen in coat pockets or lunchboxes: "Most of the theft is by employees.... Quite commonly security personnel are involved.... There is an increasing propensity to steal finished goods, such as computer disc drives and personal computers, which have become smaller in size ... and more easy to steal." There were also burglaries, truck hijackings, and armed robberies.[23] Because high-tech companies had grown so quickly, proper inventory systems had not been implemented; the philosophy was "speedy, inexpensive production and a quick product turnover." On numerous occasions stolen chips have been recovered and confessions given when the company involved could not even prove that anything was missing. Some companies considered security to be more than it was worth. "A number of the largest companies have, to my knowledge, never reported any integrated-circuit thefts."[24]

Southard went on to tell senators of the 1979 theft of Intel memory chips worth more than $1 million, stolen from a locked storage room in Santa Clara. They were known as 2732 EPROMs and were capable of storing thirty-two thousand "bits" of information or, more usually, a computer program. Used extensively in all types of product, especially microcomputers, they were well known to the

gray trade and could be sold for as much as $100 each when legiti-
mate supplies were low.[25]

An undercover deputy from the Sheriff's Department had approached a suspect and offered to sell some of the chips. In September 1980 the suspect took the bait. He told the undercover deputy he
wanted to buy them for his "German connection in Monaco," and
offered $10,000 in cash. As soon as he got possession of the chips, he
took them to San Francisco International Airport. The Customs
Service was notified. But the case was bungled. The shipment was
seized before it was collected by the freight forwarder in West Germany; it never reached the final customer.[26]

Douglas Southard described the U.S. chip broker to the congressional committee. He said the man was "hardly a back-alley crook."
He was a handsome, three-piece-suited president of a successful
parts-distribution firm. "He had a fine home in one of the exclusive
hillside residential areas in Santa Clara County. He and his beautiful wife drove a Mercedes and sent their kids to the best private
schools. He was an armed forces veteran and a member of the reserves ... all in all, a typical American success story. And yet, here
he is, selling stolen integrated circuits to an internationally known
fence. The reason is always the same — greed." But the real revelation was the identity of the "internationally known fence"; this,
claimed the deputy D.A., was none other than Werner Bruchhausen, whom he described as "a notorious international chip broker"
who was "widely reputed to be a Soviet East German agent."[27]

Had this case succeeded, Bruchhausen would now be behind bars.
One of the investigators involved in the case pointed out that "receiving stolen property would be a violation over there, and that's
why he wanted to track it. The Germans would have a case and the
Attorney General would have a case: goddam certified stolen property, no question about it."[28] Southard said they had tried to go all
out to prove the chain of evidence in the case, tracing the parts from
Germany all the way back to the theft source in California, but it
would have required the entire witness budget for Santa Clara
County for a whole year. "Frankly, the public, who is more concerned about violent crime, doesn't want us chasing all over the
world after white-collar crime."[29]

It was a disappointment for two deputies from the Santa Clara

County Sheriff's Department. In July 1979 the department had increased enforcement to try to stop high-tech crime in the area. One of the deputies put on the job was Wayne Brown, an outspoken man who now works for a local security firm. He had specialized as an undercover narcotics agent — and he pursued technology thieves with gusto. He was soon working on the case involving the stolen Intel 2732 chips, and he came to the conclusion that the man who had pulled off the theft was a West German called Brendt Werner; some of the stolen chips were being bought by companies controlled by Werner. What Brown wanted to know was why the FBI was not involved in the case. The Sheriff's Office ought to be the last to know about it, he claimed.[30]

By April 1980 — just under a month after the major Bruchhausen inquiry began — Brown and his partner, Lieutenant Bob McDiarmid, came to believe that Werner was, in fact, Bruchhausen. McDiarmid complained later that no other government agencies were interested in their conclusions. He said that the FBI told him that blackmarketing was nothing more than property crime. However, five months later — in September 1980 — the two deputies were taken to Terminal Island, Los Angeles, where they received a briefing at Customs headquarters. They were told that the FBI and Customs had started a major investigation into the Bruchhausen case.[31]

"There is no need for spies," Maluta once said. "You can get all this stuff without any intrigue." In 1983 he told reporters Pete Carey and Steve Johnson from the *San Jose Mercury* that it was common knowledge in the electronics industry that high-technology products were being shipped overseas in violation of Customs laws. Many integrated circuits, he told them, were available from American subsidiaries in Europe. Later that year he was interviewed by a British television crew. "You show up with the money and they're going to sell you anything you want, no questions asked."[32]

The inexplicable indifference of most law enforcement agencies was underlined when Doug Southard, in his testimony to Congress, observed that only once had another agency taken any interest in one of his high-technology cases or in the information he had to offer. That had been the case of Peter Gopal. One Customs agent had spent a day going through Gopal's personal and company files in the Santa Clara County Clerk of Court's Office. Otherwise, there had never been any curiosity on the part of a U.S. agency — not Commerce, the CIA, nor the FBI.[33]

At the beginning of the 1980s, Bob Lambert was a Southern California businessman who exuded success. He was a well-known consultant in the high-tech industry. He was a member of the Foreign Trade Association, and, as an export-import specialist, he held seminars for new companies and advised on the problems of commercial legislation. He taught export control at the Fullerton campus of California State University. He had a Presidential Medal for his services to exporters. His house was worth $250,000 and his export business was lucrative.[34]

In April 1982, Bob Lambert phoned a division of the Hughes Aircraft Corporation in Torrance and ordered half a million dollars' worth of high-tech equipment of a kind that could be used in satellites, missiles, and for various communications applications. This hardware was sold widely, but it could not be licensed for export to the Communist bloc countries. But that was no problem, because Bob Lambert simply wanted it for a customer in San Diego. It was a good day for Hughes Electron Dynamics Division; this was the largest commercial order it had ever received. The equipment would have to be specially built, however, since its military uses were limited and it had never been manufactured for stock.[35]

Dave Meisner, the Operation Exodus manager for Los Angeles, based there in the monolithic Federal Building, was the sort of Customs agent who kept in close touch with what was going on in the high-tech industry. He had met Lambert several times when Lambert was seeking advice on export controls for his clients. Now, when he got news of the Hughes order, he could not help being suspicious. The equipment was of a very sophisticated sort, and senior Hughes officials had already concluded that there was a very good chance that Lambert was intending to ship it overseas. The possible legitimate customers in the United States were very few. From the first, the Hughes company was most cooperative with the Customs Service.

On Wednesday, May 26, 1982, the company informed Customs that some of the equipment was about to be picked up. The next day at lunchtime, agents watched as Lambert's teen-age son, Michael, collected nine boxes sealed with white tape bearing the Hughes logo. Michael loaded them into his Chevrolet truck and drove to a company in the El Segundo area, near Los Angeles International Airport. The boxes were unloaded and taken inside.[36]

As Customs agents were keeping watch on the airport at 5:30 P.M., a silver Mercedes with Arizona license plates drove up to the loading dock in El Segundo. The boxes were put into the Mercedes. With agents following discreetly, the car drove to the Paseo de la Playa in an exclusive part of Torrance and at last pulled into the red-tile driveway of number 631. The house was near the crest of a hill and had a superb view of the ocean. It was Southern California–Spanish in style, with a beige stucco front and a white rock roof. Ornate wrought-iron fences surrounded a garden full of trees and shrubs. Two men unloaded the boxes from the car into the garage and then went inside the house.

The surveillance continued. But a little later in the evening, the Customs agents suddenly discovered that they had a problem. A police squad car pulled up behind them and they found themselves looking at the gun of one policeman while the other pulled them from their car. The agents were duly embarrassed — they thought they had cleared the action with the local cops, but one of them hadn't got the message. Luckily, the inhabitants of the house seemed to be unaware of the commotion outside.

The next day shortly before dawn, the two men came out of the house. One was carrying a gray Samsonite suitcase that appeared to be heavy. The Hughes packing cases were nowhere in evidence. The men got into the car and drove to the warehouse of a company called Uni-Data International. The agents watched the warehouse until midafternoon, when one man emerged, put two suitcases into the car, and drove to the airport. He checked the suitcases at curbside and left the car in a parking lot. The baggage tags, the agents, noted, were for a Zürich flight.

It took a little while for the agents to locate the suitcases again in the baggage area of TWA, but when they opened them, they were rewarded. The cases contained 107 pieces of electronic equipment.

Before long, the Zürich flight was called at the departure gate. The agents waited until their man was about ten feet from the plane door, and then they stopped him and arrested him for removing equipment from the country without the required export license.

His name was Franz Albert Kessler and he was a Swiss national, according to his passport. In his briefcase, the agents found a round-trip ticket for Geneva to Belgrade.[37]

Kessler was taken to the Los Angeles police station at San Pedro and booked. The agents noted that two things seemed to horrify him: one, the two drunken punk-rockers who were being booked at the same time, and the other, the thought of losing his right to do business in the United States.

When Kessler was questioned and investigated, it became clear that he had no idea of the capabilities of the equipment he had been carrying. He was simply the kind of broker that Customs agents call "10-percenters," from the amount of commission they get. According to government officials, Kessler had been given a detailed shopping list of equipment by the Soviet embassy in Belgrade and had then requested Lambert to get him a catalogue of the desired Hughes technology. Kessler was sentenced to six months for the offense and deportation after that.

The man who owned the silver Mercedes and the hill house at 631 Paseo de la Playa was one Dierk Hagemann. The Uni-Data International warehouse was his, and he was reported to be one of the most experienced exporters of specialized high technology in the Los Angeles area. Hagemann was a German who had arrived some time in the mid-seventies and become a millionaire by 1982. He was rather contemptuous of Americans, especially American officials.[38]

Ironically, just before his arrest, Hagemann had been interviewed by a BBC reporter on his opinions about the effectiveness of export controls. Said Hagemann, "I think it's more or less a drop in the bucket. If you look at the Los Angeles situation, with five inspectors on a daily basis controlling several hundreds, if not thousands, of flights in and out of the city, I would think it's very, very difficult to do an effective job."[39]

Lambert lost a lot of weight during his six months in prison. Hagemann and Kessler were bitter about the deportation that followed their imprisonment. Special Agent Dave Meisner's final comment was "It's those who know the law and use the loopholes — they think they are smarter than us." This time, at least, there were three who weren't.

It was very cold in church on this day and the younger of the two agents shivered in his parka.[40] It is usually bitter in Kansas in December, and the draft from the partly open window made things even worse. The agent bent down again and peered through the tripod-mounted binoculars across the open ground to the UCSO warehouse, rented by the Allen Electronics Company. This was their second week of freezing at the observation post in the unheated church, and Melville Schloss, a Commerce Department agent, imagined that he was gradually turning blue. There still seemed to be no chance of taking action, making the switch he and his partner had planned.

"Better get the door," he said to the other man. "Here come Chuck 'n' Chuck."

The other agent crossed the church to the front door, unlocked it, and admitted two men in heavy overcoats. They were U.S. Customs Special Agents Charles E. Brisbin and Charles L. McLeod. McLeod brushed the condensation from his ginger beard and walked over to the lookout. He was a New Englander by origin, but he and his men came from the San Francisco office of Customs, and Kansas in the dead of winter had been something of a nasty surprise.

"You'd have a better chance against frostbite if you'd shut the window," Brisbin said.

"Well," said Schloss, "you know the problem." He gestured at the window with his gloved hand. It was stained glass, made up of many small segments, and there was just no chance of seeing anything through it with the binoculars.

"That's stupid," Brisbin said.

"Yeah," said McLeod, "but don't worry. I can fix it. Look here, we'll get a pane of glass the right size and just slip it in the open space below the window."

Within a few hours, the new pane had been put in place, the temperature in the church had risen, and morale had been restored — to a certain extent. The main discomfort now was the no-smoking rule. The minister had been generous about allowing the agents to stake out in his church, but he had been firm about smoking.

McLeod and Brisbin returned to their own surveillance duty on the Kansas City home of Paul Allen, owner of the Allen Electronics Company.

The story began back in February 1975, when Gerald M. Starek took a business trip to France. Starek was the thirty-three-year-old director of a Sunnyvale semiconductor production firm properly called II Industries, Inc., but known in Silicon Valley as Triple I. His company was going through a lean period, and Starek was both worried and hungry. It seemed, therefore, like something of a godsend when he got a piece of good news from his European representative, Jerry Gessner.

There was a trader named Müller in Hamburg, Jerry said, who wanted to place some big orders for semiconductor equipment. And the man was talking in millions of dollars.

Starek was delighted. He immediately got himself a plane reservation for Hamburg to meet Gessner's contact. And he was not disappointed when he met Richard Müller. The German was cordial. After some discussion, he told Starek that if the right arrangements could be made, he could give Triple I an order for $1.5 million worth of equipment. And there was even more than that down the road — his client had a total planned expenditure of some $6 to $8 million.[41]

There was one notable detail. Müller's client lived in Moscow. Müller wanted to make no secret about that.

Gerald Starek swallowed hard, but, in the end, he shook Müller's hand on the deal and, a few days later, flew back to Sunnyvale.

Starek very quickly went into a huddle with Carl E. Storey, Triple I's vice-president for sales. The question was not quite so much whether the deal was legitimate, but how it could be made to look legitimate. The scheme was that Müller would set up a U.S. front company to act as purchaser of the Triple I products. Then the German would sign an undertaking, saying that he would be responsible for obtaining U.S. export licenses for all equipment to be sent abroad. To the Triple I men, this seemed a reasonably good safeguard.

In March 1975, Müller flew to California and met Starek and Storey in the Hilton Hotel at San Francisco International Airport. Things were progressing well, Müller reported. He had already helped set up a U.S. company, of which he became vice president. It was to be known as Semicon and was to be located at Mays Landing, in New Jersey. And he was pleased to sign the undertaking about the export licenses.

On April 2, Starek and Storey brought the proposed deal to the Triple I board of directors' meeting and argued strongly in favor of accepting it. The directors were convinced, and though there is no available record of how the discussion went, some idea of their reasoning comes from the statements of Jack D. Melchior, a director who wasn't able to attend. Melchior had a separate meeting with Starek and Storey and later testified in court that he had then consulted "friendly contacts" in the State Department, Customs, Commerce, and the CIA to sound them out on the legitimacy of Müller's scheme. Melchior insists that he was told that as long as the sale was within the United States, Triple I had no worries.[42] That vague report seems to have been the extent of the company's inquiries.

Triple I's next move was to enlist the services of John D. Marshall, an old friend of the firm, who would act as consultant on the design of the semiconductor-manufacturing plant. Marshall was told that the plant was going to be built in Hamburg. To share the production, another Silicon Valley supply company, Kasper Instruments, was cut in on the deal.

On May 1, Gerald Starek received a phone call from a man named Eugene Oakes. Oakes introduced himself as an officer from the Department of Commerce's Compliance Division. He seemed to be surprisingly well informed about the Müller connection and he warned that the Mays Landing company was a dubious customer. There was a good chance, he said, that any technology it bought from Triple I might end up behind the Iron Curtain. And, furthermore, he knew about Richard Müller's connection with Semicon.

What Starek probably knew and Oakes didn't was that one shipment of Triple I products sold to Semicon had already left Norfolk, Virginia, en route to Hamburg. So Starek was on the spot, and his only protection was to play dumb. He assured Oakes that the company had no intention of selling equipment outside the country. He also promised that he would take Oakes's warning to heart and cancel the contract with Semicon. And he meant what he said. Semicon was obviously a little too well known.

To meet the emergency, Müller flew to California in June. He discussed tactics with Starek and Storey in the North Mary Avenue offices of Triple I, and eventually a new plan evolved. It was, rather surprisingly, based on the advice of one of the shipping clerks at Triple I. Semicon was to be replaced by two new front companies located in Montreal. One was to be called USA Trade and the other — with depressing unoriginality — Semitronics. Actually, both companies were letter-drops in the offices of Kuhn and Nagel, a major Canadian shipping company.

John Marshall, the consultant, took three trips to Hamburg in 1975 in order to confer with Müller about the proposed plant — which, he soon learned, was not going to be built in Hamburg after all. On two of these trips, he went on to Moscow with Müller to discuss matters with representatives of the Soviet purchaser. In Hamburg, Marshall had overheard certain enigmatic conversations between Müller and his close business associate Volker Nast, but, he testified later, the full import of the affair dawned on him slowly.[43] It was only after he learned that Technopromimport was the buyer, after he had met Mr. Pavlov of that foreign trade organization, and after he had ascertained that the Russians did not intend to make digital watches with the Triple I equipment, that he began to guess what was up.

On December 17, 1975, a West German traveling under the name of Paul Reimer, the head of Reimer Klimatechnik of Hamburg, boarded a Chicago-bound plane at Kansas City. Once at O'Hare, he went to the international terminal and checked in at the Lufthansa counter for his flight to Hamburg.

The Lufthansa clerk looked at him and then looked at the display screen, on which there was a somewhat unusual message. It requested the clerk to ask for Reimer's passport, then to remove the stub from the I-94 — outgoing — immigration form. He was then to take careful note of the name in the passport. All this he did while the German waited.

The number of the passport was D4935F53 and it had been taken out in the name of Volker Nast. When the passenger departed with his boarding pass, the clerk went to a telephone in an inner office and made a call.

Nothing out of the ordinary happened from then on. The Lufthansa flight was called on the loudspeaker. Volker Nast boarded it and settled into his seat to wait for takeoff. He was going to have a happy Christmas in Germany, because his business affairs had been finished much to his satisfaction. He had personally observed the microchip-manufacturing plant packed and ready for shipment to Europe. By the end of the coming January, the cargo would have reached Hamburg by sea. It would then go by truck through East Germany to the Soviet Union. What could go wrong? The new channel that his partner Richard Müller had set up with the Americans was working very well. Three Triple I shipments had already passed through it and had reached Moscow. Now, all he had to do was to look forward to the Weihnachten celebrations.

Nast had never heard of Charles McLeod and Charles Brisbin, and he had no idea that they and the Commerce agents were now in freezing Kansas, preparing an ambush on the supply channel.

That new line went by highway from Sunnyvale to the small town of Lenexa, ten miles outside Kansas City, where the obscure company called Allen Electronics was situated. From the outside, Allen Electronics didn't look like much, but it did have a satisfactory credit record. It was run by a tall, good-looking blond man named Paul Allen, who lived in Kansas City. Local people in Lenexa thought he might be an Englishman or some kind of a European; he certainly spoke with a foreign accent.

A few days before Volker Nast caught his flight out of O'Hare, Paul Allen did some painting in his storage area. He painted out the shipping details on several cartons and gave them a new address. They were now destined for "Reimer Klimatechnik, Hamburg, Germany." Inside the carefully packed cartons were such exotic goods as infrared ovens, wafer scrubbers, and other chip-manufacturing equipment. When the paint dried, Allen loaded the cartons into a yellow rental truck and delivered them, on December 16, to Clement International Van Lines in Grandview, Missouri. There they were packed into a big container, which was then sealed and readied for onward shipment. Time was running out for McLeod and his team. They had to make their switch now or risk never getting another chance.

Clement International Van Lines is run by three brothers of the kind who are sometimes described, in these parts, as good old boys.

They are all ex-Marines, and they look it. Charles McLeod, as he sat in their office telling his story, thought he was going to get along with them just fine.

Mike Clement was the first to answer. "Are you telling us this asshole Allen is using us to ship computer stuff to the Communists?"

"That's about it," said McLeod.

"Okay. Don't worry. We'll fix him." The other Clements nodded.

"What do you mean?" asked McLeod.

"No problem. We'll just kill him."

McLeod felt a little stunned. He needed the Clements' cooperation, though, and he had to be diplomatic. "Look, fellas, that's a very kind offer. We really appreciate it. But it's very important to keep him alive, at least for the time being. Now, we have to make this switch before the shipment goes through, and we have to do it so that the other side doesn't get suspicious."

"How do you want to work it?" Mike Clement asked.

"Well, we have to take this electronics hardware out of the cartons and replace it with sandbags of the same weight. Then everything's sealed up again and the shipment goes off. Our people along the route watch how and where the shipment goes, and we learn something. And the Russians end up with about fifteen hundred pounds of good Missouri sand. By the way, can you get the sand around here?"

"Sounds like 'Nam all over again. Sure — there's a local sand and gravel company."

"But the big problem is that we have to get Allen the hell out of the way while we're doing the switch. His buddy just left the country, so he's no trouble. How do we get Allen off the scene?"

The room was quiet as more cans of beer were opened. Then Mike spoke. "Why not invite him to the party?"

"Sure, but what party?"

"Every year we have a company party on December seventeenth and invite all our buddies, our business contacts and such."

McLeod was interested. "Sounds great. But what if he shows up just to be polite and leaves early?" McLeod thought for a minute and then answered his own question. "Not if we gave him a good reason to stick around. Maybe a pretty secretary could sweet-talk him until, say, about one o'clock in the morning?"

The brothers nodded. Then one of them said, "No trouble finding a volunteer just for that. But what if she has to screw him in order to keep him around that long? I don't think I could ask that much — even on Uncle Sam's account."

"Hmm," said McLeod. "Isn't there a good-looking hooker we could pass off as a secretary?"

Everybody laughed. "We'll get the motherfucker yet," said one of the Clements.

"But who's going to pay the hooker?" asked another.

Without thinking, McLeod said, "U.S. Customs, of course," and immediately regretted it. How would he list those services rendered on his expense account?

Resourceful as ever, the Clements had the answer. They knew the sand and gravel company owner. He'd pad his bill by $300 and pass the cash back to be handed over to the girl.

Here, a few minutes ago, we were talking about killing Paul Allen, McLeod reflected, and now we're talking about how we can get the U.S. taxpayer to buy him an evening full of fun.

Exactly at 8:00 P.M. on the night of December 17, two cars and a truck made a small procession down a Grandview street on their way to the darkened depot of Clement International Van Lines. There was just one security guard on the gate, and he checked their identification and then opened up. An agent climbed out of one of the cars and remained at the gate as the truck rumbled into the building and backed up to a loading bay next to the container.

Ed Backer, one of the agents, broke the Customs seals and unlocked the container doors. The agents all crowded behind McLeod's flashlight to look at the prize they had been waiting for. On the nearest case was a rectangle of dark blue paint with the legend CLIMATE EQUIPMENT INTERNATIONAL stenciled in white. Next to that was the address of Reimer Klimatechnik. The truck driver — a Clement employee — turned on the lights in the bay, and McLeod pointed to the truckload of sandbags.

"It's nearly eight-twenty," he said. "Let's get moving. We've got just four and a half hours."

As the long, hard work of the switch began, Chuck Brisbin took some Polaroid shots of the inside of the container. It was important that all the cartons be repositioned in their original places in case Nast/Reimer decided to check the container in Hamburg.

The sequence of the switch was important. The first crate had to be opened and the machinery swapped for the sandbags. It was then shifted by a forklift some distance away from the container so that it could be replaced last. Then, on to the next crate.

The work went faster than McLeod had thought possible. By eleven-thirty, they had hefted the last crate back into the container. McLeod raised its top for, it seemed, one last look at the sandbags. But instead, he reached into his pocket for his business card, which he pinned to the underside of the lid. There was a little gleam of gold from the seal of the U.S. Customs Service embossed in the top left corner.

"That's against regulations," Brisbin said. "Got another thumb-tack?" Customs agents have to buy their own cards, but Brisbin considered the cost of this card money well spent. He pinned his alongside McLeod's.

The lid was secured on the crate, a final check was made, and the container doors were resealed. The agents drove back to their motel for a celebratory drink.

As for the truck with the high-tech equipment, it was parked, ready to be driven to Kansas City the next morning. The ovens and scrubbers and the rest of it would end up not in Moscow but in a cool limestone cave that U.S. Customs uses as a bonded warehouse.

While all this was happening, Paul Allen was having the kind of luck he couldn't believe. The Clements' Christmas party had turned out to be a real bash, and the secretary from the trucking company was something else. They'd fallen into conversation by the bar and she'd taken to him. At first, she had played hard to get, but after a few drinks and some smooth talk on Allen's part, she began to give him signals. Eventually, she suggested her place and so, about 1:30 A.M. on December 18, they left the party together.

On January 6, 1976, a Clement truck took the sealed container by road to Norfolk. It was then loaded on a U.S. Lines freighter. Later the same month, the ship made port in Hamburg, and the container was unloaded for pickup by the Gonderan und Gebr. trucking company, which took it to the border of the German Democratic Republic.

The shipment of "air-conditioning pumps and industrial ovens" was cleared without much formality by West German and East German Customs. In due course, it arrived at a Technopromimport warehouse. Later, unofficial reports confirmed that the Techno-promimport people were less than amused by the McLeod and Brisbin business cards.

At about the same time, the Customs agents were searching the offices of Starek's II Industries and Kasper Instruments in Silicon Valley. Other agents in Kansas City were searching the home of Paul Allen, rather to the consternation of Mrs. Allen. When the agents left, she asked her husband for an explanation, but he said that he had to go out on urgent business and that he'd explain later. The next time she heard from him, it was on the telephone from Flensburg, in West Germany.

Paul Allen, as Customs now knew, was actually named Friedrich Linnhoff. He was a German Air Force fighter pilot who had disappeared from his F104 training course in El Paso, Texas, some years before.

While the government was preparing for the trial of the electronics company officials, Agent Charles McLeod made a trip to Germany to interview Linnhoff and try to persuade him to appear as a witness. Linnhoff agreed. But about two weeks before the trial was to begin, his American lawyer called McLeod and said that he didn't think Linnhoff was going to show.

In the end, it didn't matter. On March 11, 1977, Starek and Storey were sentenced to eighteen months' imprisonment and fines of $10,000 each.

The only person who went to jail because of that trial, however, was the court reporter. He failed to produce a proper record of the proceedings that had cost the government $200,000 to carry out.

There followed a fresh grand jury indictment, and a retrial was ordered. When the case came to court again, Starek, Storey, and an officer of Kasper Instruments changed their pleas to guilty. Each was given the maximum five-year term along with a fine of $25,000. But the sentences were suspended and the men were put on three years' probation. They were even allowed to go back into business, but without export privileges.

Richard Müller, Volker Nast, and Friedrich Linnhoff remain fugitives, although their troubles in the Triple I affair did little damage to their techno-bandit operations, and Müller and Nast have since been successful in diverting more American technology to the East.

They had missed one chance, however. The day before McLeod and his men made that switch in Grandview, Missouri, a check for $495,810 had been drawn on the Bankhaus Wölbern in Hamburg, payable to II Industries. It represented the U.S. Customs' first big payoff in the war against the techno-bandits. Nearly half a million dollars is a lot to pay for fifteen hundred pounds of sand.

10

CRIME WITHOUT PUNISHMENT

IN MARCH 1982, the U.S. Customs Service laid hands on a sleek new airplane, a Mitsubishi MU-2 Marquise. It is a twin-engine turboprop that carries ten passengers, is registered as N4TN, and has a range of sixteen hundred miles. That range is just enough for a non-stop flight from Los Angeles International Airport to Mexico City. Many of the boats or planes the service seizes are scruffy and battered, and the new craft was a definite step up.

On March 18, when the Marquise was still private property, Customs agents in Los Angeles watched from a distance as five packing cases were loaded onto the plane. They were, very likely, wondering whether the flight plan the pilot had filed — southeast to Mexico City — was the one he actually intended to follow.

More men from Customs, along with their Mexican opposite numbers, were waiting at the other end. When the Marquise did, indeed, come in for its landing at Mexico City, the agents were faced with another question: Should they move in on the shipment there?

They watched intently as a truck from a cargo-handling firm drove onto the apron and its crew unloaded the packing cases, which were then taken to the general cargo area. Here, there were more Mexican agents on watch as the pilot signed various entry documents. When the pilot left to fly back to Los Angeles, the agents learned that the cases had been booked onto a KLM flight for Amsterdam. A quick look at the schedule showed that the Dutch plane would, however, make a stop en route in Houston. One of the American agents immediately got on the phone.

The Texas stopover for KLM planes is usually ninety minutes, but on that day it was a little longer. The five packing cases were taken from the plane to a Customs shed. They were carefully unpacked and the delicate instruments inside were removed and weighed. Then, in the switch that was now becoming a Customs trade-mark, the instruments were replaced with sandbags of equal weight. The cases were then carefully resealed and again loaded onto the KLM Boeing 747 for the flight to Schiphol.

A little later, another team of Customs men raided a company known as Land Resources Management in Orange County, California. In one of the two buildings, they found a number of engineers at work on some complex sets of circuit boards. They also found quite a few electronic products, but they were looking for one in particular. It turned up, already crated for shipment, in a corner of a storeroom — a special piece of equipment known as an LRM Series-100 multispectral scanner.

In the other building, the agents found a large computer room that contained a number of complete systems, including a new Magnuson M80/43 mainframe, which is compatible with the IBM 370 range. From the LRM engineers and programmers, the agents learned that the equipment was in the process of being checked before shipment, and a look through the company accounts showed that the computer and many peripherals were part of an order from Elorg in Moscow. All of this was seized. And when it arrived back at the Los Angeles Airport, so was the Mitsubishi Marquise.[1]

"If ya gonna do it at all, ya gotta do it right. No bullshit." The American voice was loud in the hotel room, and all the Englishmen listening gave body-language signs of much discomfort. One folded his arms, another puffed heavily at his cigarette, and a third hid his face behind his whiskey glass. The scene was slightly reminiscent of Jabba the Hutt's court in *The Return of the Jedi*. The six-foot-three, three-hundred-pound American sat deeply wedged into the armchair. He had heavy jowls and a crewcut, and his head joined his shoulders with no neck in between. He had been introduced as a professor of mathematics at an American university and a former pro football player. The first attribution seemed a bit incredible to the Englishmen.[2]

The time was mid-September of 1976, and the place a luxury suite at the Heathrow Hotel on the perimeter road of London's main airport. Through the second-floor windows could be seen departing jets as they pushed through the gray drizzle and lifted off Runway 28-Right toward their airlanes. The room's décor was a blending of tans and yellows, with the contrast of an off-white shag rug. The bar was very well stocked.

Charles J. McVey Jr., may have looked like a middle-America stereotype, but his deepest interests lay in Communist Russia. He had reportedly made a satisfactory and profitable deal with Elorg for two IBM System/370 Model 145 mainframe computers. It was said that McVey had bought them on the used-computer market in West Germany, shipped them to Switzerland, and then sent them on to the Soviet Union. By doing it that way, he had avoided the tedious and obstructive procedure of trying to get validated licenses from the U.S. Department of Commerce.

These computers were now installed at the Scientific Research Institute for Electronic Computers at Minsk, one of the country's first training and research centers in its field. (This was the facility that, in due course, would be accused of stealing the IBM operating system software for use on the Russian Ryad machines.)[3]

On that gray September day at Heathrow, McVey had just returned from Moscow. He was about to fulfill the next clause in the contract, which was to arrange for Russian computer people to get training courses in the use of the IBM software that McVey had delivered with the system. The most convenient source for specialists was England, so McVey had requested Roy Gibson, vice-president of McVey's London company, Vanguard International Ltd., to set up a meeting with some likely recruits.[4]

Gibson found the timing ideal; that very week, a major conference on computer technology and systems was being held at the Heathrow Hotel. He had been able to get the use of the conference hospitality rooms, Suite 1011, for the discussions. People came and departed in the course of the lengthy meeting, and those present at various times were McVey, Gibson, the conference organizer (a friend of Gibson's who ran his own computer services company), a university lecturer from the conference organization, a computer consultant, and a fifth Englishman, who owned two London companies that contracted to give computer training courses.[5]

After the introductions, McVey explained his understanding with the Russians. The Soviets now had the computers and most of the software they needed in Minsk, but there was still some to be furnished, and McVey was responsible for a certain amount of maintenance support. But the main purpose of the Heathrow meeting was to make arrangements for the training staff. "This has just gotta be done right, with no fuckups. The contract's worth a helluva lot of money to all of us. And there's plenty more where that came from," McVey barked.

The computer consultant had acquired a deep and instant distaste for McVey, who reminded him of a redneck U.S. Marine officer — a Marine officer who, in this case, had gone over the hill. He might even be a spook from the dirty-tricks side of CIA, and then how could you know what devious game he might be playing? Later research turned up little information about McVey's background prior to 1976. Nothing seemed to substantiate the math professorship story, and the National Football League records do not include his name.[6] Along with that, the consultant had a heavy workload already.

For several of the Englishmen, there was an ethical factor in the situation. They had no fundamental objection to doing business with the Soviets — with one specific reservation. Most of the men were members of the British Computer Society, and the society was campaigning for the release from detention of Anatoly Shcharansky, a Russian computer specialist accused of dissident activities.

In the end, the computer consultant declined the assignment and departed. The owner of the computer services company and the owner of the training company agreed to supply the needed staff.

Eventually, when the actual courses were given, the instructor for all but one was Edgar John English, a partner in the computer services company that had been represented at the Heathrow meeting. John English is a man with a varied and interesting background. He is a qualified meteorologist and he had served for twenty years in the British Meteorological Office — usually called the Met Office — which is part of the Ministry of Defence. The ministry is, of course, an extensive user of computers, and in the early 1980s it acquired an American Cray-1 supercomputer.

English rose to the position of operations manager in the computer department of the Met Office and acquired an expertise in the gathering and processing of meteorological data and in the use of the METEOSAT weather satellite.

In the mid-seventies, the Saudi Arabian Government got interested in the kind of systems in which English had so much experience, and when it became clear that the Saudis were about to offer a tempting contract, English left the Met Office, teamed up with the computer services company man later to appear in McVey's Heathrow conference, and went into business.[7] They did not get the contract.

In order to keep the small company afloat, English's partner took on consulting work, and English himself took on the McVey job. The courses in Minsk began on May 16, 1977, and continued through the summer and autumn. At the institute, the two very current IBM mainframe computers were installed side by side with Ryad-1 machines. The lectures were attended by about a dozen Soviet technicians, who listened through earphones to a simultaneous translation of English's remarks.

The seminars included introductions to the OS/VS1 and VS2 operating systems, and programming VSAM (the software used to access the disc stores). There were introductions to TSO (the program that allows several terminal users to access the computer simultaneously) and to CSM (which does the same thing but in a more user-friendly manner). Also included were courses relating to the design and programming of the IBM 370 3704 and 3705 communications controllers and the APL programming language. Everything went very well, and the Soviet technicians got a thorough grounding in their newly acquired software. The only hitch seems to have been a small one over the course schedule; English's partner, on May 4, wrote a letter to Gibson, saying, "I must emphasize at this late time we can make no further changes to the first two lecture trips."[8]

There were more serious hardware problems reported by the institute, and McVey had to find an engineer to solve them. In November, he was able to hire Allen C. Croall, a Rhodesian who had been working for IBM in South Africa, and the two went off to Minsk.

At just about this time, McVey offered English a permanent job that required him to be based in Los Angeles. That fact did not, however, remove him from McVey's Russian business. On July 27, 1981, McVey introduced him to his major Soviet contact, Yury Boyarinov, senior consultant with Elorg. Boyarinov had a background very much like that of John English. He had been seconded from his permanent post at the Moscow Institute for Space Research in order to give the foreign trade officials in Elorg the benefit of his special knowledge of satellite systems and applications.

Boyarinov took his new acquaintance to a meeting at the Space Research Institute. The officials they talked with were much impressed by English's experience in the use of computers and satellites in the field of meteorology, and they began to discuss the kind of technology they would like to have. It soon became clear that there was going to be a $10 million contract in the offing for McVey.

The result was that, on March 8, 1982, McVey was able to ship to Moscow an IBM-compatible computer system for use in the acquisition of meteorological data from satellites. It was remarkably similar to the one that had been proposed some four years earlier to the Saudi Arabian Government. McVey was now getting into the big time.[9]

One of McVey's companies, located in Neuchâtel, Switzerland, is called SATS, for Société Anonyme Technologie Spatiale. Without giving up the computer trade, McVey seems to have acquired a strong interest in space technology after the deal with the Soviet institute in 1982. That year, John English was dispatched to Beijing to try to work out a similar contract with the Chinese.

McVey even set up a meeting with NASA officials in the United States to test the possibility of letting the Chinese have access to the LANDSAT earth resources satellite.

A senior NASA official later confirmed that NASA had agreed to allow McVey's Land Resources Management company to carry out a series of tests to ensure that LRM equipment could pick up the signals satisfactorily. He said, "McVey told us that he was in competition with GE [General Electric] to sell the Chinese 'remote-sensing ground stations' that would enable them to use LANDSAT. We were not approached directly by the Chinese, but we knew all that was going on. McVey was quite open about it." A NASA staffer who attended the McVey meeting reported that the man "looked like Sidney Greenstreet" and that she had deep suspicions about him. With touching innocence, the NASA official added, "However, we knew that Land Resources Management would have to go through the usual licensing procedures and that the Department of Commerce would consult with us before giving the go-ahead."[10]

The deal with the Chinese was blocked when the Customs Service moved in on the American end of McVey's trading complex and seized the cargo from the Mitsubishi Marquise and the plane itself. The crated LRM multispectral scanner that the agents found in the storage room of the Orange County company became the subject of somewhat conflicting claims a little later. This device is a part of satellite systems and is used for high-resolution photographs of the earth that are of benefit to meteorologists and geologists as well. Those photographs furnish a good deal of information about the areas of mineral deposits and are excellent for telling analysts something about crops in the field. Anyone who has wondered how the CIA can make educated guesses as to the size of the Soviet harvest long before the fact should reflect on the multispectral scanner.

One of the claims came from Defense Secretary Caspar Weinberger, who said that the case was typical of the Soviet use of legal and illegal methods "to raid our technology base [by trying] to steal a multispectral scanner which is indispensable to military, air, and satellite reconnaissance."[11]

The LRM device can, from its place in orbit, resolve an object that is about half a kilometer in diameter. That is good but is not the best; quite *unclassified* technology used by NASA can resolve objects in the range of fifty meters to five meters in width. That is, the LRM scanner can identify a fair-sized lake, and the NASA equivalent can make out a barn. One manufacturer said of the McVey affair: "We sold a multispectral scanner to the Chinese during the

Carter administration that was better than the one the Russians wanted. I don't understand what all the fuss was about."[12]

Regardless of that, McVey, Boyarinov, and a Swiss freight agent named Rolf Lienhard were indicted by a grand jury in Los Angeles on March 9, 1983, on a total of twenty-three counts. The charges against all included "conspiracy, false statement to a government agency, illegal exportation of war materials, aiding and abetting." Arrest warrants were issued and bail set at $1 million each.

The Department of Commerce issued denial orders against the three and cited all the companies involved: Facilities Management Ltd., Land Resources Management, Inc., SATS, Frank AG (the freight company McVey used), ICOHAGE International, and Interprojekt Gesellschaft (the last three are Swiss).

There was an interesting omission in the grand jury indictments. There was no mention of McVey's having sold IBM computer systems to the USSR. Perhaps the nearest thing was the noting of the Magnuson M80/43 mainframe computer with peripherals (disc and tape storage units, a color printer, four graphics display terminals, and a number of communications units that allow the computer to use telephone lines).

McVey now lives in Neuchâtel, where SATS is located, unable to visit his luxurious home in the Villa Park suburb of Los Angeles.

In the 1976 meeting at the Heathrow Hotel, McVey had put great emphasis on the importance of the software involved in his deal with the Russians. There was a clear implication that he had not been able to buy in West Germany all of the software Elorg wanted. One such package was IBM's IMS, or Information Management System. This is normally called a database management package, and it allows large amounts of organizational information to be stored in the computer in such a manner that it can be manipulated in a variety of ways.

For example, the usual way to retrieve the account record of a customer would be to type in the customer's number. If the customer's number is not known, his or her name can be typed in with the same results. In another operation, an operator can make a simple inquiry about one manufactured product and that inquiry would automatically chain to every component used in the manufacture of that product. Database software of this kind is nowadays almost essential to the workings of any large, complex organization, whether it is in manufacturing, distribution, retailing, or government.

The same British computer consultant who had declined to get involved in McVey's Minsk seminars had, on February 23, 1977, met in the coffee shop of the Heathrow Hotel with a Belgian named André Marc de Geyter. De Geyter had just flown in from New York, and his briefcase bore the distinctive blue and white baggage tags from the Concorde flight. He suggested a quick dinner, and the Englishman agreed.

The consultant had not been told beforehand the purpose of the meeting, but de Geyter wasted no time in coming to the point. "I hear you have quite a few clients who are IBM users." The consultant looked up from the menu and nodded. "Look, I do a lot of business in Russia. I need a copy of the standard distribution tape for IMS, no matter which version. Do you think you could get one for me?" The Belgian spoke English very well, with a marked accent but with a liberal use of American colloquialisms. He'd obviously spent quite some time in the United States.

The waitress appeared with a carafe of red wine and de Geyter took it from her, waved her away, and poured. "How about it?"

The consultant shrugged. "Why not get it direct from IBM?" Then he was immediately struck with the naïveté of his question. That was the last thing de Geyter would want to do. On the other hand, though software tapes are sometimes copied from one company to another to avoid the substantial license fees, that is almost never done among IBM customers. The larger companies tend to be honest in this regard, and in any case none would want to risk discovery by IBM. The consultant's curiosity was aroused. "How much are they prepared to pay?"

"Whatever. I suppose something like twenty thousand dollars."

"How much of that would be for me?"

"All of it." The steaks had just arrived, and de Geyter prodded his suspiciously. "You English do not know how to cook steak."

"It was probably cooked by a Filipino or a Greek." The consultant needed a little time to think, so he turned the conversation to de Geyter's business with the Soviet bloc customers.

The Belgian talked freely but revealed very little. He said that he'd been in the USSR a good deal over the past year, about one week in every month. He had an office in Moscow with telephone and telex numbers. He also traveled a lot in the United States. Eventually, he came back to the IMS tapes.

"Do you think you could do that for me? If necessary, I suppose we might come up with as much as thirty thousand."

Now the consultant was sure that he was being asked to steal the tape. The $20,000 would not be enough to induce a company to make an illicit copy. The options seemed to be two: either steal the backup copy from a company, or bribe a computer operator to steal one, perhaps during a night shift. Neither was hard to do; the main risk would be approaching the wrong person. In all of this, Marc de Geyter would be in the least danger, because he would undoubtedly be far away from the action.

What about the national security implications? The consultant thought about that and almost began to laugh. At the time, the IBM package was of such poor quality that giving it to the Russians *could* be interpreted as an act of sabotage against the USSR. It was so slow in operation that for critical military functions it might even be a liability.

In the end, the consultant was noncommittal, saying he'd think the offer over. He did not hear from de Geyter again.[13]

The Scientific Research Institute for Electronic Computers did eventually get its copy of the tape. De Geyter was able to buy it — along with other IBM software packages — from John English and his partner. This deal displays some of the queer paradoxes of the whole techno-bandit trade. De Geyter told English and his partner that he wanted "public domain" material only — that is, out-of-date software that IBM was no longer interested in supporting. This he was going to sell in India. The partners thereupon made a call and learned from IBM that it had no objections. In fact, IBM considered that such a deal might even pave the way for more IBM computer use in India.

After some time, English's partner discovered that the tapes he was sending to Bombay were being forwarded immediately to Moscow and Minsk. At this, he refused to have anything more to do with de Geyter. De Geyter still owes him $20,000.[14]

The Belgian's financial standing must have improved by 1979, however, when he surfaced again with a $150,000 offer for some software. Software AG of North America, Inc., is the marketing arm of a West German firm that develops high-quality systems software for IBM computers. One such product is ADABAS, a database management system often considered superior to the IMS system. Development costs for ADABAS are estimated to have been some $10 million, and a license to use it costs about $125,000.

Jim Addis was the senior technical specialist in ADABAS, and he worked at the company's Reston, Virginia, headquarters. On May 21, 1979, he had a call from de Geyter, who said that he wanted to discuss some software matters and would Addis meet him for cocktails at the Sheraton Hotel? Addis agreed.

After the first drink, de Geyter began to talk about what he really had in mind. He had been retained by the Soviets, he said, to obtain a copy of the program source code for ADABAS and he would be willing to pay Addis $150,000 for a tape. Jim Addis nodded and said that he'd consider the matter.

The implications were obvious. The source code was not normally sold, because it gave access to all the design secrets of the package. For $150,000, the Russians would get a shortcut to $10 million worth of development.

The following morning, Addis reported the conversation to his boss, John Maguire, president of Software AG of North America. Maguire called the FBI and a plan was made.[15]

When de Geyter called again, on May 24, Addis told him that Maguire was interested and wanted to talk with de Geyter directly about the offer. After several postponements and telephone conversations between the Belgian and Maguire, the two finally met face to face at the Washington National Airport on July 20.

Again, de Geyter laid all his cards on the table. The Russians wanted the source code and were willing to pay $150,000. "Want a check in Zürich?" asked de Geyter. "You got it. I couldn't care less. It's a one-shot. No paper; no contract."[16]

Maguire said he was worried that the source code might get leaked to Software AG's competitors in America and Europe. No problem, said de Geyter; it would go to the Soviets and nowhere else. He said he'd call Maguire as soon as everything was worked out, and the men shook hands.

Maguire had, of course, been wired, and the FBI listened to the recording of the airport conversation with considerable interest.

When de Geyter called again, on August 7, he proposed that Maguire fly to Brussels with the tape. There, it would be verified at·a Belgian computer facility. Payment would be made in Zürich.

Maguire balked at this. He said that he wanted payment in cash, in the United States.

De Geyter said that he didn't carry large sums of cash for fear of Customs searches.

"If you're worried about cash, what if they catch you with the code? Do you know about export licensing?" Maguire asked. He was doing an excellent impersonation of a tempted but worried man.

De Geyter was nonchalant. "I'll take the whole responsibility. You're not supposed to know where it goes to and what I'm going to do with it."[17]

As negotiations dragged along, Maguire began to play hard to get. And the more reluctant he got, the more de Geyter raised the ante — to $200,000 and then to a quarter of a million. He even offered to throw in some California real estate. But the matter of the payment was nonnegotiable — no cash. The money would have to be transferred to a Swiss bank account.

There were more telephone calls, but the two men did not meet again until October 3, when they had breakfast at the Reston Sheraton. De Geyter said that he was going to make the stakes richer — the Russians had authorized him to increase the offer to $450,000. If Maguire wanted that verified, he could talk directly with an official of Techmashimport at the Soviet embassy.

Maguire was still playing a canny game, and he asked whether exporting software without a license was legal. De Geyter said that it was. Maguire said that he'd like to verify that with Commerce and State.

This kind of talk made de Geyter distinctly nervous. He replied that he could overcome any objections and legitimate the deal by having one of his own California companies licensed to use the ADABAS package. But — again — the transaction must not take place in the United States, because the tape would have to be verified by a Soviet programmer in Brussels.

Maguire said that he hadn't changed his mind: he would not fly to Europe and he wanted cash only.

"Look, I'm taking all the risks and I do not want to go to jail," said de Geyter.[18] He pleaded that if he lost his deal, he might lose millions of dollars in Soviet business. He was sure that if he failed, the Soviets would just get the tape somewhere else.

On February 4, 1980, there was a knock at the door of Marc de Geyter's room in the Sheraton City Squire Hotel in New York. The two men in the hallway showed their FBI identifications and asked to interview him regarding allegations that he was acting as an agent of the Soviet Union without having registered with the Attorney General.[19]

He asked them in. Completely deflated, he sat down and told them everything. At least, the de Geyter version of everything.

Marc de Geyter's career in techno-banditry has a number of things that are more or less typical of many other men's stories. He combined sufficient knowledge of computer technology with a manipulative instinct and a flexible morality. It could be said that he was just a bit too clumsy at playing the clandestine game. But, on the other hand, it could also be said that more often than not he landed on his feet after a fall. He had first established his connection with the Russians when he was working for Memorex in West Germany. Memorex is an American manufacturer of IBM plug-convertible peripherals, and the Soviets were interested in updating their technology so that it continued to be compatible with U.S. systems. Taking advantage of a good thing when he saw it, de Geyter resigned from Memorex in the 1970s and set up the Commercial Engineering and Sales Agency (CESA) on the rue de Genève, Brussels, as an import-export intermediary.

His version of the ADABAS attempt was, at first, fairly simple. The Techmashimport representative had approached him in February 1979. De Geyter had not been offered any sum of money, nor had he offered Maguire any. The Belgian said that he was just a go-between; if the deal succeeded, he would expect to get a 15 percent commission. Maguire would have to handle the application for a Commerce Department license for the sale.

It was not a very good try. The agents came back the next day with questions that were rather more pressing. Under their interrogation, de Geyter grew progressively more truthful. He acknowledged increasing the offers to Maguire and he admitted holding a Russian letter of credit for $450,000. He also confirmed the fact that Maguire had raised the export license question — but then he insisted that Maguire had taken the responsibility for following up on that, because Maguire had a contact in the State Department.

De Geyter must have been astonished that the FBI did not arrest him. From his point of view, the interrogation had been unsettling but salutary — it warned him that he had to change his tactics and that he had to move fast. Now was the time to get to work on his alternative route to the software.

The next morning, he put in a call to Charles Matheny. Matheny was the board chairman of a company called CENTEC, which, not coincidentally, had its offices in the same Reston building as those of Software AG. Not that de Geyter wanted to be seen in Reston again right away — so he asked Matheny to meet him at the National Airport the following morning, February 7.

As Matheny drove from National to a hotel, de Geyter described a deal he was putting together for a Saudi sheik who headed an Arab bank. The bank wanted to install a massive computer system for accounting and administration, and de Geyter was putting together a team of technical specialists for the work. One of the software packages the Arabs wanted was ADABAS, and de Geyter was willing to pay Matheny a $25,000 finder's fee in cash for an introduction to somebody in Software AG who could obtain the source code and other software — as much as possible. Matheny was supposed to keep a low profile and under no circumstances let Maguire or Addis know about the deal. Matheny answered that all of it might be feasible. He would explore.

When de Geyter phoned again, on February 21, he said that the Arabs were putting on the pressure and he needed an introduction as soon as possible. Matheny had good news. An employee of Software AG had agreed to talk it over with de Geyter.

On April 16, 1980, de Geyter was back in Virginia, this time at the Holiday Inn in Rosslyn, and a rather unenthusiastic man named Timothy B. Klund came to see him. When Klund heard the requirement, he said that stealing the source code might lose him his job. He was somewhat interested, but there were a lot of risks involved. . . . De Geyter used all his powers of persuasion to induce Klund to meet him once more, at the airport just before de Geyter was to leave for Europe. He raised the ante to $250,000; Klund countered with an asking price of $500,000, to be handed over in the United States. A frustrated but unbeaten de Geyter went off to catch his plane.

He called Matheny on April 24 to say that he was buying Klund an air ticket to Europe. He then went to Vienna, Moscow, and back to Brussels. On May 15, he called Matheny again to say that he was arriving in New York the following day with a check for Klund. Matheny reminded him that Klund would take cash only. De Geyter rang off, then called back later to say that he now had the cash and that Klund was to meet him at JFK International Airport.

Klund was on time to meet the Brussels flight, and as soon as the two men could find a secluded spot, he produced the tapes. At long last this deal was going to be closed. De Geyter, with a broad smile, reached into an inside pocket, produced a check, and extended it toward Klund. The check was accepted by an FBI man who moved in just at that point.

De Geyter's sad fate had been to strike a heavy deposit of honesty and patriotism in Reston, Virginia. Like Maguire's before, Matheny's first reaction to de Geyter's approach on February 6 had been to call the FBI. Timothy Klund was an FBI agent. One other striking thing was the high quality of the role-playing by three amateur actors. Each one had assumed, with great conviction, the part of a character in whose mind greed was contending with fear and thus breeding procrastination. They might have come straight from an Eric Ambler novel.

De Geyter was held in custody and bail was set at $500,000 — cash.[20]

On May 21, a search warrant was issued enabling agents to open de Geyter's combination-lock briefcase. What does a techno-bandit carry with him? What kind of a profile can you draw of this mysterious man simply by looking at the contents of his briefcase?

First, there were nine used or unused airline tickets for travel to or from Los Angeles, Washington, New York, Brussels, Zürich, Tehran, Athens, Vienna, Moscow, London, and the Isle of Man. These included (1) a prepaid Air France ticket numbered

3020678553, of June 28, 1978, open for any route on the airline, and (2) a Sabena ticket for a round trip from Brussels via London to the Isle of Man. (Explanations for the last item are worth twenty points. The Isle of Man is noted for A. a breed of tailless cat called the Manx; B. not being a part of the United Kingdom — it is an off-shore tax haven with personal and corporate rates as low as 20 per-cent; C. almost no discernible high technology.)

Other briefcase items were:

A green telephone-number book embossed with the name Metal-lurgimport, Moscow.

A letter from Roth Western Corporation of Janesville, Wisconsin.

The business card of Yuvenaly A. Shelakov, vice-president, No-voexport, Moscow.

A piece of paper bearing the handwritten name of Günter Caval-lar, Sony GmbH., Austria.

Two copies of a consulting agreement for a "radio production li-censing program" between de Geyter and Radio Semiconductor, Inc., of State College, Pennsylvania.

A letter in French concerning the Cloudless Trading Company SA, Panama, dated April 20, 1979.

A letter of the same date in German, concerning TVS Television and Broadcasting SA, Panama.

Telexes dated August 1979 between de Geyter and a certain Bol-shakov in Moscow.

A document titled "Delivery Acceptance Protocol" between de Geyter and Techmashimport.

A notepad with a printed heading from the Hotel Metropole, Moscow.

A ten-page contract between Techmashimport and de Geyter's CESA company, numbered 46-04/92211-113 and dated February 14, 1979.

A CESA packing slip for that contract, noting three pieces of an item listed simply as "LDH 8800" and valued at $250,000.

A credit notification from the Swiss Volksbank, Zürich, for the amount of $450,000.

A TVS (Panama) proposal for short- and medium-wave broad-cast systems, addressed to the government of Iraq.

But the most fascinating document in de Geyter's possession was what may well have been one of the few Soviet shopping lists of high tech ever to fall into Western hands.

It consisted of a single page, listing ten items. The first was ADABAS. The last was ADA BASICS V.4.1. ADA is the name of a programming language that has been developed internationally under the sponsorship of the Department of Defense and is intended for use in programming "embedded computers" — particularly microcomputers used in real-time control applications. That is, ADA would be used, for example, to program the navigation and control systems of guided missiles. There is nothing very secret about the structure and syntax of the language, but the Defense Department would be very unhappy to learn that the Russians were in contact with any of the working compilers.

From all indications, the FBI was not aware of the significance of this list (the other eight items were never disclosed), and it, along with the other papers, would have been routinely returned to de Geyter on his release from jail.[21]

The accused was charged with "interstate and foreign travel in aid of an unlawful activity"; that is, commercial bribery, in violation of the laws of the State of New York and the Commonwealth of Virginia. De Geyter's lawyer managed to get the $500,000 bail reduced to $100,000 — over the objections of Theodore S. Greenberg, the assistant U.S. district attorney. The eventual public recounting of this part of the story came in Greenberg's testimony before a Senate committee in April 1982.[22]

Just as de Geyter's lawyer was handing over a cashier's check for the $100,000, Greenberg said, "I received information from the New York office of the FBI that de Geyter had indicated that he was a KGB agent and that he would flee the country if he was able to raise the bail money."

Asked how he had obtained the information, Greenberg replied that it had come to him from the FBI and, since it was informant information, its source was not disclosed in court. When de Geyter, on the witness stand, denied ever making such a statement, reported the lawyer, the judge believed him. Pleading guilty to the lesser charges of violating the Export Administration Act and the Virginia commercial bribery statute, he got off lightly: he was fined $500 and made to pay a civil penalty of $10,000, and he served a four-month sentence in a federal correctional institution in Petersburg, Virginia.

Greenberg was asked at the hearing why the charge was switched from felony to misdemeanor and answered that there were government considerations that he could tell the committee only in closed session. But de Geyter's lawyer had included a statement in the "Defendant's Sentencing Memorandum" to the effect that the government had simply accepted his client's plea of guilty to the two misdemeanors and that "Mr. de Geyter is not and has not agreed to become a spy or agent for the United States, Belgium, or any other foreign power."

Senator William Cohen of Maine pointed out that a man in Washington was facing a fine of $1000 and a year in jail for stealing a tire from a car, yet surely his crime represented "a different level of threat to our society." How could de Geyter's sentence act as a deterrent? All Greenberg could reply was that "there were interests which required us to dispose of this case other than through a trial." Senator Cohen acknowledged that the prosecution, in such a case, may fear disclosure of the methods it used in acquiring its information.[23] But the situation was hardly clarified when de Geyter's attorney, told about the senator's remarks later, said, "It was more a question of government sloppiness than plea-bargaining. The case was overblown to begin with."[24]

On August 1, 1980, the Department of Commerce sent a standard form letter to Marc de Geyter, warning him that it was considering the issuance of a denial order against him. He did not reply, and no further action was taken. This means that de Geyter can still buy all the technology he wants from sellers in the United States.

In fact, the Russians did not readily take no for an answer in their efforts to get ADABAS from Software AG. In 1981, less than a year after de Geyter served his jail sentence, a Russian approached the company's staff at two trade shows in the Washington area. His name was Georgy V. Veremey, and he was from the Soviet embassy. His interest was far from casual; on September 25 he turned up unannounced at the Reston office. In speaking to Software AG executive Sunday Lewis, he made no secret of who he was and what he was looking for. He wanted a complete list of all the firm's products and the available supporting documentation. He left with the list and an order form.

Lewis reported the approach to her boss, John Maguire. He said that it was company policy not to sell to the USSR and reminded her that export licenses would be needed from the Department of Commerce in any case. Veremey returned on October 2. When the receptionist told him that Sunday Lewis was out to lunch, he said he did not mind waiting and was invited to take a seat. But he did not remain stationary for long and began to wander in and out of the offices. The receptionist insisted that he be seated. When Lewis arrived, the Russian gave her a completed order form for a full set of manuals and other documentation valued at $400. Lewis said that she could not fill the order because the sale would have to be licensed by a government agency. Veremey laughed and said, "What license was issued for the U.S.–USSR wheat deal?" But he left emptyhanded. Software AG did not see him again. It was later suggested that he had been identified by the FBI as an officer in the GRU.

11

A SUPERBANDIT

In 1973 the Soviet Union opened bidding on a substantial contract. The Russian objective was to upgrade the air traffic control system at Moscow's Sheremetyevo International Airport, at Mineralnye Vody in the Caucasus, and at Kiev in the Ukraine. The equipment the Soviets were using was obsolete and, with airline flights on the increase and safety guidelines becoming more stringent, the Soviets required state-of-the-art Western technology — faster, more accurate radars and high-resolution display screens, all run by high-speed processing computers. The contract was worth $40 million.

Sperry of the United States, the French firm of Thompson, and the partly state-financed Swedish company Stansaab all made bids. The Swedes won. In September 1975 Stansaab had signed a contract with Elong for technology, and for the training of over a thousand Soviet air traffic controllers. Training was to take place at the Saab facility at Järfälla, near Stockholm, and at the Swedish state air control school at Sturup Airport, near Helsingborg. But it was not the training that caused the problems.

To fulfill what became known as the Aeroflot contract, the Swedes needed American components. Stansaab applied for licenses for the integrated circuits to be used in the radar extractors and the six large computers that the Swedes would build themselves. The licenses were not forthcoming. Indeed, the contract was causing political problems in Washington. The Defense Department and the National Security Council were against U.S. equipment being used to upgrade an air traffic control network that had obvious military applications. In April 1977 the King of Sweden, with his experienced Washington ambassador, Wilhelm Wachtmeister, visited President Carter at the White House. On the agenda for the talks was the Stansaab contract. "It was," said a senior Commerce Department official later, "a subject of intense political pressure. The initial request for components was much broader than we were willing to give."[1]

By September 15, 1977, at a meeting of the Stansaab board, the company's chairman, Gunnar Wedell, was telling his codirectors that a new application for licenses had been submitted to Washington, with certain items omitted. Five members of the board were none too pleased. They had not been consulted, and this new step could mean that the contract conditions with the USSR might not be met. A further problem was that the company had not received re-export licenses for integrated circuits bought from Advanced Micro Devices (AMD), a supplier in Silicon Valley.

What later took place turned the Aeroflot contract into one of the most extraordinary and sensitive technology-transfer investigations. The AMD integrated circuits were sent, allegedly for testing, to another Swedish company, Radio Industries Factories Ab (RIFA), where the markings R/ were added to the AMD serial numbers. Then, according to one of the American investigators in the case, there was "an unexciting commercial shipment" of the circuits, now embedded in the radars, to the Russians. No re-export licenses had been granted.[2]

What subsequently became known as the Datasaab affair (Stansaab had changed its name in 1978) first surfaced publicly in Sweden on October 30, 1980, in a Swedish TV current-affairs program called "Aktuellt." After four weeks of intensive investigation, one of the program's reporters, Aake Rangborg, discovered that in January of that year a secret report on the Aeroflot contract had been compiled by two civil servants from Sweden's Department of Industry. The report was a damning indictment of the way in which the Stansaab — now Datasaab — company had evaded U.S. export control provisions. It revealed that the strictly controlled AMD chips had not only been shipped to Moscow disguised as Swedish components; in some cases they had been re-exported separately to the Soviet capital by direct delivery to the USSR embassy in Stockholm for transshipment in the diplomatic bag.

The day after the TV broadcast, Minister of Trade Robert Nilsson claimed that the "Aktuellt" reporter's allegations were untrue and that the internal report had, in fact, been compiled by the two officials "in their spare time." Shortly afterward, the reporter received a visit at his office from two American trade attachés, who asked him for a copy of the secret report. He answered their questions, but declined to hand over the document. The Datasaab employees who had been interviewed by him alleged that Gunnar Wedell had mistreated — or fired — anyone at the company who protested what was happening. The reporter had kept one of the re-marked AMD devices given to him as a souvenir. At the time, he was criticized for what many believed was unpatriotic reporting, but his misgivings were vindicated when it was learned that during the Soviet invasion of Afghanistan in December 1979, the air traffic control system at Mineralnye Vody had played a crucial coordinating role.

But it was not until early 1981, not long after the massive Swedish telecommunications company Ericsson Information Systems had taken over Datasaab, that an internal inquiry began. Ericsson's director for trade policy looked into the whole case as a result of behind-the-scenes pressure from the Swedish Government. Ericsson was insistent that the transfer had not been its responsibility.

According to the man behind the inquiry, the Soviet Army newspaper *Red Star* had not helped the situation by referring to the contract in a 1980 article that questioned Swedish neutrality. The paper pointed out that the country was heavily dependent on U.S. technology and that the Swedes had been able to fulfill the air traffic control contract only by purchasing critical components from the United States.[3]

In 1981, Defense Secretary Weinberger, on a visit to Sweden, met with government officials and socially with some members of the Ericsson board. He was reportedly given assurances that no further U.S. technology would be sent on for the Soviet TERCAS — terminal en route control automated system. But the Americans, it was reported, had decided to get tough, and the Swedes were told that vital electronic equipment for Swedish Grippen, Viggen, and the new GAS fighter planes would be withheld. A secret U.S. Customs investigation into the affair was also set in motion.

Over the next two years there were top secret negotiations between the Justice Department and Swedish diplomats and lawyers, but behind-the-scenes maneuvers were to no avail. The Americans were not willing to settle for just a denial order, and the embarrassing affair ended in a Washington court. In April 1984 Datasaab was fined $3.12 million, the largest criminal penalty ever imposed for violation of the Export Administration Act. The criminal charges were a result of an investigation by the U.S. Attorney's Office and the Departments of Commerce and Justice. Datasaab agreed to offer no defense; the case against them was damning. Evidence showed that the company had knowingly breached license regulations and had provided the Soviets with sophisticated technology. The government believed that the equipment and software the company had illegally exported had enabled the Soviet Union to upgrade its military air traffic control system.

But before the final outcome, the Swedes were caught up again in the war against technology transfer. One of the most mysterious and successful techno-bandits was about to start operating on Swedish soil. From a Swedish point of view it could not have come at a worse time.

Born in Giessübl, West Germany, in April 1942, Richard Jürgen Müller would, from his outward appearance, be regarded as a personification of the postwar German economic miracle. Müller is a millionaire who rose almost from nowhere. He has been known to the American and West German authorities since 1974, but neither country is able to furnish much detail about his personal background. Friends and employees stress his consideration for his business associates and generosity with his money, but he guards his activities by spreading them across several continents and many companies.

For some time he lived in a modest house in the village of Jesteberg, near Hamburg, but by 1974 his fortunes visibly improved so much that he became known to the villagers — who accepted a rumor that he owned chemical factories — as "Mr. Millions."[3]

Soon he bought a much bigger property in the nearby village of Wiedenhof and began to restore it. After investing in land in the area, he even established a stud farm. He engaged a team of employees; the land was fenced off and Dobermann pinschers were set to patrol. For transport, he could choose from two Rolls-Royces, a big Mercedes, and a Porsche. The Müller real estate investments extended to Belgium, Switzerland, the Seychelles, and Sweden, where he acquired a villa not far from Stockholm on Björnö Island (Bear Island), to which he often sailed for vacations on his yacht.[4] A West German who was a neighbor of Müller's, and attended the housewarming at his new house, confirms the picture of Müller as a generous and softspoken man who paid his employees well. What the inhabitants of the normally quiet village did remark was the number of large cars parked at the house during the party — many with Swiss number plates.[4]

In 1980 Müller was looking for a place where he could stay during his frequent trips to South Africa. He contacted the divorced wife of the heart specialist Christiaan Barnard, who had a villa for sale near Cape Town. According to Barbara Barnard, Müller did not even view the property. He took one look at some photographs and concluded the deal on the spot. The price was 300,000 rand. He hardly used the place; within a year he had moved on to even grander things.

At Constantia, a select spot near the coast less than ten miles outside Cape Town, stood a historic Dutch colonial house called Buitenverwachting. On its land was one of the Cape's half-dozen most prestigious vineyards. Müller bought the lot for two million rand and set about renovating the old farmhouse. He also began a five-year modernization plan for the vineyard, with the objective of improving its wine production. The estate expanded to include an adjoining farm, where he had a modern villa built for himself and his family. As with his Wiedenhof properties near Hamburg, he employed a manager and a large staff to run the big estate. According to reports, he moved his family there from West Germany at the end of 1982.[6]

Richard Müller had built his impressive fortune by being one of the first and most enterprising techno-bandits. The U.S. enforcement agencies learned of his activities when he was involved with an employee of the German subsidiary of Honeywell in using the company's name to try to obtain embargoed technology for shipment to the Eastern bloc.[7] The employee was caught by the West Germans and appeared in court in Stuttgart, accused of offenses causing damage to the nation's security. He was sentenced to four years in prison. Müller was neither charged nor convicted. Evading arrest was to become a Müller trademark.

Less than a year later, Müller masterminded one of the best-known technology-transfer cases, involving Gerald Starek's company, II Industries, Inc. (Triple I). Although a warrant was issued for the arrest of the absent Müller when that case broke, he evaded the U.S. authorities.

In 1975, when the Triple I deal was being put together, Müller was involved in yet another scheme. He had managed to persuade the owner of a small West German company to order semiconductor-manufacturing equipment from U.S. firms. He had described himself as an original equipment manufacturer who put together items from different sources to make up complete custom-built systems. This scheme resulted in the shipment to Technopromimport in Moscow of three consignments that, together, made up a semiconductor-manufacturing plant. The Commerce Department in Washington found out about the shipments too late. On September 21, 1976, U.S. consular officials interviewed the Müller contact, who denied any involvement. But Commerce persisted with its inquiries, and denial orders were issued in August 1981 — five years after the shipments had reached Moscow.[8] Müller is estimated to have made $2 million from the deal.

The American authorities believe Müller to be responsible, in all, for tens of millions of dollars' worth of technology illegally shipped to the Eastern bloc. They claim to have identified up to sixty front companies through which he has operated.[9]

One of them had been acquired in a typically fortuitous way, and the little-known story behind it illustrates Müller's ability to turn an unlikely prospect into a successful vehicle for his illicit activities. In late April 1982, he was visited at his home in Jesteberg by a man named Gerhard Schaal, part-owner of a small company, Gerland Heimorgelwerke, that made electric organs for the home. In the two years it had been in business, the Gerland company had gone from strength to strength and had opened up a good market for its products. By the spring of 1982, however, sales were beginning to drop in the face of a saturated market and increasing competition from Japanese imports. The Gerland factory, in the town of Mölln, faced bankruptcy, and a hearing had been scheduled for the following Monday. In desperation, Schaal decided to go north to visit Müller, who, so he had heard, was inclined to be generous.

· Schaal's visit was so successful that he returned with a check for DM 25,000 ($12,000), and the company was rescued. The following week, the now-solvent Gerland Home Organ Company was transferred to Müller's ownership. He had asked his business lawyer to go through the company's accounts and give him an opinion on its suitability for inclusion in the Müller empire. Several weeks later, the implications of the takeover were made bluntly clear to the staff and directors at the Gerland works. One of Müller's men visited the small factory and announced that from now on the organs would just be a sideline. His boss had other plans for the company.

Within a few weeks truckloads of large packing cases began arriving at the Gerland loading dock. Müller himself helped to offload and shift the heavy containers into the warehouse, where they were unpacked. The palleted cases contained computer systems and peripherals. Some of the packages of equipment bore the distinctive blue markings of the Digital Equipment Corporation of Maynard, Massachusetts. In all, four or five complete VAX 11/780 computer systems were delivered. The telltale Digital packaging was stripped away and the hardware recrated to await collection. Most of the old packaging was destroyed. New shipping documents itemized the equipment as air conditioning plant, office furniture, light fittings, or PVC foam filling. Much of the repackaging was done in such a way as to disguise the computer units beneath items that matched the new descriptions. The name of the purchasing firm was given as Technimex Import and Export in the town of Harmstorff. This was a subsidiary of Müller's Semitronics GmbH.[10]

According to three people who worked at Gerland, the first inkling of what was to happen next came on the night of October 29, 1982, when a long-haul truck and trailer pulled up at the yard. It bore Hungarian license plates YP-40-56 and the logo of a trucking firm in Budapest. After being loaded with one of the recrated VAXs, it drove off again into the night. A few hours later it reached the

Helmstedt crossing point into East Germany. It passed unhindered through West German Customs and headed off on the deserted autobahn to the East.

The clandestine shipping operation was repeated four more times that autumn. Disgruntled staff at Gerland had by now begun to keep copies of key documents and shipping papers. They contacted their local Customs office and told the officials of their suspicions, but it took some time before they persuaded the agents to take them seriously. When they did act and search the premises, the Customs officers discovered an advice note, dated December 27, 1982, promising delivery of a system. It was addressed to Technopromimport, 35 Mosfilmovskaya Street, Moscow.

One Gerland employee, Roland Weidhas, had kept some sketches that the company had been given by one of Müller's people. They showed the plans for a twenty-two-room office with designated areas for computers and various pieces of ancillary equipment. Werner Schmidt, another Gerland employee, told a West German TV interviewer: "They showed the design for a complete office complex. From the wall-to-wall carpet down to the last screw — and to the computer that was to be installed there." Those who saw the sketches were told that the design was for an office being built "near Moscow."[11]

Subsequent investigation turned up more papers, documents, delivery notes, and telexes that confirmed the suspicion that the VAX computers had indeed gone to Moscow. The way in which the VAX 11/780s came to be shipped to the Gerland factory in Mölln emerged some time later. In September 1982 a West German firm called Deutsche Integrated Time bought several of these computers from the state-owned Norwegian munitions firm, Kongsberg, at a total cost of between three and four million kroner ($400,000 to $500,000). That is about one-tenth the price of the equipment bought new. This bargain price charged by Kongsberg Vapenfabrik was explained by the vice-president, Rolf Erik Rolfsen: the computers had been water-damaged because of poor storage. Kongsberg had applied to Digital for clearance to re-export the damaged hardware. "We were aware that there was a Mr. Müller connected with that company," Rolfsen said, "but Müller is not an uncommon German name. We checked up on Deutsche Integrated Time and they were not on a blacklist of any kind. And so we sold the equipment in good faith with the blessing of Digital's offices in both Norway and in Germany."[12]

By the time this information became public, the West German authorities had begun a number of investigations into Müller and his part in the Gerland operation. Misleading information had been entered in the shipping documents and the Customs declarations. That is an offense under German law, and the prosecutor's office in Lübeck opened a case file on the matter. The federal attorney in Karlsruhe also began an investigation into Müller to determine whether there was evidence of his acting as a secret agent. The Wiesbaden headquarters of the Bundeskriminalamt (BKA), the West German equivalent of the FBI, also showed an interest in what had happened in Mölln. Word reached Müller. In December 1982 he threw a grand party at Jesteberg, and before the empty bottles reached the trash can, he was out of the country.

Müller's destination was South Africa, where, apart from his large estates, he had a network of high-technology companies. One of them — the largest — was the Microelectronics Research Institute (MRI), which he had helped to establish in 1980. MRI started buying computers and advanced electronic equipment. In 1983 alone some $8 million worth was licensed to MRI from the United States.[13] Among the suppliers approached was the Digital Equipment Corporation, a company that has strict rules about trade with the apartheid regime in South Africa. Two VAX 11/782 systems were ordered; they were shipped with Commerce Department licenses that stated their permitted destination as South Africa.

Dr. Athol M. Harrison acted as the business consultant in setting up both MRI and several other Müller companies in South Africa. He describes this as a straightforward business-consulting deal.[14] MRI had an office address in central Cape Town on the seventh floor of the Motor & General building, but the main MRI facility was located on Banhoek Road in the select white town of Stellenbosch, twenty-five miles east of Cape Town.

Using the Swiss-held finance he had accumulated from previous deals, Müller also founded Optronix Pty. Ltd. in Cape Town. This was the first of his South African companies network. In all, some half dozen have been identified. Their names reveal that they are mostly concerned with the electronics industry. All were based in the Cape Town area, though one also had a box address in Rogge-bual, a small town near Cape Town. Most of these operations were fronted by people whose names would not attract the attention of the South African authorities or of Customs inspectors elsewhere. It was only in the company registration documents that a link might have been made to Müller. The formal connection to Switzerland lay in a company called Dancontrol, based in Zug, to the south of Zürich. The informal connections were through long-time business associates of Müller — men like Detleff Heppner, a go-between in his dealings in Germany, and Manfred Schröder, who had once worked in the Digital offices in Hamburg before joining Müller's Deutsche Integrated Time company. One person who could throw light on the interconnections is Clive Whitton, a South African who acted as Müller's accountant, but the glare of publicity that was to descend on Müller's South African operation originated with the departure from Cape Town of an ordinary freighter on a routine trip to Europe in October 1983.

The voyage of the Swedish roll-on, roll-off twenty-one-thousand-ton container vessel, *Elgaren,* unknown to the crew, was the subject of intense international surveillance from the moment she entered European waters in early November 1983 from her port of departure in South Africa.

On November 9, a police automatic-camera speed trap by the side of the A1 autobahn to Hamburg caught a gray Mercedes 190 E heading north at high speed. The U.S. Customs agent at the wheel liked to drive a car that would "haul ass"; his fellow agents attached to the Bonn embassy preferred the bigger but slower Mercedes 230. The only thing he did not like about the car was the interior trim. His boss had been right on the mark when he had described it as "O.D. Green."[15]

That morning he and the special agent in the passenger seat beside him had received a telephone call: if they wanted to see the Swedish ship dock, they would have to be in Hamburg not later than 2:00 P.M. Once off the Cologne ring road, the agents hit the north-bound lane of the autobahn and covered most of the three-hundred-mile trip at more than 100 mph. Germany's excellent freeways have few speed restrictions, and that was one of the reasons the agent had chosen the car. Throughout the trip the two men talked about the case. There had been weeks of preparation, and neither wanted to miss out on the bust. Their boss in Bonn had decided to stay behind and look after liaison with the German Government, the American ambassador, and communications with headquarters in Washington. Commissioner von Raab had asked to be kept posted on developments.

Their boss, Victor Jacobson, was one of the most popular men in the U.S. Customs Service. He had been in Bonn for so long that he spoke German like a native; the standard joke on meeting him was to ask whether he had remembered to renew his American citizenship. There was relief that he was on this case, but it would put all his diplomatic skills to the test.

The Justice Department had entered a formal request for assistance from its West German counterpart, but it was still essential to go through the formalities of applying to the court for appropriate warrants. By the time the hurried American agents had met up with German Customs in Hamburg, there was only fifteen minutes left before *Elgaren* docked. The agents headed straight for the state attorney's office on Karl Muck Platz, in the heart of the old city. The procedure was not normally a problem, but today was different: the ship was due to be turned round in eight hours and leave at ten that evening.

The hearing was scheduled before a judge in the lower court. By the time the German and American agents walked into the courtroom, it was already dark. They had worked on the court application together, but the presentation was made by the German case officer, in suitably formal language: "Your honor, a vessel has docked here in Hamburg today. We have received information telling us that it has a computer aboard which has been illegally re-exported from the Republic of South Africa, contrary to regulations of the United States of America. Furthermore, we have good reason to believe that the computer is destined for the Soviet Union."

With some judges, that would have been enough. This one nodded to the case officer to continue. Based on intelligence that had been passed to the Americans, he began to sketch out the details. *Elgaren* had left South Africa at the end of October, bound for

Scandinavia. She was to call at several other European ports on the way. According to intelligence, when she docked at Cape Town, she had picked up containers filled with components for a complex and expensive computer system. They had been shipped quite legally from the United States to South Africa earlier in 1983. The U.S. export license had specified that the equipment should be shipped to that country only and must not be exported to any other country without a new license from the U.S. Department of Commerce. Furthermore, the American Customs office in Bonn believed that the computer was a Digital Equipment Corporation VAX 11/782, which had strategic military applications.

The judge looked hard at the agents. He asked for evidence. "Perhaps I could see some shipping documents?" It was a question the agents feared most. Although their sources were good, they were very short of documentary evidence. They tried a flanking move: "Your honor, it is precisely because we cannot obtain the documents that we need the *Beschlagnahmeverfügung* — the seizure order. This will enable us to search the containers and prove things, one way or another."

But the judge did not buy the argument. "And if the containers do not contain what you say, could there be some difficulties?" The case officer was nervous. "We would, of course, have to offer our sincere apologies for any inconvenience caused to the shipper and the captain and owners of the vessel. But we do have the support of the Ministry of Justice in Bonn. And the American embassy and Customs Service in Washington. This request for a seizure is not being made at the request of an individual Customs officer."

The two U.S. agents exchanged glances; the judge was not going to give the order. Talking about the Justice Ministry probably sounded as if they were trying to pull rank. Their assessment was right. The judge continued: "And the Swedish authorities? You say this is a Swedish-registered vessel? And the ship will be berthed in the Hamburg free port, the Customs-free zone, when you carry out the seizure? There will surely be a protest. *Das ist was Ernsthaftes —* that is a serious matter." He stared across the bench at them, but they had nothing more to say. *"Also, es tut mir leid, meine Herren —* I'm sorry, gentlemen, but I am unable to grant the order on the basis of the evidence you have laid before me."

The men walked through the maze of alleyways back to the state attorney's office. Time was running out. But an immediate appeal was lodged with the circuit court. There were just three hours left before *Elgaren* was due to cast off, but it was going to take one hour to convene the three judges needed; two of them had already left for home.

While they waited, the two American agents called Jacobson in Bonn to fill him in. He was disappointed with the outcome but told them that the operation had to be a German one and that they should push ahead with the appeal. He had spoken with Commissioner von Raab, who had given his full support.

The appeal was held in a different courthouse and started only a few minutes after eight. Again, the German case officer spelled out the arguments. Some initial discussion took place between the judges about the presence of two U.S. Customs agents in the court. Eventually, the case officer came back to them and asked them to please wait outside; there was no time to explain why. For the two Americans, this made the tension worse. Inside the courtroom the legal arguments went on for an hour, but when the case officer came out, there was a smile on his face; the decision of the lower court had been overruled and the seizure order had been granted. There would be another delay while the warrants were prepared for signing by the clerk. It was now after nine; there was less than sixty minutes left.

The warrants took longer than expected, and it was after nine-thirty when the documents were handed over to the German agent. He held the papers in one hand and his personal radio in the other. He thumbed the transmit button and raised his controller. He was still talking into the radio as they all left the courthouse and headed for their cars. It was nine forty-five when the *Wasserschützpolizei* — the port authority police — received the message in their station at the extreme end of the pier across the water from the Africa wharf. *Elgaren* had been berthed at an outer east berth of the pier, where it could be easily observed by the police. Within seconds, one of their patrol boats was streaking across three hundred meters of dark, oily water to the berth of the container ship. With blue lights flashing and the howl of the siren cutting into the night, the small boat heaved to under the looming bow of *Elgaren,* effectively blocking her passage.

By this time the Customs team had turned onto the Versmann-strasse, which would take them across the bridge over the River Elbe and into the free port area. The case officer was now speaking into the car radio microphone and coordinating the dispatch of standby agents to the quay. Move in, but do not board the ship. Within minutes they turned off the main access road and drove down the pier. They cut across between sheds 62 and 63 and pulled to a halt on the dockside opposite the ship. Her lights were on and the engines running in preparation for departure; the lights of the police boat flashed an eerie blue cast on the scene. Faces looked down at the agents from the bridge as they walked up the gangway and boarded the ship. As it turned out, they were in good time. She was behind schedule, and her stern ramps were still down.

One of the ship's officers was on deck to meet them. He introduced himself and took them to the wardroom, where the captain was waiting. As usual, the Swedes were correct and polite. Captain Bexelius was a distinguished-looking, white-haired man in his mid-fifties. There must be some misunderstanding, he said as he passed the warrant to a man standing beside him, whom he introduced as the Hamburg lawyer for the owners. The Customs agents were amazed: How did the crew of *Elgaren* find out that a raid was going to take place? The wardroom fell silent as the German lawyer leafed through the papers. After the bitter cold of the quayside, the cabin was stuffy. It did not help that most of the ship's officers, the two Americans, and four German Customs agents were all crowded into the limited space. The atmosphere was tense and then broke into anger when the lawyer asked the two Americans to leave the ship. "This is a Swedish vessel," he reminded them, "and this document does not permit you to carry out a search. Only the German Customs Service is mentioned here." They protested, but to no avail. Harsh words were exchanged as the two withdrew, but they were unwilling to be the center of an international incident.

Once more they had to wait. The two agents stood on the dock with their collars up and their hands thrust deep into their pockets. The day had started bright and sharp, but now a blustery wind whipped the freezing drizzle around their legs. Suddenly, tiredness overcame them and depression set in. Between the drive from Bonn, the court hearings, and the meetings with the local officials, there had not even been time to eat.

By now a search had started, and the German Customs team soon homed in on a group of containers that had been stowed on the upper forward cargo deck, exposed to the elements. The Americans, using their own radios, listened in on the local Customs frequency. Most of the exchanges were in a terse jargon that was difficult for them to follow. Shortly, there was a sudden roar behind them as the engines of a dockside crane started up.

A team had been mustered to off-load the three containers specified in the warrant and set them down on the quay. As they came over the side, the case officer joined the U.S. agents and gave them an encouraging nod. It was a straightforward operation. By 2:00 A.M. on Thursday, November 10, the seized shipment had been moved into a nearby Customs shed and *Elgaren* had raised her stern ramps and was heading downriver to the Elbe estuary and the North Sea.

By this time the two Americans were so cold that they could hardly feel the lower half of their bodies. But the operation had been such a tense one that, as one agent confessed later, "I sweated nickels when the containers were unloaded. Remember, there was a lot hanging on this. It went right up to ambassador level. And we had a system worked out with Washington. They were calling us direct every fifteen minutes and, at one stage, every ten. 'Habeus Grabbus,' we called it."

When the doors to the Customs shed had been secured, one of the German Customs agents took the Americans to their hotel on the outskirts of the city. They arrived at 2:30 A.M. but after only a few hours' sleep they were conferring again with their Hamburg counterparts. They drove back to Bonn to talk with Jacobson later that morning. It was an early start again on Friday, November 11. This time only one of them flew with Jacobson to Hamburg. They were met at the airport on arrival and went straight down to the dock area and the Customs warehouse. Inside the shed they found that the Customs agents had been joined by two lawyers acting for the owners' company.

The containers had by now been unsealed and the double doors at the back of each stood wide open. Inside were twenty to thirty refrigerator-size packing cases. When the heavy-duty cardboard was stripped off, they found themselves looking at an unmistakable array of computer peripherals. "When we found the mainframe," the junior agent recalled, "I just about kissed it. I'd been over in Germany eighteen months doing embargo cases, and this was the biggest seizure of the lot — two million dollars' worth of the stuff" The Germans decided to transport the computer and its peripherals to a more secure location at a police barracks in the small town of Alsterdorf, about thirty kilometers outside Hamburg. Then there would be negotiations with the Americans to decide what to do with the equipment. The two U.S. Customs men went to Bonn to receive commendations and congratulations. But the heady mood was soon to fall flat; the embassy received information that *Elgaren* had sailed from Hamburg to Sweden with four other containers that were also packed with high-tech systems.

When *Elgaren* left Hamburg, she headed north around Denmark and east toward Sweden and her home port of Gothenberg. After a short stop there, she put to sea again and steamed toward the southern tip of Sweden, heading for Malmö, her easternmost port of call. But heavy weather in the Skaggerak passage forced her to put instead into the nearby haven of Helsingborg, where there is a free port.[16]

During her stopover there, *Elgaren* off-loaded a number of containers originally bound for Malmö. It was only after the weekend of November 12 to 13 that Swedish Customs was alerted by the Germans to look out for a shipment of electronics hardware from South Africa that might be on the vessel. By then the ship had already passed west through the Kiel Canal and called back at Hamburg. She carried on west, down the coast to Bremerhaven, and then across the North Sea to Tilbury on the Thames estuary, where she arrived at ten on the evening of the 16th. Her Majesty's Customs and Excise had also been alerted to watch for the containers and was prepared to impound anything arousing suspicion. Nothing was found.[17] *Elgaren* put out from Tilbury on November 18 and by the beginning of December was back in South Africa.

Because of the ship's unscheduled stop at Helsingborg, it was several days before the Swedish Customs — expecting her at Malmö — noticed that four large containers unloaded by *Elgaren* at the Helsingborg free port had not been collected by their consignee. Agents conveyed their suspicions to Stockholm headquarters, but it was some time before anything happened. The four containers were officially "frozen" on Thursday, November 17. Carl Johan Aaberg,

Permanent Under Secretary at the Swedish Foreign Trade Ministry, told the press: "It would be too strong to say that we have impounded the shipment. We have not received a request to do so. But everything has been frozen and the containers may not be moved until we are satisfied of their contents." Declining to reveal more details, Aaberg went on, "The owner and the country would be in serious trouble with the United States if this became known, and Swedish policy in this sort of instance is to keep quiet."[18]

The following Sunday, the telephones at the Customs office in Helsingborg began to ring. The Americans had now formally requested that the containers left in the free port be seized and opened. This posed an immediate problem for Gosta Ekdahl, Customs superintendent at the local office. His men had no legal authority to seize what was essentially unclaimed cargo. The containers, weighing twenty-five tons each and marked "Electrical Equipment," were consigned to a Swedish destination. Ekdahl had no concrete evidence that any Swedish law had been broken. What is more, the containers were in the free port area. What had begun as a quiet Sunday for the Custom's man soon took on the dimensions of an international row.

There had already been inquiries to Helsingborg Customs concerning the cargo from Sven Haakansson of Sunitron, a firm in Stockholm. He claimed that the cargo was being shipped to him and that he had already ordered a fleet of trucks to go down and collect the containers. The Helsingborg office put Haakansson off with the excuse that it had not received the required forms proving his ownership. As far as it was concerned, the cargo still belonged to a Swiss firm called Integrated Time. But the next day a Stockholm lawyer, acting for Richard Müller — Integrated Time's owner — called to confirm that the containers could be released to Haakansson.

Pressured on one hand by the Americans to seize the containers and on the other by the legal consignee, the Swedes found themselves in a dilemma. In the uneasy diplomatic climate following the Datasaab affair, they were reluctant to seem obstructive to U.S. demands. But their neutrality and trading reputation could not be compromised.

To resolve the impasse, Swedish Minister for Trade Mats Hellstrom called on the services of the government's inspector of war materials, Carl Algernon, to examine the seized equipment and determine whether it had possible military application. Algernon decided that the goods at Helsingborg did have such possible application and could thus be confiscated under Sweden's War Materials Act, because there had been an infringement of neutrality. To stress the point, the government immediately issued an announcement to the effect that Sweden was banning all arms' imports from South Africa. In the welter of publicity that followed, the Swedes declared that the seized equipment should be returned to the manufacturer in the United States.

The Americans had succeeded. U.S. Customs believed that Richard Müller, via the companies in South Africa, had been in the process of diverting Digital VAX 11/782 computers to Moscow. Following the Helsingborg seizure, Customs searched a number of other premises in Malmö and Stockholm. They found more equipment from a variety of sources. The U.S. authorities had tipped them off to look out for another fifteen containers of electronics.

Haakansson and Müller disputed the American claims. The equipment from South Africa was destined for a computer-aided design office that they were going to open jointly in Stockholm at the end of January 1984, because Müller was winding down his Cape Town operation and moving to Sweden. (Swedish experts agree that there is a big potential market for computer-aided design services in Sweden.[19]) Haakansson had already paid half a year's rental for three hundred square meters of office space in the Stockholm suburb of Täby; the hardware from South Africa was to have been installed there.

Haakansson's story did not cut much ice with the Swedish authorities. Customs agents had already inspected the proposed site for the new company and were skeptical that it would be suitable for computer equipment. There was no obvious sign of air conditioning, and the place was in a poor state of repair; a few pieces of office furniture and some half-empty cans of paint were not entirely convincing. The head of the Customs Service, Björn Eriksson, explained that the identification markings and serial numbers on some of the devices had been obliterated.

Haakansson was later arrested and held by the Swedish authorities. He was charged with tax fraud, currency offenses, and illegal importation of electronic equipment. Müller seemed to have evaded the authorities yet again. After he had boarded a London-bound plane in Durban at the end of October 1983, his trail went cold.

The Richard Müller case was considered so important that a Washington press conference was called. The seized equipment was to be displayed; Defense Secretary Caspar Weinberger and Treasury Secretary Donald Regan were to attend. The conference was a golden opportunity for publicizing Operation Exodus and for reinforcing the United States Government's contention that crucial technology was still being shipped to the Soviets.

The first journalists to arrive at the main Treasury building on 15th Street took seats right in front of Richard Müller's VAX 11/782. The latecomers had to stand behind the platform that the maintenance staff had constructed for the television cameras. As the cameras would see it, the central processor and the magnetic tape units were directly in front; a three-hundred-megabyte disc drive, two Tektronix graphics displays, and two Digital VT-180 terminals were positioned to the left. To the right of the central processor was a speaker's rostrum; behind that, chairs for the VIPs. Tables showed various circuit boards and manuals bearing the logo of Systems Industries, Inc., and display panels showed photographs of the scenes at Andrews Air Force Base when the system arrived back from Germany on a massive USAF C-141 cargo plane.

It had taken several weeks of diplomatic maneuvering to get the equipment back for the December 19 conference. After their success in persuading the Swedes to seize the systems, the Americans thought they would try Stockholm first. A considered reply came back: technically, the computer still belonged to Müller, who had not been convicted of breaking any Swedish laws. The issue was also sensitive at a political level. Müller, in the first interview he had ever given, pointed out to *Svenska Dagbladet* that his new business operation in the country was intended to create new jobs.[20] An informal approach was then made to the Germans, but the legal system dictated that such matters be resolved through the courts. The VAX seized in Hamburg had been originally shipped out of Kennedy Airport, which is in the jurisdiction of the Brooklyn U.S. attorney's office. The local federal prosecutor made a formal application for the return of the equipment; it would be needed as evidence in any case that might be brought. The German court agreed to the request.

Secretary Weinberger told the assembled reporters that the VAX could have helped the Soviets increase the accuracy of their missiles. All of the equipment on display was totally embargoed to the Eastern bloc, and the seizures had been "much too close a call." He said the Pentagon wanted to review license applications, such as those granted for these shipments, but had not been allowed to. They were West-West cases. Had Defense been involved, the licenses would never have been granted.

Twelve journalists later attended a background briefing at the Pentagon. They were told that as many as three VAX 11/782 systems were believed to have been involved in the shipment from South Africa to Europe. The officials also suggested that the consignment may have included eleven small computers. It was their best guess that the Soviets wanted to use a lot of this equipment to produce integrated circuits for the military. Something on the scale of a large microchip factory would have been possible. The resulting chips would have made Soviet weapons smarter, given them improved targeting, and made them more effective in avoiding countermeasures. The look-down targeting radar of the F-15 fighter included 4,778 MSI chips. The average failure rate was one every hundred hours. By 1990 the Americans estimated that they could reduce the number of chips to forty-one and, at the same time, bring the failure rate down to one every ten thousand hours. This was what the Soviets wanted to be able to do, but they were still fifteen years behind the United States in this field. The Pentagon wanted to keep it that way.

The Defense officials said that the main weakness of the Soviet Union was not in research and development but in producing adequate quantities of the chips. As many as twelve to fifteen of the country's integrated-circuit production lines had been bought or stolen from the West.

The Müller case had confirmed a Pentagon belief that the Soviet Union was determined to import as many VAX machines as possible. Although not really compatible with its sixteen-bit predecessor, the PDP 11, this thirty-two-bit machine does have a lot of storage and peripheral devices in common with the older systems.

At this time many other VAXs were being shipped to the East by rings allegedly operated by Brian Williamson in the U.K. and by another Englishman, Alan Simmons, in Greece.

Although Digital would argue to the contrary, the VAX system is not state-of-the-art for that type of processor. It is, however, well established and supported extensively by Digital and by many suppliers of alternative peripherals and software. The Soviet Union cannot yet make the advanced VLSI chips needed to construct an equivalent computer or the essential flow of spares. But apparently the Soviets needed the VAXs for certain essential applications in the short term — and thus they ignored the long-term problems.

The power and capacity of the VAX makes it suitable for a wide variety of applications — commercial, academic, and military. Its strong points include communications — it can be used as the switching node in networks — and for graphics and computer-aided design. Although it is not built specifically for graphics applications, it can do the job well enough and its software library contains many programs for specialized tasks. The machine is so versatile that it could be used for the design of microchips, and the same hardware could be used to set up a new military communications network. It would also be an excellent machine to provide researchers and students in universities with interactive computing facilities.

But perhaps one of the more startling revelations of the Müller case will surface when the government investigates how millions of dollars' worth of computers came to be licensed to the network in the first place. Commerce's Compliance Division had been investigating one of the companies in South Africa at the same time that licenses were being issued for the sales.[21] There was obviously something wrong with procedures.

On November 30, 1982, an American manufacturer had written to Commerce of his suspicions about MRI. The letter lay on the file for several months. In March 1983 a cable went from the State Department to the U.S. embassy in Pretoria, passing on the information and requesting that a check be carried out. The cable was acknowledged in April, but it was not until the beginning of July that a detailed message came back to Washington. It reported that members of the consular staff had visited the premises at 101, Connaught Road, Parow, and had seen the VAXs, installed and running.

But a subsequent visit met with some resistance, and the U.S. consular staff had some difficulty getting inside. On this occasion they found that MRI appeared to be closing down its operations and the computers were gone. Inquiries showed that they had been sold to one of Müller's other companies, Optronix, which appeared to have resold all the equipment to a Swiss company, Integrated Time AG, based in the town of Malthers, near Lucerne.[22] Integrated Time AG was a subsidiary of Müller's German firm, Deutsche Integrated Time. But by the time this was discovered, the VAXs were on *Elgaren*, steaming northward toward Hamburg and a confrontation with Customs.

12

A BANDIT FAMILY TREE

THE CHARGES that Republican Representative John Ashbrook of Ohio leveled against the Department of Commerce on March 12, 1980, were indeed grave. High officials, he said, had suppressed evidence about just what technology the Soviets had acquired from the United States — technology that had been put to use in Russian factories building intercontinental ballistic missiles and their launchers, chemical warfare laboratories, and secret weapons' research plants.

Then Ashbrook produced his evidence, a Commerce Department document that detailed illegal transfers between 1974 and 1980. It was a total anticlimax.

To anyone but a specialist, the document was meaningless, because it consisted of a maze of export control numbers and model numbers of equipment with all names of manufacturers and techno-bandits removed. True, there were Soviet bloc consignees named, but that was not much help. For Ashbrook, however, it was proof that Commerce had been caught in a serious lie. He pointed out that during the debate on the renewal of the Export Administration Act in 1979, Congress had been told time and time again by Commerce that no such information existed.

"What my colleagues will find in this document is computers, computer parts, advanced electronic devices, and even lasers, going to ... organizations like Mashpriborintorg, Technopromimport, and others," said Ashbrook. Commerce's cover-up had not only affected the renewal of the act; it had had a bearing on the SALT negotiations and the Defense Department budget. Commerce had shown contempt for Congress, he thundered, and guilty men should be removed from office.[1]

It should be remembered that John Ashbrook was a right-wing Republican. The nature of his views had no particular relevance as to whether or not his charges against Commerce had merit. But his attitude was certainly affected by his antagonism toward the SALT talks and his advocacy of larger Defense budgets. In any case, he died in 1983, without receiving any real answer to his accusations.

Indeed, until the authors of this book obtained certain documents under the Freedom of Information Act, Ashbrook's evidence remained indecipherable. Now, at last, it is possible to fit the congressman's information to names and thus reveal networks of techno-bandits who have been operating, in some cases for almost twenty years, without ever being brought to justice.

The newly available official papers show a consistent pattern of a kind that would have made Ashbrook despair. Time and time again, the Russians have gone to many of the same traders to obtain the desired technology. And time and time again, these traders have been caught or identified and then forgotten by U.S. enforcement authorities. It was as if computers with information storage and retrieval did not exist.

Over a twenty-year period, with adjustments for changes in dollar rates since 1962, the following cases alone account for a total of some $12 million in embargoed technology known to have been shipped to the USSR or her satellites.

In the 1970s, one of the most sought-after pieces of equipment was the oscilloscope, an electronic instrument that displays on a video screen the wave pattern of an electrical oscillation. In the 1970s, Ulrich Schneeman was the general manager of a Viennese company, Rohde and Schwarz-Tektronix GmbH, that imported and exported technology manufactured by American firms. The company had an annual turnover of $35 million, and most of what

Schneeman sold required export licenses; requests for 281 were filed in 1979.

On February 12, 1980, a letter from the U.S. Department of Commerce was hand-delivered to Schneeman. It accused him and the company of having illegally exported a COCOM-listed oscillograph, made by Tektronix, to the Soviet Union. And that was a true cause for concern. The Commerce Department can penalize a company by denying it the right to import or export any U.S. goods. Lawyers were hired immediately to represent both the manager and the firm.

Commerce charged that Schneeman had knowingly sold the instrument to Franz Eggeling, a man who had been on the Commerce blacklist since 1967 and had been investigated again in the mid-seventies. Eggeling had promptly shipped the oscilloscope to Mashpriborintorg.

Schneeman denied it. But the story he told was so confused and incomplete as to produce shudders in the executive offices of his firm. He said that in September 1979 an airline representative had come to the company offices late one afternoon and, "because most of the employees had gone for the day," had been directed to Schneeman. The airline wanted to buy four oscillographs to use in servicing aircraft instruments at the Vienna airport. Subsequently, Schneeman believed, a purchasing agent had been brought in to represent the airline. The instruments were delivered to a Vienna warehouse.

A few months later, Schneeman went on, a man from a transport company came to him with an invoice itemizing the cost of carrying one of the instruments to Moscow. "I had no knowledge or reason to know ... that the equipment listed in this order would be exported to the Soviet Union and I had no knowledge or reason to know that Franz Eggeling ... was directly involved," protested the manager.

Apparently, Schneeman knew a good deal more than he was saying. He left Vienna abruptly in 1981, and when a U.S. embassy security officer called at his last known address, the American was told that Schneeman had moved to the Seychelles. Commerce wrote him there, and after getting no reply, placed him on the denial order list — or blacklist — for fifteen years.

As for Eggeling, he came to the attention of Commerce shortly afterward, when he illegally re-exported a Tektronix amplifier from Austria to the USSR. The department extended his blacklist term to 1990.

Eggeling and his Liechtenstein company, Memisco Anstalt, had first come to attention in May 1967, when both had been accused of illegal export of strategic goods — some of it carried over the border in Eggeling's own luggage. Commerce, getting no answer from Eggeling, and deciding that it would be "impracticable" to subpoena him, simply put him on the list.

He had surfaced again in 1971, when he approached a British manufacturer of electronic and scientific instruments with orders for oscillographs worth over $130,000. Alfred Greenup, director of Greenup Scientific (International) Ltd. of Manchester, may well have known — according to Commerce — that Eggeling meant trouble. He nevertheless ordered the equipment from the U.S. manufacturer, telling the manufacturer that his company would be the end-user. Shortly after the equipment arrived, Greenup turned it over to Eggeling, who trucked it to Dover and smuggled it out of England.

Greenup was fined £3000 by the British Government and put on the blacklist indefinitely.[2]

The Information Magnetics case showed how easy it is, even for an American company, to get away with high-tech smuggling for a long time. This Goleta, California, company was first caught in 1972 and again in 1973 for illegally exporting $800,000 worth of disc heads, testing devices, and other magnetic recording and reproducing equipment for analog computers. But the company promised not to do it again, and got off with a warning.

Information Magnetics kept its word until March of the next year, when it tried shipping similar equipment, all unlicensed, to its subsidiary in Weybridge, England. Company employees carried many of the parts in their hand luggage on transatlantic flights. In the U.K., the equipment was hand-carried to the Bulgarian legation in Queen's Gate, Kensington, where it was put into a diplomatic bag and sent on to Bulgaria and the government trade organization known as Isotimpex.

Later in 1974, Information Magnetics exported a ferrite slicing machine to Poland. Finally, when the counts against the company had risen to fifty-five, action was taken. The firm's president, Daniel Gillum, pleaded guilty in California federal district court to violations of export controls. He got a fine of $10,000 and a suspension of export rights for five years.[3]

Another company with a very devious history was a trade agency called Caramant. In February 1965 the firm and one of the partners, Manfred Hardt of Wiesbaden, were accused by Commerce of diverting electrical test equipment from West Germany to Budapest. Hardt pleaded ignorance of the control regulations and managed to get Commerce to let his company off with only one year of export suspension.

Five years later, Caramant reappeared in the records when a German trader named Gustav Dieter Pese bought some controlled test equipment in the United States and sold it to Caramant, which promptly shipped it eastward. Pese, however, was the one who suffered. Commerce banned him from U.S. trade as long as export controls are on the books.

About the same time, Caramant made itself known in another quarter. A company executive named Christopher Brand had made a deal with the Mexican owner of a musical instruments store in Tijuana. José Resnicov was in the business of exporting radios, record players, amplifiers, and so on, and that seemed to be good cover for the export of $175,000 worth of banned American electronics equipment. It turned out that Brand, when caught, was able to dissociate himself — at least technically — from Caramant by pleading that he was acting as a purchasing agent. In 1976, he was blacklisted for two years.

In the same year, however, Manfred Hardt and Caramant applied to Commerce for their removal from the denial order list. Rauer Meyer, director of the Office of Export Administration, was obliging, and the removal was effective from January 1978. But in the meantime, something very interesting had happened. Hardt had been caught on another charge by another agency.

On November 11, 1977, after a fifteen-month FBI investigation, Manfred Hardt, along with Carl John Heiser III and Carl Lutz

Wieschenberg (a.k.a. Ron Lutz) were indicted by a grand jury in the Southern District of Florida under the U.S. Munitions Act. They had conspired to export illegally a Litton Industries inertial navigation device to the USSR. The other two men got jail sentences, but Hardt remained at liberty abroad.

The Department of Commerce apparently then came to its embarrassed senses. A few days after the sentences were handed down, it sent Hardt a letter, saying, in the quaint language of bureaucracy, that he had violated his denial order and was being given fifteen days to answer the charges. A failure to do so would be seen as an admission of guilt.

In October 1979, the verdict against Hardt, Heiser, and Wieschenberg was overturned by the appeals court on grounds of insufficient evidence to prove conspiracy.[4]

One of the most active technology diverters in the 1970s — as the FOIA-obtained documents show — was a German named Peter Lorenz. Between 1971 and 1972, he used a number of companies in Germany and one in Vienna to supply the Soviets with two strategically related computer systems worth $3 million. Lorenz had shipped the second computer while Commerce was investigating him in connection with the first one. He was also charged with having sold two oscilloscopes to the Soviets.

In September 1972, Lorenz requested a hearing before the Commerce Department and was granted immunity to come to Washington. He did not show up but, instead, sent Hans Jürgen Filter, his executive officer. It was to no avail — both Lorenz and Filter were blacklisted until 1990.[5]

Commerce moved with all the speed of an elderly tortoise in its pursuit of an elusive Frenchman named Albert Rolland. As owner of a French company called Seurolec, Rolland received a letter from Commerce, in August 1971, alleging that he had made false statements in order to buy U.S. goods. What Commerce seems to have overlooked was that Rolland was busily shipping oscilloscopes, spectrum analyzers, plug-in units, a crystal-growing furnace, bonders, four-loop electrodes, and an automatic electronics system to "unauthorized destinations."

In September 1973, Rolland replied to Commerce with the admission that its charges "correspond[ed] more or less to what actually happened." But it was not until April 1975 that he was permanently blacklisted.

"Permanently," it soon appeared, was a word that Rolland did not understand. He at once set up another company, called Sopex S.A.R.L., in the same offices that had housed Seurolec, and he was back in business, importing from the United States. One of his channels was a New York City company called National-Tronics, run by a man named Albert Goldberg. Commerce eventually discovered that Goldberg had sold transistors and integrated circuits to Rolland at least twenty-five times; the department consequently blacklisted the New Yorker and gave him a civil penalty, a fine of $25,000.[6]

Commerce decided in December 1977 to restore conditionally export privileges to Rolland and his French company, Seurolec. Stipulations included that Rolland report monthly to the department about all his transactions with American commodities for a period of two years. Records of such business activities had to be available to "authorized agents of the U.S. Government."

In the mid-sixties, Rolland served as European representative for William Bell Hugle of Mountain View, California. According to a story later told by Hugle, the Soviets once tried a double approach to the Hugle-Rolland team. In 1966, Hugle attended a U.S. Specialized Electronic System and Instrument Trade show in Tokyo and was approached by a representative of Technopromimport who was hoping to procure full equipment for a large integrated-circuit plant. At about the same time Rolland, in France, was being queried about the same kind of purchase. Hugle further said — for the benefit of anyone who could believe he was this innocent — that he had queried Commerce about it and was told that such equipment could not be exported. In any case, there is no record that Hugle-Rolland ever attempted to follow through on the Russian offer.[7]

This, then, is a sampling of representative cases from the Commerce Department files; of course, it does not include the many smuggling operations the department was not even aware of. The route through Canada has, for example, always been an easy one, simply because the United States requires no export permits for goods going to Canada. Millions of dollars' worth of computers have reached the Soviet Union that way, according to a March 4, 1984, story in the *Buffalo News,* which reported that the Canadian External Affairs Department was looking into new enforcement measures.

All in all, there is little doubt of two things: the United States has suffered from heavy technology spill in the 1970s and eighties. And the Commerce Department has not provided a very effective dam. Techno-bandits have regarded the civil penalties as not much more than a small tax on doing business. In fact, getting on the public denial order list can even be a kind of advertisement. As one controls enforcement officer explained, the Soviet technology-shoppers can simply use it as a kind of Yellow Pages.

The denial list does, however, give Operation Exodus a basic guide, and it was equally useful to British Customs in 1983, when it launched its counterpart operation, Project Arrow.

On the night of December 11, 1983, a team of U.K. Customs agents seized a truckload of computer equipment at Poole, a sleepy harbor town in Dorset, shortly before it was due to be loaded aboard a ship for France. The shipper was Datalec Ltd., a bureau doing computer-aided design in the new Ferndown Industrial Estate in nearby Wimborne (a town more noted as the burial place of King Ethelred I than for high tech). The next day, Datalec directors Brian Williamson and Christopher Carrigan were charged in the local magistrates court with evading the British Export of Goods legislation.

Williamson is a tall, neatly dressed man of fifty-one, with thinning sandy hair and a well-trimmed beard. The two directors were remanded for trial, released on bail of £6000 ($10,000) each, and ordered to surrender their passports.

The Project Arrow raid was, however, only the culmination of a series of events and associations going back about twenty years. Williamson's name first entered the history of high-tech evasion in the early 1960s, in connection with the enterprises of an old West-East trading hand, Edward George Bajzert, who is always called Eddie. In 1961, Bajzert founded the Uni-Export Trading Company in Britain. Five years later, he had acquired several subsidiaries, and in 1967 he expanded into the fields of shipping and travel. One of the companies he bought was a small electronics trading and manufacturing enterprise founded by Williamson and a man named Anthony Young. Bajzert promptly appointed a number of Soviet citizens to the board of the company (now called Charter Travel), and the Anglo-Soviet Shipping Company bought many shares. Anglo-Soviet Shipping — to complicate matters further — was owned by the Russian shipping concern Sovfrakht.

The Commerce Department began an investigation of Bajzert, Young, Uni-Export, and Williamson in 1967. It found that Williamson (now using the name Byron Williams) and Young were running a company called Bay Laboratories in Dublin. On August 20, 1968, Commerce declared that everybody involved had engaged in illegal export, and denial orders were issued.[8]

Williamson got on the record again when he was implicated in the dealings of another shady trader. Jacob Kelmer of Haifa, Israel, had been blacklisted — on the usual charge — in 1972. In 1976, he and a Canadian named Peter Virag had shipped a number of GCA/David Mann chip-manufacturing machines valued at more than $1.5 million via Canada to Moscow — and, most likely, Zelenograd. By 1978, one of Kelmer's shipments had been intercepted and confiscated, and the result was an extension of the denial orders against both Williamson and Kelmer. (Bajzert admits business dealings with Kelmer, but denies strongly that he has ever shipped proscribed equipment to the East.)

Never one to be downhearted in adversity, Williamson had, in the meantime, set up the new company, Datalec, in England. In June 1981, Williamson's blacklist status was renewed by Commerce. In the fall of 1982, however, he was able to get hold of two Digital VAX 11/780 computers from the United States and ship them via West Germany to Bulgaria. He bought these machines with no apparent difficulty — especially surprising for a man who had been on the list for fifteen years.

The story of those VAXs is interesting and circuitous. Williamson used a Cologne company called Datagon GmbH to buy the machines from Computer Maintenance in St. Paul, Minnesota. Three of them were flown to Cologne, trucked to Le Havre, and sent to Poole on the Channel ferry. From Poole, they were taken to Datalec at the Ferndown Industrial Estate, unpacked, and assembled. Then a team of Bulgarian technicians was flown in to inspect them before at least two were consigned for Sofia. (The Bulgarians were reported to be almost as interested in buying up spare parts and accessories for their cars back in Bulgaria as they were in looking at the VAXs.)[9]

What happened to the third VAX is something of a mystery. But there is no mystery about what happened to Datagon as a result. The Cologne company, apparently an innocent party in all this, had made the mistake of putting Brian Williamson on its board of directors in 1981 (although the action was unavoidable, because Williamson had done much to revive the nearly moribund firm). The company president, Martin Coyle, is still bitter about what happened after the VAX shipment. The third VAX was never paid for, and as a result, Datagon had to go into bankruptcy. The next development came when the West German police raided Coyle's home and offices and confiscated all his records — though these have now been returned and no charges have been brought. Coyle blames both Williamson and two Datagon employees, who, he says, gave the police false information about Datagon's involvement. One of those employees, Uwe Schumann, had once done work for the well-known techno-bandit Richard Müller.

Another interesting connection of Williamson's — through Datagon — was with Michael J. Winkler, the techno-bandit arrested by Bob Cozzolina and Dick Curci in 1979. After his trial, Winkler had returned to Germany and changed the name of his company to Syscom. Winkler did business with Datagon, handled personal computer sales at the U.S. Air Force bases in Frankfurt and Darmstadt, and, according to one business associate, re-established his equipment sales to the Eastern bloc.[10]

Just seven months before Williamson was charged in the U.K., a company called Electrocom opened its doors close to the Signal Corps headquarters at Fort Monmouth, New Jersey.[11] The local Yellow Pages and some electronics trade magazines carried ads for the new firm on Shrewsbury Avenue, but otherwise the debut was quiet. It was scarcely an unusual event, because the area around Monmouth has in recent years become a kind of mini–Silicon Valley.

Electrocom was in the business of brokering and negotiating contracts for the purchase of military-related microwave surveillance and test equipment. During its first year, Electrocom established good credentials in the field.

In October 1983, it acquired a new potential customer, a Chinese businessman who lived in New Jersey. Mr. Kuang-shin Lin explained to the Electrocom president that he wanted to buy a Watkins-Johnson 3108. This piece of equipment has the technical description of "defense electronic countermeasure traveling wave tube," and its specifications are classified. It is employed in B-52 bombers to jam the guidance radars of incoming surface-to-air missiles.

The conversation about the Watkins-Johnson 3108 took place over the telephone, but there was a meeting shortly after. Lin explained that he ran a company called East Star Enterprises from his home in Lincroft, New Jersey, and that there was quite a list of equipment he wanted to buy. The trouble was that it was all subject to export controls. Not that Lin objected to export controls — he wanted to trade legally, but he just couldn't get the necessary licenses. If Electrocom could get what he needed, well, "the sky's the limit," he said inscrutably.

Now, Mr. Lin had a friend who owned six companies in Hong Kong — though he traveled on a People's Republic passport — and he would be arriving in New Jersey soon. The friend, said Lin, had excellent connections in Beijing party and government circles. Perhaps a meeting could be arranged?

On February 10, 1984, the friend, Mr. Zheng, and a group of other Chinese arrived at the Electrocom offices. They wanted to discuss buying an initial order of transverse-wave tube amplifiers.

Electrocom's president explained very carefully that there were licensing requirements for this equipment. Electrocom would be taking a great risk. He therefore would have to charge an extra 20 percent. The Chinese said they understood.

The president then asked Zheng for his technology list, and the man reached into his briefcase, produced a paper, and handed it over. He explained that Electrocom shouldn't be concerned with the first six items — they had already been obtained elsewhere.

It was a historic moment. For the very first time, a Chinese technology shopping list had fallen into the hands of U.S. authorities.[12] Electrocom had been the front for Operation Scotch, a Customs sting set up to net Soviet traders. Ironically, it had netted the Chinese first. The offices had been wired for audio and visual recording. When the Chinese group left the meeting, twenty Customs agents were waiting for them.

The Chinese shopping list made fascinating reading. It was typed in English — with many spelling mistakes — and handwritten in Chinese on the right-hand side of the page.

Item one was a Calma Model II computer-assisted design system. Items three, four, and five were pieces of equipment produced by GCA/David Mann of Bedford, Massachusetts. Two of these were figure generators, and the third, a GCA 9400, was a full design system for VLSI microchips.

Item five specified two Varian Instrument Division power-supply sources, one for 440 KeV and the other for 220 KeV. There was also a military specification PDP 11/43 from Digital Equipment.

The remaining seven items had applications to microwave communications of the sort used by the West in satellite ground stations; they were, for the most part, traveling wave tubes for various parts of the spectrum. They are manufactured by such companies as Hughes, Raytheon, and Watkins.

Operation Scotch had already produced some interesting intelligence about Soviet operations. When the Chinese walked into the parlor, Dick Curci — with Pat O'Brien's approval — had to make a decision whether to blow the operation or to let the Chinese leave the country. But the last thing Operation Exodus wanted was another group of escapees. So the five Chinese ended up in custody, charged with conspiracy to violate the Arms Export Control Act.

From now on, it would be harder for Customs to mount such successful ambushes. But on the other hand, there was one benefit. As Pat O'Brien pointed out, "No one is going to trust anyone anymore in the industry. We may have stopped more than we know."[13]

13

THE POLISH CONNECTION

TUCKED AWAY in one corner of the Villa Park Shopping Mall in Orange County, the Fling is the kind of bar where a serious drinker can concentrate on his work. The management keeps it open most of the day and half the night. No food is served. The décor consists entirely of dark wood, lit by ten-watt bulbs. In short, the Fling offers a good deal of basic relief from the Southern California sun. William Dougherty, when he stepped into the bar on a hot October day in 1981, wasn't looking for relief, however; he was looking for the answer to a minor mystery.

Dougherty was a criminal lawyer and something of a maverick who did a lot of his business not in paneled offices but in bars or coffee shops around the county. Many people who know him by reputation alone call him Wild Bill. Most of his friends call him Doc. Both nicknames have a certain truth.

He stood and waited for his eyes to get used to the half-light, peering around to assure himself that none of his legal colleagues happened to be in residence. The Fling had been chosen on very short notice as the venue for a discreet meeting, and he didn't want a chance encounter with anybody who knew him by sight.

Dougherty had no notion of the looks of the man he had come here to meet, but that was all right, because nobody could ever miss

Dougherty. He is six feet tall or more, has an imposing presence, and a haircut about three quarters of an inch longer than the boot-camp look. None of that is coincidental, since Dougherty is an authentic ex-Marine fighter pilot and a colonel in the Marine reserves. He walked over and stood by the bar.

The man who got up from a chair in a far corner of the room and made his way among the customers was, in the dim light, something of a lookalike, because he too was tall and sturdy and he also had a cropped head. "I'm Jay," he said, holding out his hand.

With a coffee for Dougherty and a Bloody Mary for Jay, they sat at a corner table, and Jay began to talk in a low tone. "I want you to get me out of trouble," he said. "I've been spying for Polish Intelligence." Just like that. But Dougherty was less than completely astonished.

He had caught a few hints beforehand. A stranger — identified in time as someone calling himself Jay — had telephoned three or four times over the past two weeks, saying that he would like to do something to help Christopher Boyce. Boyce was one of the two young men arrested in 1977 in the "Falcon and the Snowman" case, and Dougherty and the other lawyers had fought a determined but losing battle in his defense. Finally, Dougherty had agreed to a meeting.

In the course of the next twenty minutes, Jay incriminated himself desperately and thoroughly. He said that he had been selling secrets from a Silicon Valley Defense Department contractor to Polish Intelligence agents. Dougherty nodded and listened, anticipating what was going to come at the end of the story, as, indeed, it did. Jay wanted Dougherty to get him immunity from prosecution if he agreed to become a double agent for the government.

That, Bill Dougherty pointed out, was not something he could promise. He'd ask some questions in the right places, he told Jay; he'd try to see what he could do. They agreed to keep in touch.

Driving home, the lawyer pondered what he'd heard and tried to weigh it on some imagined set of psychological scales. There was the chance that Jay was a fantasist or a paranoid case — but Dougherty's instincts told him that neither was true.[1]

Dougherty's reputation as a maverick is well and truly earned. For instance, he took the Boyce case — an unpopular defense and one that must have grated a bit on the nerves of a former Marine officer — and charged no fee. Unlike other successful lawyers in Southern California, he has no office; he runs his practice out of his rambling, red-roofed home in Villa Park. His study, next to the kitchen, might be that of an absent-minded scholar. Files spill from desk to floor, and the floor is loosely stacked with magazines from *Aviation Week* to *Soviet Life* to *The Architectural Digest*. A spare bedroom occupied as a temporary office by an assistant is called "the church room," after a civil case the assistant is working on. The church in question is quite as unorthodox as Bill Dougherty — the Church of Religious Science has made a property claim against the Utsava Rajneesh Meditation Center. The garage is a kind of book depository, with shelves on which volumes of the California Code stand side by side with the garden tools. Outside is a garden thick with olive and lemon trees.[2]

In the courtroom, Dougherty is known as a tough opponent and a brilliant legal strategist. He graduated from Cornell Law School in 1950, worked in the Justice Department in Washington, and in 1959 moved to California, where he was a part of the department's Organized Crime and Racketeering Strike Force. He ranges from case to case and court to court in his Seneca private plane. He had defended a good many strange characters, but Boyce was his first spy.

Christopher Boyce — indicted with Andrew Lee — had worked for the Defense contracting company TRW, and the satellite surveillance secrets he sold were so sensitive that the trial was held under conditions of strict security. America's most secret intelligence organization, the National Security Agency, was deeply interested. Dougherty had to sign a secrecy oath before the trial, and much of the evidence has never been revealed. He lost, and Boyce was sentenced to sixty-eight years in prison.

Dougherty has also appeared for the defense in one of the earliest technology-transfer cases, that of Walter and Frances Spawr, accused of illegally exporting laser mirrors to the Soviets. They were prosecuted by Ted Wu, were found guilty, and Walter Spawr served a six-month term.

Such cases appealed to Dougherty's delight in the odd and unusual, and perhaps, as Robert Rickles, a former law partner, says, there is "a little bit of the James Bond in him."[3] After the Boyce case, Dougherty used to say as a joke, "If you know any double agents, just send them around." Now, in the Fling, he had met somebody with ambitions to become a double agent.

A few days after his meeting with Jay, Dougherty got in touch with what he calls the old boy network — friends or acquaintances who work for the FBI, the CIA, or military Intelligence. He set up a meeting with two CIA men, and they all went out to lunch at a Chinese restaurant near the Los Angeles Federal Courthouse. Dougherty explained the situation but said firmly that he hadn't any idea of Jay's identity and that he wasn't going to let the agents meet him.

Dougherty says that the agents' response was "highly professional — they were not going to buy a pig in a poke."[4] The best compromise was to have the agents prepare a list of twenty questions that the lawyer would put to Jay the next time he saw him.

That next time was in early December 1981, at the Orange County Airport. Jay, dressed in a jogging suit and running shoes, got off a flight from San Francisco, met Dougherty, and drove with him to a local bar. As they rode in the lawyer's Mercedes, Jay read the CIA questions. He nodded and put them in his pocket, but he told Dougherty that he wasn't ready to reply yet.

It was a month before he did. At a meeting in early January 1982, he handed Dougherty a cassette tape. Dougherty took it home, transcribed it, and then burned it. "There might have been fingerprints, or something," he explained later.[5]

Dougherty describes the CIA men's response after a reading of the transcript as "ecstatic." They had — like stout Cortez's company — a look of wild surmise. From then on, Dougherty says, the senior of the agents "almost haunted me." There were many telephone calls and five or six meetings. The agents prepared another list of twenty questions, and the answers came in March 1982. Dougherty, by this time, had been given two "clear" telephone numbers, one in Los Angeles and one in Washington, either of which he could call at any hour.[6]

By this time, the CIA had sketched out a tentative plan in which Jay — in the classic double agent role — would pass disinformation to the Poles and, as reward, get to keep their payment. But the Justice Department in Washington was not impressed with the idea. When the CIA approached it, the department replied, in effect, No deal. John L. Martin, head of the Internal Security Section, wrote Dougherty on June 22, 1982, to say "It will not be possible for the government to reach agreement on the ultimate disposition until he identifies himself."[7] The main reason for this attitude was that the FBI wanted to arrest Jay. When Dougherty had lunch with an FBI agent one day, the man told him that the agency was searching for his client.

Dougherty was able to talk Martin into letting him have a little more time for persuasion, but Jay was hard to move. "I did my level best; with all my heart I tried to help him," Dougherty says, but Jay still held out for immunity before he surfaced.

At the end of 1982, Justice got tired of waiting, and Martin wrote the lawyer, "My responsibility for national security requires that I act on the information already in my possession." The FBI, he continued, was about to get the go-ahead sign.[8]

The Bureau did not, however, move with gangbuster speed. It was ten months before a team of twenty FBI agents from the San Francisco regional Counterintelligence Squad began its Silicon Valley stakeout. A beautiful autumn day was just dawning as they took up positions around Montclair Le Parc, a two-story block of apartments at 1931 California Street, Mountain View. Several of the agents woke four Stanford University students in a house opposite and set up an observation post. Other agents were sitting in parked cars along the street and around the block.

Inside Montclair Le Parc apartment number 8, the occupant was sitting in his bathrobe, drinking a cup of coffee and reading the morning paper. His wife had left a few days earlier to attend her father's funeral in Eureka, California. There was a sharp knock at the door.

It all happened very quickly — the identification, the arrest, and the preliminary search. The occupant was not allowed to dress, but he was permitted to put on some shoes. He went to a closet, and the agents saw some twenty pairs of running shoes inside. The apartment was small and shabby, but there was a computer in a hall closet and other electronic equipment scattered throughout. As they left, the agents sealed the place in order to keep it intact for a later search.

The four FBI men escorted the suspect down the path through the scrubby garden to a waiting car. Little was said during the four-hour drive through Silicon Valley to the Federal Court Building in San Francisco. The suspect was kept in the FBI offices over the weekend and interrogated about spying, but he refused to say anything.[9]

That same Saturday morning as the arrest, an FBI agent knocked on Dougherty's door and handed him a subpoena to appear before a grand jury at 9:00 A.M. on the following Monday. "Which division are you from?" he asked the agent. When the man replied that he was from the Internal Security Division, Dougherty at once knew what was happening. "Maybe I should have got him [Jay] immunity before anything was handed over," he observes, "but my client wanted me to keep fighting."[10]

Bill Dougherty did not pilot his own plane when he flew to San Francisco on Monday. The commercial plane was late and he was in a rush when he arrived at the Federal Court Building and went to the sixteenth floor. In the corridor, he met his two FBI acquaintances. Near the courtroom door, Dougherty noticed a middle-aged man talking with a blond woman, and he guessed that this might be a man Jay had mentioned in one of their talks — a Silicon Valley consultant who had introduced Jay to the Polish Intelligence agents. One of the CIA men confirmed it.

While the grand jury was convening secretly in San Francisco, William H. Webster, director of the FBI, was announcing in Washington that James Durward Harper, Jr., forty-nine, a retired engineer from Mountain View, California, had been charged with espionage.

Webster told the press that Harper had allegedly sold secrets of the Minuteman intercontinental ballistic missile and classified information on ballistic missile defense research and development programs for more than $250,000. The FBI was sure that the Poles had been the cat's paw for the KGB.[11] For substantiation, the FBI released a rather curious document, a thirty-three-page affidavit sworn to by Special Agent Allan M. Power. Parts read like a plot-within-plot Le Carré spy story — others, like a farce. True to George Smiley tradition, it raised more questions than it answered. The document implicated a well-known Silicon Valley electronics entrepreneur. Many of the characters were known by code names — "the Big Man," "the Minister," and so forth. It revealed the existence of "the Source," a mole planted in Polish Intelligence. At the FBI press conference, the engineer was prematurely tried and convicted. Special Agent Robert Gast told reporters that what Harper had done would "damage his country beyond calculation."[12]

Of all those revelations, that about the mole was the most fascinating. It appeared that the FBI, through his reports, had known since early 1979 that vital American military information had been leaking to the Soviets. The KGB had been so warmly gratified by what they were getting that the then-head of the organization, Yury Andropov, had sent a personal commendation to the two Polish agents responsible for the American operation. What the Source didn't know and couldn't pass on was the origin of the leak. Now, things had become a bit clearer.

Harper had apparently installed a photocopier in his apartment, and the FBI now had some fifty documents he had copied and sold to the Poles between 1975 and 1981. One was "Minuteman Defense Study (Final Report)" and another was "Report of the Task Force on U.S. Ballistic Missile Defense."

All of these documents had been traced back to a certain Silicon Valley electronics firm where Harper's wife, now dead, had worked as a secretary and bookkeeper. U.S. Attorney William McGivern told the assembled press, "One reason we're glad this case broke is we hope it will focus attention on what we've attempted to emphasize is a high priority — and that's the protection of classified material in Silicon Valley. We hope that this is an exceptional case, but we know this type of stuff is going on."

James Harper walked into Court 3 on the seventeenth floor of the San Francisco Federal Court Building on February 3, 1984; he had come from a secret location where he had been held in custody for four and a half months. He looked trim in body, but his eyes seemed sunken and his complexion was sallow. He no longer had his hair cropped; it fell to his collar. As he stood facing the court, he was wearing pressed jeans, polished black shoes, and a dressy shirt with a white collar. Throughout the hour-long hearing, he kept his hands behind him and occasionally rocked backward and forward. He did not say a word.

The judge facing him from the bench was a short man wearing small, gold-rimmed spectacles. He was known as "Slammin' Sam"

Conti, and he had a controversial reputation in the Bay Area. He ruled his courtroom firmly, and some lawyers considered him the toughest judge in Northern California. As a Richard Nixon appointee, he held appropriately strong law and order views, observing on one occasion that the death penalty is a necessary deterrent. In a faraway echo of Winston Churchill, he once said, as he refused bail to draft resisters awaiting trial, "I didn't become a judge to preside over the decline and fall of the American public." In 1975, he declared Sara Jane Moore — a Charles Manson disciple and the would-be assassin of President Gerald Ford — fit to stand trial. After she pleaded guilty, he sentenced her to life imprisonment.

Samuel Conti had been characteristically hard-nosed with Harper's lawyer, Jerrold M. Ladar. He had already said that he could not rule out the death penalty for the offense. That day, when Ladar applied to see some of the evidence — copies of ninety-nine reels of tape recordings, tape of some three hundred hours of wiretap from Harper's telephone, made in the spring of 1983, and transcripts of twenty taped interviews that the FBI had conducted with Harper — Conti turned him down on the first, agreed to the second, and released no more than a summary of the interviews.

The speculation around the courthouse was either that Harper would be fatalistic about getting a life sentence from Conti, and thus would stay silent — or that he would confess everything in hopes of mercy

The accused man had come a long way from the Silicon Valley life of money and pleasure that had been one important factor in putting him into his present fix. In 1974, there had been a time when James Durward Harper, Jr., might have made the quantum leap from the status of small-time engineer to that of someone very tall in the Valley. Seemingly, he had everything it takes — the company, the capital, the business, and the product. He had invented something called the Accusplit, an electronic digital stopwatch. The idea for its split-time function had come to him when he was frustrated with a stopwatch he'd been using to time his daughters' performance in swimming time-trials.

In 1972, Harper found an angel. Albert Nelson, founder of *Track and Field News,* the leading running magazine, thought the watch could be a huge commercial success, and he backed Harper's company with capital and with his presence on the board of directors. The company's total resources amounted to $250,000 in working capital and a line of credit with the Wells Fargo Bank.

Things looked very good that year. The new watch — which sold for $199 — was publicized in *Playboy* and was endorsed by several racing drivers. "We believed that we were at the beginning of an entire revolution in timekeeping," says one of the original Accusplit employees.[14] Starting in a two-story office building in Mountain View and producing 50 watches a week, Harper's enterprise was soon producing 150 a week, and the small staff was working seven days. The business grew to a volume of $1.5 million a year.

But, as it often does in Silicon Valley, everything had grown too fast. A lot of the early watches were returned because they were defective. Then came the wolves. By 1974, competitors began to flood the market with cheaper imitations. By the time Accusplit had reduced its price to under $100, it had lost the leading edge of the marketing.

What was equally worrisome for the directors was the increasingly whacko behavior — even by Valley standards — of the founder-president. He decided to go to Switzerland to launch Accusplit in the very home of precision watchmaking and there got himself involved in a drunken brawl. He took a Swiss mistress, whom he visited on many trips before installing her in his California home in 1974. He covered the walls of his office with nude pinups. Sometimes he slept there; sometimes he disappeared for long spells. He was rude to his staff. "He was not a polite drinker," Bert Nelson observes, "and his personality changed."[15]

Harper shaved his head, began wearing T-shirts, jeans, and jogging shoes without socks. His colleagues thought he looked like Telly Savalas gone hippie.

Then came the Internal Revenue Service, demanding immediate payment of $54,000 in unpaid taxes. A special board meeting was called to deal with this problem, but Harper refused to attend. Instead, he sat outside in his car, listening to radio news bulletins on the possible resignation of President Nixon.

The end came quickly in 1975. It was discovered that Harper had spent some $80,000 of the company's money on personal luxuries.

Shortly after the directors persuaded him to resign, Accusplit went into bankruptcy. "We considered a lawsuit against him," says Bert Nelson, "but there were no assets."[16] In all, the investors lost nearly $400,000.

Ironically, within the year, two Santa Clara businessmen took over the bankrupt company and successfully relaunched it. They now make the claim that their product is the dominant stopwatch in the American market.

Harper turned to a new profession — selling paper to Poland — and the man who apparently set up that venture was one of Silicon Valley's earliest and most colorful pioneers, William Bell Hugle. Or, as he was later code-named in the FBI affidavit, the Big Man.

Hugle was known in the Valley as a promoter and a risk-taker. His career had begun in Cincinnati some thirty years before, when, after graduating from the University of Cincinnati in electronics, he went to work for Baldwin Pianos. He quickly moved on to become manager of Westinghouse's Semiconductor Division and chairman of the corporate committee on computers. By the time he and his wife, Frances, moved to Silicon Valley in 1959, they held fifty patents in microcircuitry and solid state electronics. In 1962 he founded Siliconix, manufacturers of integrated circuits, and four years later he started Hugle Industries to manufacture semiconductor production equipment. His wife died in 1968, leaving an estate valued at half a million dollars.[17]

Hugle began to show signs of public and political interests about that time, and he gave an interview to a local newspaper, warning that the Soviet Union and its satellites were illegally obtaining high technology and trying to get hold of the latest circuitry.

He founded Hugle International in 1972 to manufacture and distribute calculators, clocks, watches, and cordless telephones. Hugle had a dream of making Mountain View the world capital of electronic clock- and watch-manufacturing. It was, in fact, Siliconix that later bought the rights to Harper's stopwatch.

Hugle International went bankrupt in 1975. One of the contributing reasons may have been that its owner had discovered a new and more public career. He set up an influential high-technology trade association. Then, when he ran for Congress on the Democratic ticket in the Seventeenth District, it was one of the loonier campaigns in California history — which has seen quite a few. Hugle announced a platform that called for the legalization of marijuana, an end to the war in Vietnam, big cuts in military spending, and boosting overseas opportunities for U.S. manufacturers. None of these was especially outré, but Hugle's method of bringing his views to the attention of the Seventeenth District was. He embarked on a worldwide fact-finding tour and regularly cabled his supporters back home with news of his progress. He was, he said, nearly killed by an angry mob in Belfast. He was banned from the U.S. embassy bar in Warsaw. Once, he sent an urgent cable, telling his staff to put out a call for demolition of the local high school, because it was built on an earthquake fault. Finally, midway through his world tour, he cabled from Istanbul to say that he was dropping out of the race for Congress. On his return, he loosed a public blast at the State Department for its ineptness in promoting — through U.S. embassies and consulates — the American electronics industry.

Hugle's success had been greater with his Semiconductor Equipment and Materials Institute (SEMI), which he had founded in 1970 to promote the industry and organize trade fairs. From its start, this trade group called for better relations with Iron Curtain countries. Hugle was annoyed that European competitors were able to do a better job of selling to the Communist world, and he said, "We should be able to bid in the same way; after all, the Communists are going to get the equipment anyway."[18]

In 1975, the bankruptcy of Hugle International showed that this was no mere theory on his part. The judges of the bankruptcy court were asked by the public trustee to examine the affairs of Mr. Madhu Urajmir Desai, a member of the board from Pantai Hills, Kuala Lumpur, Malaysia.

Desai, it was discovered, took part in the shipping of embargoed equipment from Hugle International and transshipping them to Poland — without the benefit of export licenses, of course.[19] The kind of equipment was almost predictable, so great was the Communist bloc's hunger for the means of producing integrated circuits and semiconductors. One of the largest creditors with a claim against the bankrupt firm was the Polish Government's purchasing agency, Unitra Ece. Hugle's company was said to owe them $648,000, a claim that was later disallowed by the bankruptcy judge.[20]

In unraveling the tangled affairs of Hugle International, the receiver came across some even more interesting clues. He stated that the U.S. Customs held certain items of merchandise "which may or may not be an asset of the bankrupt."[21] What was definitely not an asset for the company — but was for the FBI — was a receipt for $300,000 cash that Hugle had signed on October 31, 1974, in Warsaw. It was the *other* signature on the receipt that attracted the Bureau's attention and was, nine years later, to provide a link with the Minuteman case. The signatory was a certain Zdzislaw Przychodzien, a high-ranking officer in the Polish Intelligence Service, although he operated under the cover of the Polish Ministry of Machine Industry.[22] According to an FBI affidavit, Przychodzien's assignment was espionage. The authors of this book discovered that he was the man whom Peter Gopal had met in Rudi Sacher's office in Vienna in 1977,[23] the man who was responsible for taking the Hugle consignments shipped through Malaysia, and, in another, later personification, "the Minister" in the Harper case.

The collapse of his eponymous trading company didn't slow Hugle down very much. He began to take part in international affairs, and for a man whose chief previous exploit had been to get himself kicked out of the embassy bar in Warsaw, he rose to unexpected heights. Hugle's son-in-law was Ali Reza Nobari, governor of Iran's central bank, and he played a crucial role in the negotiations for the release of the American hostages in January 1981. Hugle himself acted as a State Department consultant during the crisis.

Along with that, Hugle had become a consultant to the British National Enterprise Board (later renamed the British Technology Group) and the Scottish Development Agency in 1979. The board paid him to produce technical studies of advanced microchip technology and gave him access to the design of the INMOS (Integrated Metal Oxide Silicon) factories that were being set up with British Government money. INMOS made a statement to the effect that the company knew nothing about Hugle and that he had done no work for the company. Hugle was said to have held talks with Sir Keith Joseph, Minister for Trade and Industry, when Joseph came to California in 1979.[24]

Hugle now bitterly resents the allegations of wrongdoing in his connection with Harper. "I have introduced thousands of people to thousands of others," he said in a Paris interview in early 1984. "I have not been indicted and I have been allowed to keep my passport. They have no evidence against me apart from the statements made by Harper to Dougherty. So far as I'm aware, I have only ever been investigated by the Internal Revenue Service. I have U.S. security clearances, and a lot of things people have said about me have damaged my business and my life. I believe that the FBI has made a terrible mistake."[25]

The FBI clearly doesn't believe that it has made a mistake. Its affidavit, released in October 1983, is as strongly based on fact as possible. It is derived from the information Harper supplied to the CIA, and much of it is confirmed independently by the reports of the American mole in the Polish Government. Even then, it has the elements of a classic spy thriller.

In this business of intrigue, shopping lists are of consuming interest. Harper, in his depositions, described the lists that his Polish contacts used when buying foreign technology. But these were only sublists from the master list, which never left Moscow. When Harper was given one of these sublists, he further broke it down "as a function of my contacts in government, private industry [and] freelancers."[26]

The mole in Poland confirms the procedure. Each section of Polish Intelligence had its own KGB liaison officer. Each year, he was given lists of items he was supposed to obtain. "Orders for particular items were sometimes issued from high levels of the KGB," says the FBI affidavit. Requests for military information were, of course, given priority.[27]

Hugle's defensive statement — "I have introduced thousands of people to thousands of others" — makes Harper's first appearance in the drama seem rather offhand and fortuitous. In actual fact, Harper and Hugle together flew to Warsaw in late May 1979 for the introduction to Przychodzien. After some very private discussions, they came to an agreement. The Poles would pay for the documents in American dollars. The money would be split three ways among Harper, Hugle, and the unnamed source of the documents. Harper, in one of his statements to the CIA, reportedly said something that sounds like a hungry author with an unwritten book trying to con a publisher into a healthy advance: "I gave him a copy of the front page, title page, and the table of contents. . . . The Big Man assured the Minister that I could be trusted, and the Minister said that he was very interested."[28] The role of the literary agent is easily recognizable.

At the end of the year, Harper flew from California to Vienna. With him he had fifty to a hundred pounds of documents. He also had an inch-thick stack of their title pages, which he took to a meeting with Hugle and Przychodzien. "After a drink at a hotel bar," the affidavit relates, they "went to an apartment, which, the Big Man assured us, was not bugged." That little detail was, oddly enough, confirmed by the American mole in Warsaw. While Przychodzien was away, the mole had happened into his office and had seen a telephone message from Hugle with call-back numbers in Vienna. The mole had copied the numbers, which, when later checked out, proved to belong to some friends of Hugle who had let him use their flat in October 1979. This was of no enormous significance, but it did link Hugle, Harper, and the Polish agent circumstantially — and it was one tiny verification of the mole's bona fides. The fatal, overwhelming mistakes in espionage are often no more than a few words and numbers scratched on a memo pad.

There was ampler evidence when Przychodzien got back to Warsaw and told the mole that he had met an "interesting American businessman" through Hugle. He then described a meeting in which he and his immediate superior had received from the businessman some fascinating documents. The American had asked $1 million for them, and Przychodzien, like any prudent buyer, had headed for a telephone. But it was all right. The affidavit continues, "Przychodzien determined through Soviet KGB liaison that the documents offered by the American businessman were considered very valuable [and that the KGB] was willing to make substantial payments. . . ."[29]

Harper and his Polish customers met again in June 1980 in Warsaw, when the American turned over a large number of documents relating to the Minuteman missile. The documents — for a reason unexplained in the statement — were in strangely bad condition: wet, stuck together, and out of sequence.

"A team of three to five UB [Polish Intelligence] technicians worked overnight, cleaning, copying, separating, and assembling the documents. The next day, June 6, 1980, a special team of about twenty KGB analysts and engineers was dispatched by plane from

Moscow to Warsaw to evaluate the authenticity and importance of the material the American had delivered," said the mole. Przychodzien later told the mole that the KGB had taken the papers to the Soviet embassy, where the readers became very excited, because these proved to be documents the KGB had been seeking unsuccessfully all over the world.

In fact, the purchase inspired the chief of UB to hold a ceremony to commend his agents. On the same evening, July 22, 1980, the mole was present at a staff meeting at which a commendation from Yury Andropov, head of the KGB, was presented.

"So I got this big envelope with one hundred thousand dollars in it and proceeded to count it and got about a quarter of the way through it and said, oh the hell with it, it has to be there. I can eyeball it, and it's all in one-hundred-dollar bills." That was Harper's description of his own little awards ceremony.[30]

But how and where had Harper got hold of the documents? That was a question that faced the FBI early in the investigation, and on this score, Harper was not much of a volunteer. The FBI went seeking the woman.

The future Mrs. Harper was born in Mobile, Alabama, in 1943, and she acquired a yearning to be anywhere else. Louise went to Kansas State University, and when she graduated, headed for Los Angeles. After a short time, she decided that she preferred San Francisco, and she went to work there for the Mattsom Navigation Company, overseeing its foreign business. In 1968, she married an electronics salesman named Neal Schuler, and when Mattsom shut down its foreign operations and Schuler's sales declined, the couple decided to seek their fortune in Silicon Valley. Schuler, very shortly after, met Harper, and Harper offered him a job as chief of production at Accusplit.

Some time before the collapse of the company, Schuler suffered severe injuries in a car accident and was paralyzed in both legs. Today, he recalls Harper as "a brilliant engineer and a pretty good businessman." But Schuler also noticed the increasing aberration. "He had all kinds of personalities," he observes.[31]

By 1973 Louise and Neal were divorced, and by 1979 she had a new job — at Systems Control, Inc. — and a new husband — James Durward Harper, Jr.

Systems Control, Inc., has its offices on Page Mill Road in Palo Alto, a sprawling complex surrounded by gardens and parking lots. Architecturally, it is a bit reminiscent of Stanford University, two miles away. Page Mill Road is at the foot of the San Bruno Mountains, and some of the office windows look out at cows and horses grazing on the foothills. On one side of Systems Control is the West Coast printing plant of the *Wall Street Journal* and on the other the offices of Hewlett-Packard.

The company is regarded by the Defense Department with considerable concern. It is one of those Valley Cinderellas, started by two business-minded academics ten years before and now grossing about $25 million a year. In 1981, it was engaged in sonar-signal processing for the U.S. Navy, energy-transmission planning for the Electric Power Research Institute, and advanced navigation and guidance systems for NASA.[32] When a subsidiary of the massive British Petroleum Group wanted to buy it in April 1981, the Pentagon was alarmed.

Eventually the problem was solved when the Pentagon dictated certain safeguards — a separate company, insulated from the operations of BP and Systems Control, had to be set up. As CEO of this new operation, General John W. Pauley, former commander of the allied air forces, Central Europe, struck the Pentagon as eminently acceptable.[33]

After Harper's arrest, the FBI made a careful investigation of both companies and of Louise Schuler Harper. She had worked for the president of Systems Control and there she had a good reputation for reliability. One of her fellow workers came to her defense in an eloquent statement to the *San Jose Mercury:* "If there is anybody guilty in this, it isn't Louise. The lady was true blue, a U.S. American-type of lady all the way."[34]

There is a missing piece to the puzzle here, but its outlines can be guessed. One of Louise's former bosses told the FBI that she had, on occasion, taken Harper into the company offices at night or on weekends. Then, there are four interesting lines in the FBI affidavit. She is quoted as having told a friend, "There was a reason Jim and I got married that only he and I know. I can't tell you or anyone else and I never will."

She kept that promise to herself. In August 1982 she left her job, and by the spring of 1983 she was dead of cirrhosis of the liver, unaware of the case that was to involve her name.

On Monday, May 14, Harper was sentenced to life imprisonment. Judge Conti recommended he never be released on parole, telling him: "You are a traitor to your country who acted for greed and for money." Harper had pleaded guilty to one count of conspiracy to deliver military information to aid a foreign government. In exchange for a guilty plea and cooperation with the government investigation in the case, other charges were dismissed.[35]

Harper had insisted to the FBI that he had several sources for the documents he sold to the Poles, and the FBI has confirmed that — but not with any numbers. He seems to have duped certain of his contacts into telling him where classified documents were stored in company offices.[36] Dougherty believes that Harper often used bribery. "I would think that there are at least six people they [the FBI] will pick up sooner or later. I suppose there are a lot of people in Silicon Valley who aren't sleeping too well these days."[37] The Harper trial was hardly revealing about other suppliers of documents. All that was said in court was that Harper was helping an investigation of others alleged to have been involved.

14

COCOM

"A BASIC CONCERN of the Russian Intelligence system is to steal America's classified military, technical, scientific, and industrial secrets. That's the purpose of the Russian spy apparatus."

These words do not come out of the present-day offensive against the techno-bandits; they were spoken by J. Edgar Hoover in 1962. He went on to say "The Russians are doing everything they can to make contact with friendly American businessmen. . . . It is because the Russians want to obtain — by begging, borrowing, or stealing — the industrial secrets of American business."

In a magazine article dated May 1962,[1] Hoover gave as an example the American businessman who was invited to social events at the Soviet embassy and then asked to disclose "economic conditions in the electronics industry." As for scientific and technical conventions, "Soviet officials systematically cover [them]. . . . Here they gather . . . anything they can lay their hands on . . . from telephone directories to radar devices." At one such convention, a Russian official had taken motion pictures of jet aircraft, guided missiles, and an atomic cannon, he said.

He went on to note that these Soviet activities were perfectly legal. "They buy patents by the thousands; subscribe to technical, scientific, and other journals, belong to scientific societies." All this information was shipped back to Moscow by the ton. Later, Hoover testified before the Senate Internal Security Subcommittee and said that the Soviets had developed "the best industrial spying machine in the world." In this ambiance, he made it all sound rather less legal, and he spoke of the "subterfuge and deceit as well as deliberate circumventing of customs regulations."

The Soviets had set up their Amtorg import-export firm in New York in 1924. Recently, Hoover said, it had bought $30,000 worth of electronic equipment, ostensibly for use within the United States by the company itself. Some of this equipment was embargoed for export to the USSR, but that, apparently, was where it had ended up.

Technology transfer was thus already a live issue in the Kennedy administration, when Hoover's report went on to a five-member House select committee investigating the effectiveness of the 1949 Export Control Act, which was about to expire. That act gave the President broad powers to control or restrict the export market.

The committee came up with some conclusions that are now depressingly familiar. It asked for more Commerce Department staff to carry out investigations, better detective work from Customs, more and better-trained foreign service officers to work on the problem abroad. Most important, it recommended "that our government take a firm position with our allies to extend and make more effective international control of export of strategic commodities to Communist countries, including Cuba."

Only one thing really hampered the committee investigation — a Commerce Department refusal to allow it to examine important files. Researchers had to request information formally and within clearly defined limits. There was no way that the committee, in the end, could assess how well the laws governing exports were being administered. The Commerce Department's stonewalling succeeded, and the committee was left to grumble about its "dissatisfactions with this arrangement."

In 1960, the Kennedy administration had put all exports to Cuba under strict license control, with the exception of medical supplies and foodstuffs. COCOM agreed to cooperate in regard to U.S. goods, but refused to restrict the shipment of foreign products. The United States tried persuasion, but to no avail, and Secretary of State Dean Rusk pointed out the dilemma: "We have had . . . to balance the advantages of maintaining the COCOM system in order that our influence might keep these restrictions as strong as possible, or letting that system disappear and finding that the COCOM controls might gradually wither away." Rusk believed in COCOM because it had been effective against Communist China and North Korea during the Korean War, but he knew the weaknesses of the system. He also knew that the United States could not simply threaten to cut off supplies in order to bring a COCOM colleague to heel. After the United States had made an unsuccessful try for a longer embargo list, Rusk lamented, "This is pretty heavy weather in our dealings with countries that are heavily dependent on foreign trade.... We nationally cannot do it alone."[2]

The paradox resulted in a political row between Britain and the United States in 1962, when more British ships carried cargo to Cuba than did those of any other country. Congress was advised (in testimony before the House Select Committee on Export Control, on October 2, 1962) to cut off economic aid to Britain and Greece.

One of the most knowledgeable men in this field is Theodore Thau, former executive secretary of the Export Control Review Board. Thau is now happily retired in Salinas, California, and teaches at a small college in Monterey. But he is occasionally called back to testify before congressional committees, where he is not always heeded but is always respected as a calm and objective observer.

He hears today the same arguments as the ones he heard in 1969 and again in 1979, when new export control legislation was being introduced. In 1983, he told Congress that it was almost impossible to get COCOM countries to make sure that American shipments to them ended up where they were supposed to. A COCOM treaty (something more binding than the present ad hoc understanding) would be impossible to get, he thought, short of war conditions. "Business has always had a predominant say, rather than any security agency." And as for the Commerce Department's enforcement record, Commerce had always been interested in promoting exports, not in stopping them.

Thau remembers a rather nice example of some of the complexities contained in the problem. In the early sixties, the Russians were seeking color television technology, and three American manufacturers asked Commerce about getting licenses for their products. No, Commerce replied: video tape recording, machinery for the manufacture of integrated circuits, and some other equipment were considered strategic. The West Germans, through their COCOM representative, agreed with the U.S. position.

De Gaulle at once took advantage of the situation by selling the Russians the French SECAM color system — only to have the United States discover that the integrated-circuit technology the French were about to sell wasn't French at all: it had originated in America. Whereupon the French began to demand licenses for the sale, saying that their contract with the Soviets was binding. On the lower levels of the administration, there was a desire to hold the line. But when the matter was finally bucked up to the National Security Council, Thau recalls, Henry Kissinger decided to withdraw our objections, observing, "like the fox about the grapes, that the integrated-circuit-making technology wasn't very important militarily, anyway!"

During World War II, export controls were handled by the Board of Economic Warfare and a few other agencies. When Thau joined Commerce as an attorney in charge of the legal aspects of export controls in 1948, the department had been in charge of this activity for no more than two and a half years, yet there were already criticisms from Congress. To Thau, Commerce is a kind of a Willy Loman, too much "the nation's salesman" to be "a good judge of human nature." If you were a controller at Commerce, you got depressed. If you were a promoter, you got better pay, better chances for promotion, and even a better office and furnishings.

As for Congress, it has not grown more trusting in the course of time. The Commerce export control mechanism has had, over the years, more congressional reviews than any other regulatory agency.

Thus, the roles have remained more or less unchanged for a long time: a critical Congress worried about controls, a rather reluctant Commerce enforcement agency, a European COCOM fraternity that would rather sell more to the Soviets than less.

In Thau's view, the big break in COCOM began just after the Korean armistice. COCOM had loyally supported the United States until then, but soon the British wanted the controls on trade with China relaxed until they were like those on USSR trade. Washington opposed the idea, but Britain went ahead, and France followed suit. "From then on," Thau notes, "things went downhill and never stopped."

As sometimes happens in the history of bureaucracies, COCOM is the coordinating committee of an organization that has ceased to exist — the Paris Consultative Group, which vanished through sheer inaction in the 1950s. COCOM then became the only forum for international policy decisions on trade with the Communist countries. Because of its peculiar ancestry, COCOM had no legal status in national or international law. It was an informal body, not created by any treaty. Its rules required unanimous agreement before any action was taken. COCOM discussions weren't even reported back to the parliamentary bodies of the member nations for debate.

The last fact created a peculiar situation that was explained in a U.S. Department of State telegram of February 15, 1950, to heads of mission in Europe. The telegram said, in part:

NEARLY ALL EUROPEAN COUNTRIES HAVE TAKEN STRONG POSITION THAT SECRECY BE MAINTAINED OVER MULTILATERAL ASPECTS EXPORT CONTROL ARRANGEMENTS.... THUS ... AGREED ON BEHALF ALL COUNTRIES INCLUDING US THAT SECRET MINUTES OF NEGOTIATIONS COVERING EAST-WEST TRADE CONTROLS . . . COULD NOT BE MADE PUBLIC EXCEPT WITH CONSENT OF ALL. IF THESE COUNTRIES FORCED PUBLICLY TO ADMIT EXISTENCE OF MULTILATERAL ARRANGEMENTS ... STRONG LIKELIHOOD EXISTS THAT THEY WOULD WITHDRAW . . . FROM PROGRAM.

From this rather strange and shaky establishment, COCOM was to suffer many of the ills of illegitimacy. There were questions that would never have a final answer. Was COCOM supposed to deal with identifiable military technologies alone? Or was it to regard anything that contributed to the Soviet war capability as subject to embargo? Should COCOM decisions be binding on member governments that had bilateral trade agreements with the Soviet Union?

The broad outlines of COCOM history are known, and, in general, they follow the course of thaw or freeze in the cold war. A slightly less important governing factor — in the case of the United States — has been the attitudes of succeeding administrations toward free trade. Thus, the Truman administration took a tough attitude toward selling to the Russians; Eisenhower, who was committed to free trade, was far more lenient. The least restrictive pressure came in the détente years, under the Nixon, Ford, and Carter administrations.

The British, too, have had their changes of viewpoint — the major one being a gradual trend toward a permissive attitude. In the immediate postwar years, when Britain was America's senior partner in Europe and in a special-interest relationship, the two allies dominated COCOM. In the course of time, as Britain joined the European Economic Community, that has altered.

Just as COCOM debates have always been secret, so have the resultant lists of the strategic technology to be denied to the East. National lists, likewise, are usually secret. This makes it difficult for a manufacturer to know what he can sell to an Eastern bloc buyer or what he may be able to sell after getting a special exception from the rules. The trade ministry in a COCOM country has had the tricky job of trying to pick its way through a mass of decisions while trying to increase its country's trade rather than stifle it. As the COCOM members have been drawn deeper and deeper into the workings of the secretive committee, it has become harder for them to make public the difficulties in which they have become enmeshed. To do so would be to admit a history of secret collusion. Rather surprisingly, what little we do know about the inner workings of COCOM comes from the close-mouthed British, who, in January 1984, declassified some secret Foreign Office papers relating to events of 1953. (U.S. foreign policy documents up to 1955 have also been released — but on a very selective basis.)

In 1953, the situation was this: the Churchill government, two years back in office, was eager to expand trade and ease restrictions on every form of business. With Stalin dead, the Soviet Union looked more benevolent. Now that a truce in the Korean War had been declared, there might even be a chance to open up trade with China. On November 16, 1953, Stewart Crawford, a Foreign Office official, put together a long draft memorandum on his country's position in COCOM. As a kind of *plus ça change* document, it has more than a historical interest.

Crawford wrote that the United Kingdom needed to expand its trade, no matter what the source or the destination. Security controls on products should be kept to a minimum, "consistent with strategical requirements and the necessity for maintaining an agreed control system with our allies." The United States, he noted, was ready to stop adding items to the embargo lists and to take a "more flexible and liberal attitude."[3]

On the other hand, said Crawford, evasion was taking place "on a large scale." Both the United States and Great Britain were in agreement that controls should be made more effective. He believed that Washington nevertheless "has moved a long way from its previous view that trade with the Soviet Bloc is bad in itself. . . . [It] is most anxious to get out of its present unpopular position of international policeman and to reach agreement with us and the other main countries of the Paris Group."

One of Crawford's important points was to advise his government to accept the application of controls to "transaction and transshipment." By this time, shippers who wished to evade the COCOM rules knew enough to run their shipments through several countries on a zigzag route to some Iron Curtain destination. "Large quantities of goods which simply transit continental ports such as Antwerp and Rotterdam are not controlled," Crawford observed. Posting controls on transshipment would not only stop some leaks but would help to placate some of the British businessmen who compared the strict control enforcement in the U.K. with the looser one on the Continent — and so complained that "the bad hats" got all the business.[4]

Most important, he wanted Britain to back these new controls. If it did not, "We shall be abdicating from our position of responsible leader of the Paris Group, in which we have maintained a middle position between the cynicism of the Continentals and the desire for outright economic warfare on the part of the Americans." He saw Great Britain as the mediator who would hold the COCOM system together.

Among the recently released British official papers is a letter from Mr. Denzil Dunnett to Miss Rolleston on the subject of ball bearings. Miss Rolleston was in the Mutual Aid Department of the Foreign Office, and Mr. Dunnett was in the British delegation to the Paris Group. On November 18, 1953, he wrote, asking her to "give urgent consideration to the problem of ball-bearings." Indeed, the day before, British and American delegates to COCOM had disagreed rather sharply on the subject.

> The Americans [wrote Mr. Dunnett], sought to convince us of the importance of ball-bearings. They argued from the fact that illegal shipments to the Soviet bloc exceed legal shipments of ball-bearings and that the Russians regarded bearings as of vital importance and this was, therefore, a strong reason for hitting the Russians where it hurt. They even argued at one point in favour of denying the Russians ball-bearings for agricultural tractors. We said that we were not convinced from the intelligence standpoint that there was a critical shortage of bearings in Russia (except perhaps in one or two special categories).[5]

The ball bearing issue would continue to raise tempers for years to come. In a way, it was symbolic of many COCOM dilemmas, even though it concerned something that was hardly a new or sophisticated high-tech product. Did ball bearings for oil rigs contribute to the Soviet war potential? What about railways? Or tractors? We do not know what conclusions Miss Rolleston came to, but in the years just ahead, ball bearings would run and run, in a way their inventor never envisaged, as a classic example of a strategic embargo that went wrong. Congress was told: "In a period of détente and bridge-building we license the sale of precision ball bearing grinders which permit the Soviets to increase the accuracy of their strategic missiles. [Then] the U.S. taxpayer assumes the cost of upgrading U.S. ICBMs to reduce our vulnerability."[6] Dr. Stephen Bryen, Richard Perle's deputy at the Department of Defense, left senators in no doubt as to where he stood on the ball bearing debate. The statement was made in May 1982.

In fact, it was World War II that had brought home to the Allies the vital strategic role of the simple ball bearing, on whose efficient functioning so many key systems and weapons depended. It was essential to tanks, armored cars, guns, bombsights, engines, U-boats, railroads, communications, electrical generators, planes. For example, the Focke-Wulf and the Flying Fortress each used about four thousand ball bearings. The war could not have been waged without them.[7]

The company that produced 80 percent of Europe's ball bearings was the gigantic Swedish firm SKF. Because 60 percent of its worldwide production during the war went to Nazi Germany, the United States pressed hard to develop its own manufacturing base for every variety of bearing and ball race. To do this it had to develop the machine tools and metal technology that would turn out the quality and quantity the Allies required. It succeeded, and during the 1950s COCOM tried to keep a watchful eye on exports of bearings to the Soviet bloc. But the Soviet Union was aware of the shortcomings in its own production.

In 1960 the first round of a long bout of negotiation and counter-negotiation began in the United States. The story would end with senators charging that because of a classic piece of technology transfer, Soviet rocket and missile guidance ability had advanced by leaps and bounds. According to some, the MX missile program would never have been necessary but for a fatal slip in U.S. export controls.

In 1960 the Bryant Chucking Grinder Company of Springfield, Vermont, asked the Commerce Department for an export license for the sale of some of its specialized machines to the Soviet Union. The company made grinders of such high precision that all seventy-two of their Centalign-B models sold in the United States were used by Department of Defense contractors in the manufacture of miniature ball races for plane engines, synchro- and servomechanisms, and, most significant, for battlefield fire-control and advanced navigational devices mounted in planes, missiles, and spacecraft.

The Soviets wanted to buy thirty-five of the Centalign-B precision grinders. The Bryant Company, assuming that Department of Commerce license approval would be a matter of course, even passed on partial plans of their machine to Moscow as part of the contract. Commerce asked for expert assessment on license approval, and Commerce Secretary Luther Hodges subsequently claimed, "This technical information was to the effect that the [U.S.] national interest would not be prejudiced by the export of these machines by an American company, but on the contrary our national interest would be served."[8]

When called on to give its opinion, the Defense Department strongly disagreed. It asked another U.S. company — Miniature Precision Bearing Company — to back up its opposition to the Bryant deal. Commerce and Bryant both insisted that machines similar to the Centalign-B were available in Europe. They argued that the Soviets wanted to mass-produce ball bearings for conventional use and not to the rigorous standards and fine tolerances required for military applications. The Pentagon argued that with Bryant machines the Soviet Union would be able to produce smaller, more reliable gyroscopes and other fine-tune components for their missile guidance systems.

According to their own newspaper reports at the time, Soviet factories in key locations like Vitebsk, Saratov, and Voronezh were unable to match the Bryant machines, and the Soviet State Committee on Automation and Mechanization had reported very adversely on Russia's capability only the previous year. U.S. experts thought it would take the USSR at least several years to produce their own equivalents to the Centalign-B.[9]

Competitor companies in Sweden, West Germany, Switzerland, and Italy were all evaluated by Pentagon-appointed experts and found to be inferior. The Commerce Department's "foreign availability" waiver did not stand up. A Senate subcommittee looked into the whole issue in February 1961 and recommended against the Bryant contract. One consulting engineer testified, in terms that would echo in the technology-transfer debate (and would also be uncannily applicable to the silicon chip in due course):

It is necessary to distinguish between giving away secrets, know-how, and capability. Our manufacture of these small devices is no secret — even the manner is not difficult to determine — but the capability to do it well and economically has taken years to develop and should not be sold to a potential adversary. . . . The situation is not one of selling our adversary a better "club" — but machines which help to produce better "clubs," faster and cheaper.[10]

Pointing to the Soviet lead in rocket engine power and the way in which the United States had compensated by pulling far ahead in miniaturization and high-precision instruments, the report of the Senate subcommittee concluded: "Whether it would take five years or two years, or one year, our national security obviously demands that we stop helping Soviet industry, especially the Soviet defense industry, to overcome its weaknesses. It demands, on the contrary, that we inflict delays on them whenever this is in our power, that we make things more difficult for them rather than easier." The Kennedy administration agreed, and the contract was cancelled. But the topic and the deal refused to lie down and die. Indeed, a shipment of grinding machines from another U.S. company, Jones & Lawson, was licensed by the Department of Commerce and delivered to the Soviet Union in April and May of 1961 without objection. One witness to the Senate subcommittee, Joseph A. Gwyer, a senior research specialist at the Library of Congress, made an interesting observation during his testimony: "The problem of restrictions on strategic materials going to the Soviet Union appears to fluctuate with international tensions. Since the tensions in Berlin are so great it appears that the various agencies here in Washington, D.C., concerned with export control are trying to tighten up the restrictions on the shipment of strategic items to the Soviet Union."[11]

The Soviets did not give up their long-term interest in Bryant's machine tools. When Nixon and Brezhnev signed the trade agreement of May 1972 in a spirit of reduced tension and increased potential for trade between the superpowers, one of the first items on the Soviets' shopping list was, yet again, Bryant grinders. This time they wanted no fewer than 172. After initial hesitation, the Department of Commerce once more approved the necessary export licenses. This followed lobbying from the Bryant Company itself, which insisted that foreign equivalents to the Centalign-B were now on the market in Switzerland, West Germany, and Japan. A Commerce Department expert, William Clark, was sent to the Swiss company Voumard to compare notes. Clark reported that Bryant machines no longer had the edge over their competitors. According to Morris Mountain, director of Strategic Technology and Munitions Control at the Pentagon, testifying in May 1979 to Senator Richard Ichord's Armed Services Subcommittee, pressure was put on COCOM partners in 1972 to embargo their equivalents to the Bryant machines. The COCOM partners politely declined to cooperate.

Secretary of State Henry Kissinger is reported to have interceded to override objections to the deal. To judge from his statement at the time, the Soviet Deputy Minister of Foreign Trade was overjoyed when the deal went through. But controversy continued over the Bryant deal. In 1973 it was alleged that the CIA had been misinforming the administration about the accuracy of Soviet missiles and that improved ball races were heightening the USSR's MIRV capability, as well as helping it to turn out advanced high-temperature jet engines, high-speed planes, and complex steerable space antennas. In 1976 Defense Intelligence Agency officials reported to Congress that parts made by Bryant grinders "may now be used in the guidance equipment of Soviet missiles."

The Bryant case came up yet again during renewed debates about technology transfer in 1983. In testimony given on March 8 to Representative Don Bonker's House subcommittee, investigating the extension of the Export Administration Act, James A. Gray, president of the National Machine Tool Builders Association of America, argued that between 1961 and 1971, about a thousand machines comparable to the Bryant Centalign-B were delivered to the Soviet Union from such companies as Minganti (Italy), Lumart (Switzerland), Overbeck (West Germany), and Sako Seiki (Japan). In his view, the Bryant machines, which were eventually delivered in late 1973 and early 1974, did not begin ball race production in the Soviet Union until after the initial flight tests of the new generation of Soviet SS-17, SS-18, SS-19, and SS-20 missiles.

The Soviet Union, of course, has always had its corps of COCOM-watchers, and particular attention is paid to the United States and its Export Administration Act and amendments. One of the leading experts is Dr. V. L. Malkevich, a staff member of the Ministry of Foreign Trade. His 1981 monograph, "East-West Economic Cooperation and Technological Exchange," summarizes very well the official Soviet views.

There are two major — though somewhat contradictory — points in his argument. First, the American trade controls are a form of economic and political blackmail against the "Socialist nations" and against the developing countries of the third world, as well. Second, there is no technology gap, and the notion that the East is technologically dependent on the West is a myth.

The latter point is one that the Soviets like to stress in public statements, and it was repeated for world consumption by Dzerman Gvishiani, deputy director of the State Committee on Science and Technology, in an interview with a BBC television reporter. He said,

"I'm absolutely convinced that there is no technical or scientific problem that the Soviet Union cannot solve by itself. There is potential for it, there is talent for it, and so this assumption that there is such [technological] dependence ... is ridiculous."[12]

COCOM is, of course, dismissed as no more than a front organization for American interests: "On examining COCOM activity, the view that the committee is in fact an appendage of the U.S. export control system and used by the United States as a tool of its export policy is fully justified."[13]

In actual fact, there is evidence that Soviet Intelligence pays close attention to the secret COCOM proceedings in Paris and tries to manipulate certain trade matters accordingly.

Eugene Michiels, a sixty-year-old Belgian national, was arrested in August 1983 on charges of selling information to Eastern bloc countries, and he currently awaits trial in Brussels. Michiels had been head of the European Coordinating Service of the Belgian Foreign Ministry since 1971 and was responsible for EEC–COMECON relations. According to a senior Pentagon official, "He had all the COCOM stuff and it was flowing through him to the Russians. That was the way they maneuvered and worked it: when a product comes up [in COCOM] for discussion, [the Russians] like to claim they make it themselves, anyway. So why embargo it? 'We make this; it is in our catalogue [for such and such an upcoming trade show], so why aren't you selling it [to us]?' "[14]

What has happened, of course, is that each COCOM embargo discussion has centered on a certain product. The Russians — through spies — learn of that and hastily print a catalogue showing an ostensibly Russian-made version of the product.

Carlos Romulo once said, "History makes hypocrites of all nations." In the 1980s, we tend to identify the avid technological acquisitors as the Warsaw Pact nations and their prey as Japan and the NATO countries. But the nations have not always played the same roles. Just before and after the Revolutionary War, America felt compelled to use a number of measures, both legal and illegal, to close the technology gap of that era. That is represented very simply in a 1780 statement to the American Philosophical Society: "British Tyranny restrained us from making steel, to enrich her Merchants and

Manufacturers, but now we can make it ourselves as good as theirs."[15]

Despite those bold words, the technology gap across the Atlantic widened in the next forty years. Europe took eagerly to James Watt's steam engine, yet in 1820, when Daniel Treadwell wanted to run his prototype of a new printing press with power, he couldn't find a single steam engine in the city of Boston.[16]

There is an interesting parallel between the Soviet Union and the new United States. In the 1950s, the Soviets failed to make a commitment to microelectronics because their rockets were powerful enough without miniaturization. At the close of the 1700s, the United States made no great attempt to adopt the new European machinery of agriculture and manufacture, simply because there was a prodigal supply of land and natural resources available. There was no urgent need for a better technology. It was when the country had to have a large and efficient production of arms, machines, and consumer products that the catching-up process began.

Punch, at the turn of the century, found the American backwardness amusing:

> By Yankee Doodle too, you're beat
> Downright in Agriculture,
> With this machine for reaping wheat,
> Chaw'd up as by a vulture!

Things changed dramatically by the 1850s. In those "grand expositions" — the Victorian equivalent of trade shows — the Americans were beginning to display their new printing presses, mass-produced locks and clocks, machine tools, photographic equipment, the Morse telegraph, surgical instruments, glassware, and chemicals. At the New York Exposition in 1853, a single American Corliss and Nightingale steam engine provided power to all the machines in the show. At the Paris Exhibition of 1855, American agricultural machines took the main prizes. (It was also at this show that Charles Goodyear, awarded the French Legion of Honor for his vulcanized rubber products, ended up in a Parisian jail for failure to pay his debts.)

The Yankee love affair with the machine had begun in earnest. And the buyers of the world began to take notice. Displayed at the

Paris show of 1867 were the Hughes printing telegraph (a forerunner of the Teletype) and such weapons as the Winchester repeating rifle. By the 1870s, American lathes, planers, gear and screw cutters, and milling machines were at least as good as British manufactures. And so the trend began. The Bell company and the Thomas Edison company competed to install the first telephones in London in the 1870s. Edison Electric Light started operations there in 1882, the same year that Western Electric established itself in Antwerp. These and other companies were soon applying their new American technology worldwide — and a century of American high-tech leadership had begun.

In the 1980s, we often hear politicians and officials of the Reagan administration describe any form of commercial transaction with the Soviet Union as "trading with the enemy," yet during World War II, a number of supposedly respectable American citizens and corporations did quite the same thing without arousing governmental wrath or retribution. Charles Higham has recently detailed many of these transactions in a book titled *Trading with the Enemy.*[17] Government records declassified under the Freedom of Information Act involve such corporations as Standard Oil of New Jersey (now Exxon in North America and Esso in Europe), the Chase Bank (now Chase Manhattan), Ford, General Motors, International Telegraph and Telephone (ITT), and others in the traffic.

For example, Standard Oil — through its chairman, Walter C. Teagle of Cleveland — concluded deals that enabled the Luftwaffe to bomb Britain and the German U-boats to ravage supply lines across the Atlantic. It came about because of Standard's close prewar affiliations with I. G. Farben. Even after the Securities and Exchange Commission forced Teagle to resign from the board of I. G. Farben (which was Nazi-dominated by the 1930s), Teagle was able to obtain five hundred tons of tetraethyl lead for I. G. Farben in 1938. Farben got another $15 million worth from London in 1939. Without this aviation-fuel additive, Hermann Goering's Luftwaffe could not have flown.

Teagle's Standard tankers also did a brisk business carrying oil to Teneriffe in the Canary Islands, to supply both Germany and German U-boats in the Atlantic — and this even after the United States was fighting an undeclared war in the Atlantic. (Ironically, one of the freighters sunk by a submarine was the S.S. *Walter Teagle*.) It was much later, in September 1947, that Judge Charles Clark ruled that "Standard Oil can be considered an enemy national in view of its relationships with I. G. Farben after the United States and Germany had become active enemies."

In March 1942, a meeting took place in the Ritz Hotel in Madrid between Sosthenes Behn, the head of ITT worldwide, and Gerhard Westrick, the chief of its German operations. They discussed "how best they could improve ITT's links with the Gestapo, and its improvement of the whole Nazi system of telephones, teleprinters, aircraft intercoms, submarine and ship phones, electric buoys, alarm systems, radio and radar parts, and fuses for artillery shells, as well as the Focke-Wulf bombers that were taking thousands of American lives."[18] During the war, the Behn-owned ITT factories in Europe industriously supplied the Nazis with technical goods and equipment — including even parts that went into the V-2 rocket bombs. When ITT couldn't get U.S. government licenses to ship a product, the company shipped it anyway.[19]

In the end, though, it is power and powerful connections that count, and all was forgiven ITT. On February 16, 1946, at the company's New York headquarters, 67 Broad Street, Sosthenes Behn received America's highest civilian honor, the Medal of Merit. In due course, ITT also got compensation for damage done to its German factories by Allied bombing.[20]

There are equally shameful histories for the Ford Motor Company (Edsel Ford used to send Hitler a present of fifty thousand Reichsmarks every year on his birthday) and for General Motors. In 1940, Ford decided not to build desperately needed aircraft engines for the British but to build the five-ton trucks that the Wehrmacht used so successfully in its blitzkrieg. GM's German subsidiary, Adam-Opel, made half of all the propulsion systems for the Junkers JU-88, "the deadliest bomber of the German air force."[21] The financial records of Opel Ruesselsheim revealed that between 1942 and 1945, production and sales strategy were planned in close coordination with General Motors factories throughout the world. The German GM group even helped to develop the first Nazi jet fighter plane. But after the war, GM was rewarded by the United States with a $33 million tax exemption for war damage to its German and Austrian factories.

Indeed, the strong American feeling against selling an enemy the weapons he can turn against the United States and its allies probably has its roots in these dismal events of World War II. The 1949 Export Control Act came only four years after the end of the war, and it seems unlikely that any large American multinational would ever again supply an enemy with military hardware on such a large scale. The problem for the American control system has changed in character. Like the miniaturization inherent in transistor and microchip technology, the trade with the enemy is much more sophisticated and harder to see with the naked eye.

15

THE ISSUES

ONE PART OF MANKIND, therefore, is striving to prevent another part of mankind from sharing in the marvels of invention we have brought about in the late years of our century. The objectives are clear, but the motives are mixed, perhaps, and more obscure. The West submits: the Communist East has been controlled by an aggressive tyranny for sixty years or so; to sell it the technology we have developed is to arm it even more dangerously against us. It is like the wagon train selling repeating rifles to the Sioux.

The more obscure motive is a product of pride, a pride that says, Europe, Japan, and the United States have again proved the superiority of their intelligence. Why should we disperse our technological riches among nations that have not earned them and will not share them with their peoples?

The counterarguments come best in the form of questions: In a free society with an open market, how can ideas or the products of ideas be denied to another part of the world? Shouldn't technological leadership rest on a constant striving for invention and discovery rather than on hoarding what is produced?

Probably the largest question is this: Can an open society put limits on the free exchange of knowledge and still remain an open society?

All of these abstract propositions come down to concrete cases in the debates over technology transfer. For example, one leading academic critic saw, in 1983, a definite issue between the U.S. Government and the scientific community.[1] The government, he argued, has used the Export Administration Act to control university research programs, science symposiums, and even the presentation of scientific papers. Scientists perceive a serious threat to academic freedom. They contend that America's lead in electronics and computers has largely resulted from a free circulation of scientific and technological information. *That* is the operative reason for America's technological surge and, in contrast, for the Soviet lag.

When the Departments of Defense and Commerce and the Intelligence community formulated proposals for firmer controls over the publication of unclassified information, the result was a storm of protest in the world of science. The government rebuttal was put by Dr. Jack Vorona, director of Scientific and Technical Information in the Defense Intelligence Agency. In testimony before a congressional committee in May 1982, he said he knew that the Soviets have received every one of the eighty thousand government reports lodged with the National Technical Information Service of the Commerce Department — and 75 percent of those papers were from the Pentagon, the Department of Energy, and NASA.[2]

Arthur Van Cook, director of Information Security at the Defense Department, was even more dramatic in his testimony. He spoke of "this hemorrhage of information to hostile nations," and gave an FBI estimate that as much as 90 percent of Soviet collection requirements could be satisfied through open sources — and by the efforts of the several thousand Soviet technology collection officers now at work.[3]

Meetings and conventions of specialists offer one of those open sources. In the winter of 1980, the Department of Energy issued an order to its contractors: any communication between them and Soviet scientists had to have official clearance. That same year, the Commerce Department forced the American Vacuum Society to withdraw an invitation to Soviet scientists who were to attend a conference on lasers and electro-optical systems.[4]

In August 1982, the Pentagon intervened in the program of a meeting of the Society of Photo-Optical Instrumentation Engineers in San Diego. More than a hundred technical papers had to be withdrawn — a record of its kind — because they did not meet regulations concerning the international traffic in arms. The papers dealt with advances in optical technology (including the use of small mirrors in laser communications between satellites and submarines), infrared optics, airborne sensors, and other microelectronic research. The Pentagon, having noted several foreigners from Communist countries among the listed participants, sent a team of intelligence officers to San Diego to convince the authors of the papers.[5]

Exchange students in the sciences were quite as great a cause for anxiety. Senator William S. Cohen of Maine told the Committee on Government Affairs that it was nonsense to draw up a list of COCOM items "and then allow students to come in and have access to that very technology we seek to deny them." He gave an example of a Hungarian who headed his country's magnetic bubble research program. This man had come periodically to the United States to do research at leading universities, observe the findings of others, and attend conferences. The Pentagon has no way of screening the State Department student selections, he said, and added, "Surely to the extent we are training and helping through exchange programs with our allies, inevitably that information will become available to our adversaries as well."

Who are these Eastern bloc students? In 1982, an émigré Soviet engineer who used the assumed name of Joseph Arkov told a congressional committee they are carefully selected older people, usually well established in their technical or scientific fields. "Soviet students do not go to the United States to study Faulkner," he said. "Conversely, American exchange students ... might come to the Soviet Union to study Dostoyevsky."[6]

Senator Cohen later pursued this point in a hearing before another Senate committee. He submitted a list of student exchanges and the subjects studied and pointed out some contrasts. American students at Moscow State University were studying genres in Russian music, Pushkin's tetrameters, and the debates on the democratization of the Russian military. Soviet students in the United States were concentrating on technology. Senator Cohen found this an unwarranted gift to the Soviet military machine.

How did academia respond to this? In 1982, the National Academy of Sciences tried to find a balance between the administration's alarming "hemorrhage" talk and the scientific community's fears about censorship. The academy report made university research an open field, but it did find a gray area where government review and advice should be heeded. The academy panel set up just four criteria for what should be restricted: the technology in question should be something that was developed rapidly; it should have direct military application; it should provide significant military advantage; and information about it must be available from just a single source. "In comparison with other channels of technology transfer," the academy report concluded, "open scientific communication . . . does not present a material danger for near-term military implications."[7] A report from the Office of Technology Assessment in 1983 held that education was a kind of "passive mechanism" of technology transfer much less likely to help the Soviets increase technological capability than would the transfer of technological hardware.

If the university scientists felt threatened, the businessmen felt actually penalized. America had had a good run of some twenty years as the high-tech supplier to the world. But in the 1980s the Japanese, particularly, were becoming very aggressive competitors. The tougher new export controls began to pinch American exporters, and they complained. The paradox in this, of course, was that a lot of the control enforcement rests on the cooperation and good will of industry.

Predictably, the great issue was the definition of "dual use." Many things, from the simplest to the most complex, can have both a peaceful use and a war use. The grain that the United States sells to the Russians can feed factory workers in Tula, but it can also be rations for troops in Kabul. Multispectral scanners and image-enhancing systems can be used to locate American missile silos, but they are equally useful for mineral exploration or weather forecasting. The same double test applies to most computers.

There is a true story of a wonderful example of this particular enigma. In April 1982, Customs agents at JFK International Airport seized a Bell Laboratories crate destined for Moscow. The Commerce Department ruled that the cargo was "militarily significant" and could not go out.

The very disgruntled Bell Labs scientist who was accompanying the shipment protested, "That thing plays chess. That's all." Inside the crate was a machine called Belle, a master class chess-playing whiz. Kenneth Thompson was taking it to Moscow for a chess tournament.

The only way the computer could have a military application, Thompson remarked, was to be dropped out of an airplane. "You might kill somebody that way," he said.

The second key phrase in the exporters' resentment list is "foreign availability." That means, simply, that the controls often seem to keep American companies from selling products that their foreign competitors — in, say, Japan or Germany — are ready, willing, and able to supply. When the Commerce Department, in June 1983, announced that spectrum analyzers were to become subject to "special licensing procedures," the department asked for comment. One of the most stinging comments came from the Santa Clara company Genrad.

Genrad manufactures instruments that have significant applications to antisubmarine warfare, and the company wrote Commerce to say "The rule penalizes U.S. manufacturers without substantial effect on the transfer of military technology." The same kind of equipment — with equal or better performance — was on sale by European and Japanese manufacturers. Genrad even had reason to believe that similar products were already being manufactured in Eastern Europe. "If the rule is approved," Genrad noted, "U.S. manufacturers will be at a substantial disadvantage in selling to Western nations because Europe and Japanese manufacturers can quote faster deliveries . . . due to the time required to process individual validated license applications." In short, in the years of the famous Reagan deregulation drive, things were actually getting worse for some businesses, not better.

Genrad continued, arguing that there was a vast difference between strict criteria and strict controls on the U.S. side and much looser practice on COCOM's. And the conclusion was that COCOM should be forced to apply American Government standards.[8]

The complaints about "foreign availability" and the permissiveness of COCOM have been echoed many times. Because of that availability, "prohibiting U.S. exports neither meets the objective [depriving the USSR of strategic technology] nor keeps the export revenues," the Computer and Business Equipment Manufacturers Association told Congress in March 1983.[9] As for COCOM's laxity,

James A. Gray, of the National Machine Tool Builders Association, said in a hearing: "My presumption is that [the Japanese] think we're a bunch of chumps. They go to COCOM meetings and they agree not to sell things. The difference is that we're sending men like Richard Perle and Larry Brady; the other countries are sending businessmen to represent them."[10]

Finally, as a kind of bottom-line support to the exporters' contentions, the Government Accounting Office assessed the matter of waste in a 1982 report. The GAO said that Commerce reviewed 60,783 export license applications in 1981 — and about half of those had no need to be licensed at all. The products involved simply had no military significance. This whole charade cost business $6.1 million extra for applications, and the government wasted $1 million in unnecessary administrative costs.[11]

Connoisseurs of these matters, however, consider the Joyce Loebl case the classic comedy of errors in control history. It is an excellent example of the "American component" controversy. Joyce Loebl is not a lady but a subsidiary of the major British military contractor, Vickers. In August 1982, U.S. network news reported that Joyce Loebl had mysteriously shipped an American-made military computer to the Soviets, who were using it to spy on the United States. When the Soviets decided to upgrade the system, the report continued, they shipped it back to its manufacturer in Pasadena for modification. The Russians seemed to expect it back again after that — which was, according to Commerce officials, "either unbelievably dumb or incredibly brazen." The British were simply accused of bad faith and double-dealing.

That set off an angry debate: the Americans included a slide of the equipment in the CIA traveling dog and pony show, and the British accused their ally of "imperialism." The story had begun with the Joyce Loebl purchase of a Vision 8000 R at a cost of $70,000. The manufacturer was Comtal, a subsidiary of the giant 3M Corporation and a leading maker of state-of-the-art graphics systems very useful in a range of image-enhancement applications. Comtal described its technology in an ad in *Computer Graphics World* in November 1983:

Whether you're exploring the outer regions of space or exploring for oil in some remote area of the world, Comtal's new Vision Ten/24 is the only digital processing system that processes and displays ...

high-resolution images with a clarity never experienced before.... It's
a powerful tool for interpreting and analyzing images for such diverse
applications as LANDSAT, meteorology, seismology, graphic arts,
earth resource management, medical imagery ...

A California middleman had obtained a Commerce Department
license to ship the Vision 8000 R to Joyce Loebl in 1979. The
Vickers subsidiary had then incorporated the Comtal equipment
into a larger system. Before the whole system was shipped on to the
Institute of Geology in the USSR, Joyce Loebl alleges, COCOM
granted it a "national exception" and the U.K. licensed the sale.

In any case, either the "dumb" Soviets or the "brazen" Soviets (or
perhaps even the guileless Soviets) shipped the Vision 8000 R back
to Comtal for upgrading in 1981. A British engineer and a Russian
engineer accompanied the shipment. The Russian asked for a three-
week course in how to maintain the equipment, and Comtal refused
him entry to its building. The British engineer explained that the
equipment had already been used in Russia. "At that point, we just
about dropped our pants," later reported Roy Brugman, international sales manager for Comtal.[12]

Joyce Loebl, on being informed of the situation, at once applied
for a license to get the equipment back. The Commerce Department
refused. On August 24, 1982, after nine months of deadlock, Commerce officials went to Pasadena and seized the goods.

The British, who had been hoping to keep the affair secret, were
astonished at the sudden glare of U.S. publicity. A Commerce Department official went on television to inform viewers that the Vision 8000 R "would enable [the Russians] to build up their war
effort, munitions, and military capability." Ted Wu, head of the Office of Export Enforcement, wrote a congratulatory letter to Comtal.
And Ron Hendron of Comtal explained that the original export license was good for British purchase only — certainly not for Russian.
Over two hundred of the machines had been sold to France, Israel,
and Britain, but not for use in nuclear facilities, and never to the
Russians.

But then Hendron added some rather curious remarks. He said
about the 8000 R, "This was not our top-of-the-line model. We
don't sell it anymore in [that] form." He went on, "In terms of what

the Russians got, it was useless without a mainframe to attach it to. It's expensive to maintain and the boards inside are unique. The 8000 series just displays the work of the host computer."[13]

Even more curious was an internal Comtal memo written just a week after the seizure. The equipment bought by the Russians was described as "obsolete." The memo related that Comtal's German distributor had very recently tried to ship a far more sophisticated Vision One/20 to Czechoslovakia, had obtained COCOM approval, and had been turned down by the Commerce Department. The author of the memo commented, "I believe that this latest denial . . . is political, following as it does so rapidly on the heels of the seizure."[14] And to cap all this collection of doubts, one of the U.S. negotiators on the case said that the Joyce Loebl purchase had been so "low level" that the export license had not even specified postshipment-use verification — something Commerce usually demands in the case of sophisticated technologies.[15]

The Comtal case illustrated another sharp issue between the controllers and the businessmen. The American claim that any foreign-built equipment with one American component was subject to licensing resulted in the brouhaha over the Siberian pipeline. And, again, the British were horrified to think that one American microchip in a British computer would make the whole machine subject to American export controls; that seemed to threaten the survival of the British "sunrise industry" itself.

In the meantime, it seemed likely that the free and easy life style and the porous security of Silicon Valley might be far more dangerous than the shipment of a few pieces of ancillary equipment. There were, for one thing, a good many visitors with heavy accents. In his testimony, Dr. Vorona had noted that in 1979 there were over a thousand Soviet business visitors to the United States. They were obliged to make a statement about their contacts and itineraries. But the eight thousand East European businessmen, scientists, and trade officials each year go "unprocessed by the Intelligence community." He said that it would be a hopeless task for the FBI to try to keep an eye on this host of people, most of whom, he was convinced, work for the KGB or the GRU. He added, "I am just as confident as I can be that a . . . number of them are . . . scarfing up bits and pieces of advanced technologies."

There is a Washington story that illustrates Vorona's point. In the summer of 1983, FBI agents were following some Polish diplomats who had just left their embassy on 16th Street. The Poles walked *en bloc* to the Radio Shack store on 15th Street and stayed awhile. After they left, an FBI agent learned from the store clerk that they had bought a number of Tandy Color Computers — and had used their diplomatic passports to get the sales tax waived.

The Valley, though, is a far bigger target than Radio Shack. The Minuteman case — two people simply walking out of a Defense contractor's office with pounds of documents — may have alarmed congressmen, but it came as no surprise to people who know the Valley well. Competition is strong, and companies spy on each other as a matter of course. To a casual visitor driving down Santa Clara County roads, security at the electronics companies will seem tight enough. There are high chain-link fences, gates operated by remote control, closed-circuit television cameras, and security guards in evidence. In addition, the employees going into those plants have been checked and given a clearance by the Pentagon's Defense Intelligence Agency — if they are engaged in work on government contracts.

Security experts, on the contrary, feel that there is a dangerous looseness about the whole place. The companies were founded by creative, often eccentric, people — and many of the employees are of the same kind. One security company head explained, "It's a different attitude toward work, where there can be fantastic engineers who may get an idea at two A.M. and go into a plant and work for the next forty-eight hours. These people are going to want to get into restricted areas and when they forget their pass cards, they're still going to want to get in."[16]

Security people in a position to know have estimated that there may have been as many as thirty espionage cases in Silicon Valley. "And there are at least a hundred and fifty cases where there are problems," says John Shea, a consultant with Sierra Technology Group, Inc., of Tahoe City, an organization that keeps track of advanced technology trends for the Intelligence community. On the other hand, there could be even more than that. Some companies are very reluctant to admit when their security has been breached, because that might mean the loss of valuable government contracts, adds Harry V. Martin, publisher of the *Defense System Review,* a Valley trade magazine.[17] Shea further remarks that except for the major Defense contractors, the carelessness about security is deplorable.[18]

As to the general level of ethics in the neighborhood, a columnist on the *San Jose Mercury News* wrote, "In the rank jungles of Silicon Valley, swarming with venality of every shade and stripe, the spy who's driven by a simple craving for bucks has a perfect camouflage." In other words, with people selling out to the devil left and right, who's to know which one is selling out to the specifically Soviet devil?

The fact that causes perhaps the greatest anguish to honest men in government and business is that techno-bandits rarely suffer more than some inconvenience after they've been exposed. Bruchhausen, Müller, and McVey all appear to be beyond the reach of American justice — on a list that gets longer with almost every new transfer scandal. All are rich men living in luxury with only one annoyance: they cannot enter the United States. There is a well-recognized principle of international law which provides that a state refusing to extradite a certain criminal should proceed to punish him according to the equivalent local laws. Many international conventions contain such clauses. But these conventions deal with universally recognized crimes, and they do not apply to United States export control legislation. In any case, there are no more than civil penalties for breaking economic laws.[19]

Senator Sam Nunn was especially incensed about the case of Richard Müller. The senator said, "We are engaged in a military alliance with West Germany.... We are spending billions and billions of dollars.... We charge people with the [technology-transfer] crime and they flee to one of our prime allies, one we are helping to defend against the Soviets, and we can't get them back."[20] In 1983, Nunn both introduced legislation on the issue and urged the President to start negotiation with the allies. He wanted techno-bandits who had been indicted in the U.S. either to be extradited or prosecuted where they are at present. Nunn had a few tough clauses in his bill. He wanted Customs to be able to seize and search outbound passengers and cargo without a search warrant. Customs would have the right to tap telephones of suspected export controls violators. Stealing or buying technology with the intent to export illegally would be recognized as a new criminal offense. The same applied to commercial bribery for the same purpose. Penalties would be five years in prison or a $50,000 fine — either of which could be doubled in the case of export to a Communist country.

Now, there is good reason to believe that Senator Nunn's initiative is a shrewder way of going at the problem than was the behavior of Commerce in the case of Belle, the chess master, or in the case of the Comtal Vision 8000 R. Nunn was arguing for a better-defined target and a straighter shot. Coinciding with this view was the evidence of the Bucy Report in February 1976. The report — named after the task force chairman, J. Fred Bucy of Texas Instruments — was funded by the director of Defense Research and Engineering, and it concentrated on four main export areas: airframes, aircraft engines, instrumentation, and semiconductor devices.[21] Of the fifteen task force members, twelve were from the Department of Defense or from major Defense contractors.

The conclusions were clear and decisive: the Commerce Department's commodity control lists should be much shorter. The Defense Department's military critical technologies list (MCTL) should be sharply cut. Speaking of the MCTL, Chairman Bucy said, "It is the size of a phone book, but it should be on five sheets of paper." Furthermore, there was no reason to deny the sale of many high-tech products to the Eastern bloc, but the know-how or the means of manufacturing those products should not be sold, the task force declared.

Apparently, no one in power was much convinced. Commerce's control list remains an eight-hundred-page book with more than 200,000 items listed. The DOD's MCT list is reputed to be even larger.

There is some relaxation, nevertheless — and it comes in a rather odd quarter, in view of the United States' COCOM quarrels with the British back in the 1950s. Washington is being very kind to Beijing. On July 8, 1981, the Department of Commerce issued a press release announcing a liberalization of its trade policy with the People's Republic of China, specifically in regard to dual-use high technology.

Bo Denysyk, Deputy Assistant Secretary for Export Administration, explained this new benevolence in a speech to the National Council for United States–China Trade, saying "[The] new policy will reduce administrative restrictions on export to the PRC and also treat it more favorably than any other Communist nation." Approval would be automatic "for products with technical levels twice those previously approved," and anything "more advanced" would be considered on a case-by-case basis. And, Denysyk continued, to make U.S. industry competitive and to lend "certainty and predictability" to trade with China, the Commerce Department alone would process all licenses that did not require COCOM clearance.[22]

Through the murk of this bureauspeak, we can discern the outlines of a quite new policy. The fact that Commerce alone would decide on licenses — rather than Commerce together with an interagency review — meant that the waiting time could be sharply reduced.

Caspar Weinberger pursued this initiative on his trip to China in 1983 by inviting the Chinese to submit a shopping list of U.S. technology and products. Although it was not quite yet the year of the rat, the Chinese smelled one. It seemed obvious that there was much they would like to acquire, but any list they furnished would instantly show up their main areas of weakness. Instead of handing over a list, they asked the Americans to supply a list of the things they were prepared to license. In the spring of 1984, President Reagan finally signed a trade deal with the Chinese, covering many categories of previously embargoed high technology.

The whole subject of controls is, therefore, both a philosophical and procedural confusion because of its many paradoxes. There is the paradox of COCOM leniency, the paradox inherent in the dual-use decisions, the paradox of foreign availability, the paradox of the American component, and, finally, the paradox of limiting the dissemination of ideas from an open society.

More narrowly — in the control mechanism the United States has set up—there are the nagging paradoxes of the internecine strife between Commerce and Customs, the paradox of inequity as to the products embargoed, and the paradox of crime without punishment.

Some of these are inevitable; others are the result of bad thinking and bad management. But most likely much of the trouble comes from the fact that the government of the United States has never formed a clear, conscious, and consistent policy decision overall.

There are two primary viewpoints. The first, as noted before, is that we in the wagon train must do everything to prevent people from selling those Winchesters, and everything remotely connected with a Winchester, to the Indians. That is the defensive and conservative attitude.

The other view is that the technological advances we are now concerned with are *not* just hardware; they are not the secrets of making a bigger bomb. In contrast, they are informational technology that will, in the long run, pervade and shape every postindustrial society. First the East European satellites and then the Soviet monolith itself will feel the shudder. There will be an end to monotonous arrivals at "the proper Socialist solution." The political system will be forced to accommodate itself to the information age. That is the hopeful and idealistic attitude.

These are questions on which the United States and its Western allies should have a strategic and tactical agreement. What short-range controls do we really need? What relaxation is likely to contribute to a beneficial social transformation of the Communist bloc in the long run? Perhaps once the large, directive ideas can be articulated and agreed on, the specific actions and methods can be made more rational.

A clear vision of all this just might make a great difference in the course of our *fin de siècle* history.

NOTES
INDEX

NOTES

Chapter 1

1. Interview with former CIA official, Washington, D.C., November 17, 1983.
2. David M. Alpern, et al., "America's Secret Warriors," *Newsweek,* October 10, 1983, pp. 30–36.
3. Testimony of Lawrence J. Brady, Assistant Secretary of Commerce for Trade Administration, Department of Commerce, to Senate Committee on Governmental Affairs, Permanent Subcommittee on Investigations. *Transfer of United States Technology to the Soviet Union and Soviet Bloc Nations,* 97th Cong., 2nd Sess., Hearings, May 1982, pp. 262–277.
4. Interview with senior Pentagon official, Washington, D.C., November 17, 1983.
5. Interview with British diplomat, Washington, D.C., November 30, 1983.
6. *Soviet Acquisition of Western Technology,* an unclassified report, published by the Central Intelligence Agency, Washington, D.C., April 1982.
7. Ibid., p. 3.
8. Ibid.
9. Ibid., p. 1.

Chapter 2

1. Kildall's remark was reported by Professor Martin Healey, University College, Cardiff, South Wales, in an interview on January 24, 1984.

Chapter 3

1. There is no comprehensive account of the events of October 22, 1946, though many authors refer to them. Vol. 2 of Anthony C. Sutton's three-volume study, *Western Technology and Soviet Economic Development: 1917–1930, 1930–1945, 1945–1960* (Stanford: Hoover Institute Publications, 1968), contains a definitive account with supporting facts. There is much supporting additional material in histories of Soviet rocket technology. See note 6, below.
2. Michael Tatu, *Power in the Kremlin from Khrushchev's Decline to Collective Leadership* (London: Collins, 1967); Robert Conquest, *The Nation Killers* (London: Macmillan, 1970).
3. N. Voznesensky, *Voennaya Ekonomika SSSR* (Moscow, 1948), p. 42.
4. Carl Gershman, "Selling Them the Rope — Business and the Soviets," *Commentary,* March 1979.
5. For details on nerve-gas plants, see R. Harris and J. Paxman. *A Higher Form of Killing* (London: Chatto & Windus, 1982).
6. For background on Russian rocket technology and the story of Korolyov, sources include:
    A. Lee, *The Soviet Air and Rocket Forces* (London: Weidenfeld & Nicolson, 1959).
    A. Parry, *Russia's Rockets and Missiles* (London: Macmillan, 1960).
    A. J. Zaehringer, *Soviet Space Technology* (New York: Harper & Row, 1961).
    M. Stoiko, *Soviet Rocketry, The First Decade of Achievement* (London: David & Charles, 1970).
    G. Vladimirov, *The Russian Space-Bluff* (New York: Dial Press, 1973).
    D. Baker, *The Rocket: Development and History* (London: New Cavendish, 1973).
    J. Oberg, *Red Star in Orbit* (New York: Random House, 1981).
7. Four B-29s were impounded after making forced landings on Soviet territory during World War II sorties against Japan. They were never returned to the United States.
8. *Khrushchev Remembers, The Last Testament* (Boston: Little, Brown, 1974).
9. There are several general sources for this material. The most definitive is: Isaac Deutscher, *Stalin, a Political Biography* (Oxford: Oxford University Press, 1982, first edition, 1949). See also John Erickson's two-volume study *Stalin's War with Germany* (London: Weidenfeld & Nicolson, 1982).
10. For details on the development of Soviet weaponry, see C. Campbell, *War Facts Now* (London: Fontana, 1982); D. Hamlyn, "The Russian War Machine: 1917–1945," in *Encyclopedia of Russian Military Equipment* (published jointly, in U.K. by Arms & Armour Press and in U.S. by Bison Books, 1977).
11. See compilation of two Russian articles, "The Cradle of the First Computer," and "Mikhail Alekseyevich Lavrentyev Is Seventy Years Old," *Soviet Cybernetics Review,* July 1971, pp. 71–73.
12. Information on Zelenograd was obtained from interviews with Mark Kuchment and with Eric Firdman, Boston, February 11, 1984. Firdman, a Soviet computer scientist now resident in the United States, was part of the Zelenograd design team and visited the Center for Microelectronics regularly between 1963 and 1972.

13. Mark Kuchment, "Soviet Science and Technology: Eyewitness Accounts," Harvard University Russian Research Center, 1983, Paper 12, and interviews with Kuchment, November 10 and December 2, 1983, and January 10, 1984.
14. Based on interviews conducted by Mark Kuchment with émigré Soviet scientists.
15. A. P. Ershov, "A History of Computing in the USSR," *Datamation,* September 1975, pp. 80-88.
16. This section draws heavily on the work of Dr. Norman C. Davis, formerly with the Office of Scientific Intelligence, Central Intelligence Agency, and Seymour E. Goodman, now at the University of Arizona. Their main research appeared in a paper, "The Soviet Bloc's Unified System of Computers," published by the Association for Computing Machinery and reprinted in *Computing Surveys,* June 1978, pp. 93–122. These two authors were once the chief CIA advisers on Soviet developments in the field, but all ACM papers are reviewed by independent experts.
17. The Russian word *ryad* means "series," so the phrase is redundant. Bilingual redundancy, however, makes for a clearer meaning. Ryad-1 was formally announced in January 1972. See N. Novikov, "Computers: Third Generation," *Pravda,* January 12, 1972, p. 3, and M. Shimansky, "All Powerful Electronics," *Izvestiya,* January 22, 1975, p. 5.
18. According to Seymour Goodman, "Prototype Ryad-2 models existed by the end of 1978 and serial production was due to start 1979-82." See "Soviet Computing and Technology Transfer: An Overview," *World Politics,* Princeton University Press, July 1979, pp. 539-570.
19. Article in *Nedelya,* Moscow, December 4, 1967, p. 4.
20. Davis and Goodman, "The Soviet Bloc's Unified System of Computers," pp. 94–119. See also S. Goodman, "Soviet Computing and Technology Transfer."
21. Davis and Goodman, "The Soviet Bloc's Unified System of Computers," p. 111.

Chapter 4

1. The Soviet bloc nations operate numerous foreign trading organizations through their Ministries of Foreign Trade. In the Soviet Union they are called *vsesoyuznye obyedineniya,* or federal associations, sometimes abbreviated simply as V/O. There are more than sixty such associations in Moscow, generally known by their acronyms.
2. Technopromimport, Mashpriborintorg, Techmashimport, and Elektronorgtekhnika are all acronyms of the full Russian designations for Imports for Technological Industry, Machine Tool Import Trade, Technical Machinery Import, and Organization of Electronic Technology.
3. "The Soviet Need for Western Technology" (declassified document, prepared for the United Kingdom Department of Trade and Industry and available from its library in London), Appendix E, "The Electronics Industry," p. 37.
4. A full text of the decree, signed May 31, 1978, was published in Russian in late 1978. A summary in English, entitled "Decree on FTO's, Summary," was prepared for the British Embassy in Moscow, summer of 1978.

5. "Charter of the All-Union Foreign Trade Association V/O Elektronorgtekhnika," *Foreign Trade* (Moscow), January 1979. pp. 49–51.
6. Ibid.
7. Gorlenko's biography was published in *Foreign Trade,* June 1981.
8. No mention of Kedrov's name is made in listings of deputy directors of Elorg in a briefing sheet prepared for use by British embassy in the USSR, as revised in March 1983.
9. Portions of documents and materials seized at the time of Gopal's arrest on September 28, 1978, by U.S. law enforcement officers, were used in evidence during Gopal's subsequent trial. They are currently held by Santa Clara County Court clerk, Santa Clara, California.
10. "Decree on FTO's, Summary."
11. Testimony of Dr. Jack Vorona, director of scientific and technical information, Defense Intelligence Agency, Department of Defense, Senate Committee on Governmental Affairs, Permanent Subcommittee on Investigations, *Transfer of United States High Technology to the Soviet Union and Soviet Bloc Nations,* 97th Cong., 2nd Sess., Hearings, May 1982, p. 112.
12. John Barron, *The KGB: The Secret Work of Soviet Secret Agents* (first American edition published, 1974, Reader's Digest Association; U.K. edition, London: Hodder & Stoughton, 1974).
13. H. Rositzke, *The KGB: The Eyes of Russia* (New York: Doubleday, 1981).
14. Greville Wynne, *The Man from Odessa* (London: Robert Hale, 1981), p. 418.
15. Interview with East-West trader, California, July 21, 1983.
16. Interview with East-West trader, England, November 4, 1983.
17. Testimony of Edward J. O'Malley, assistant director, Intelligence Division, Federal Bureau of Investigation, Senate Committee on Governmental Affairs, Permanent Subcommittee on Investigations, *Transfer of United States High Technology to the Soviet Union and Soviet Bloc Nations,* 97th Cong., 2nd Sess., Hearings, May 1982, p. 170.
18. "To Catch a Spy: The Case of the Fat Bear," *Asiaweek,* June 3, 1983, pp. 10–16.
19. Linda Melvern, "Chernov Was High Tech Spy," *Sunday Times* (London), July 3, 1983, pp. 1–2.

Chapter 5

1. Interview with Special Agent Dick Curci, U.S. Customs Service, Newark, New Jersey, January 20, 1984.
2. Court records, *United States* v. *Michael J. Winkler,* Newark District Court, New Jersey. Transcript of court hearing, March 19, 1979.
3. Interview with Robert Cozzolina, Section Chief, U.S. Customs Service, Intelligence Branch, New York City, December 8, 1983.
4. Interview with Immigration and Naturalization Service personnel, Washington, D.C., December 1983.
5. This section is based on extensive interviews with U.S. Customs special agents in Washington, D.C., November 1983.
6. Interview with Patrick O'Brien, assistant regional commissioner for enforcement, Region II, U.S. Customs Service, New York City, December 7, 1983.

7. Interview with Commissioner William von Raab, U.S. Customs Service, Washington, D.C., November 17, 1983.
8. Court records, United States District Court, Central District of California, *United States v. Edward F. King, et al.*, November 1983. Indictments filed November 3, 1983. Affidavit, John P. Waite, Special Agent/Criminal Investigator, U.S. Customs Service. Sworn to on January 27, 1983.

Chapter 6

1. Serge Schmemann, "Brezhnev Souvenir: Vast Limping Truck Factory," *New York Times*, February 4, 1983.
2. Clyde H. Farnsworth, "The Freeze on Russia: It Hurts Both Sides," *New York Times*, Section 3, May 25, 1980.
3. Serge Schmemann, "Brezhnev Souvenir: Vast Limping Truck Factory."
4. Testimony of Senator Jake Garn (Utah) to Senate Committee on Governmental Affairs, *Proposed Legislation to Establish an Office of Strategic Trade*, 96th Cong., 2nd Sess., Hearings, September 24–25, 1980.
5. Interview with John Huhs, New York City, December 6, 1983.
6. Interview with Stanley Marcuss, former Deputy Assistant Secretary for Industry and Trade, Commerce Department, Washington, D.C., January 9, 1984.
7. Part of Lawrence J. Brady's testimony to the Research and Development Subcommittee of the House Armed Services Committee, 96th Cong., 2nd Sess., Hearings, May 1979, remains classified. This account is reconstructed from interviews with former senior Commerce Department officials and from an article, "Will Liberal Senators Hear Red Trade Expert?" *Human Events*, December 8, 1979, p. 4.
8. "Technology Transfer and Export Controls," *The National Security Record*, September 1979, p. 2.
9. Interview with Stanley Marcuss, Washington, D.C., January 9, 1984.
10. Testimony of Senator Jake Garn to Senate Committee on Governmental Affairs, *Proposed Legislation to Establish an Office of Strategic Trade*, 96th Cong., 2nd Sess., Hearings, September 24–25, 1980.
11. "Commerce Aide Lifts Lid on Kama River Project," *Human Events*, December 8, 1979, p. 1.
12. Clyde H. Farnsworth, "Soviet Trade in Review, Nominee Tells Hearings," *New York Times*, December 20, 1979.
13. Interview with Lawrence J. Brady, Washington, D.C., November 30, 1983.
14. Testimony of Lawrence J. Brady to Senate Committee on Governmental Affairs, Permanent Subcommittee on Investigations, *Transfer of United States High Technology to the Soviet Union and Soviet Bloc Nations*, 97th Cong., 2nd Sess., Hearings, May 1982.
15. Interview with Lawrence J. Brady, Washington, D.C., November 30, 1983.
16. Ibid.
17. Testimony of Senator Jake Garn, Senate Committee on Governmental Affairs, *Proposed Legislation to Establish an Office of Strategic Trade*, 96th Cong., 2nd Sess., Hearings, September 24–25, 1980.
18. Secret CIA memorandum, no. 780/79, dated December 14, 1979. Subject: Kama Trucks: Production and Uses. Declassified October 9, 1981.

19. *Technology and East-West Trade: An Update,* Office of Technology Assessment, Congress of the United States, Washington, D.C., 1983, p. 34.
20. Ibid.
21. "Three Are Indicted in Attempt to Ship Truck-Making Equipment Machines to Soviet Union," *New York Times,* January 6, 1983.
22. Testimony of Senator Jake Garn, Senate Committee on Governmental Affairs, *Proposed Legislation to Establish an Office of Strategic Trade,* 96th Cong., 2nd Sess., Hearings, September 24–25, 1980.
23. Testimony of Lawrence J. Brady, Senate Committee on Governmental Affairs, Permanent Subcommittee on Investigations, *Transfer of United States High Technology to the Soviet Union and Soviet Bloc Nations,* 97th Cong., 2nd Sess., Hearings, May 1982.
24. Report by the Comptroller General of the United States, "Export Control Regulations Could be Reduced Without Affecting National Security," General Accounting Office, Washington, D.C., May 1982.
25. Internal Report of Inspection, prepared by the Office of the Inspector General, U.S. Department of Commerce, June 11, 1982, summarized by Sherman M. Funk, Inspector General, U.S. Department of Commerce, to Senate Committee on Banking, Housing and Urban Affairs, *Export Administration Act: Oversight on the Commerce Department's Fulfillment of its Responsibilities Under the Export Administration Act,* 98th Cong., 1st Sess., February 3, 1983, pp. 124–136.
26. Testimony of Lawrence J. Brady, Senate Committee on Governmental Affairs, Permanent Subcommittee on Investigations, *Transfer of United States High Technology to the Soviet Union and Soviet Bloc Nations,* 97th Cong., 2nd Sess., Hearings, May 1982.
27. *Technology and East-West Trade: An Update,* p. 39.
28. *Foreign Affairs,* May 1981, pp. 62–63.
29. *Technology and East-West Trade: An Update,* p. 39.
30. "Export Controls: Customs Making Play for Enforcement Responsibility," *ITEX* (Bureau of National Affairs), January 6, 1981, pp. A1–A4.
31. Testimony of Fred Asselin, staff investigator, Senate Committee on Governmental Affairs, Permanent Subcommittee on Investigations, *Transfer of United States High Technology to the Soviet Union and Soviet Bloc Nations,* 97th Cong., 2nd Sess., Hearings, May 1982.
32. Ibid.
33. Senator Sam Nunn (Georgia), Senate Committee on Governmental Affairs, Permanent Subcommittee on Investigations, *Transfer of United States High Technology to the Soviet Union and Soviet Bloc Nations,* 97th Cong., 2nd Sess., Hearings, May 1982.
34. Ibid.
35. Testimony of Glenn W. Fry, Senate Committee on Governmental Affairs, Permanent Subcommittee on Investigations, *Transfer of United States High Technology to the Soviet Union and Soviet Bloc Nations,* 97th Cong., 2nd Sess., Hearings, May 1982.
36. Representative Don Bonker (Washington), House Committee on Foreign Affairs, Subcommittee on Economic Policy and Trade, *Export Administration Amendments Act of 1983,* Hearings, 98th Cong., 1st Sess., March 1, 1983.
37. Statement of Lionel Olmer, Under Secretary for International Trade, Department of Commerce, accompanied by Lawrence J. Brady, Assistant Secretary for Trade Administration, Senate Committee on Banking, Housing and

Urban Affairs, *Export Administration Act,* 98th Cong., 1st Sess., Hearings, February 3, 1983. p. 54.

38. The cases were Elder Industries, 1977, 1979; Spawr Optical Industries Inc., 1980; Bruchhausen, Maluta, and Tittel, 1981.

39. Interview with special agent, U.S. Customs Service, Los Angeles, January 4, 1984.

40. Interview with Theodore Wai Wu, Washington, D.C., December 2, 1983.

41. Testimony of Lionel Olmer, Under Secretary for International Trade, Department of Commerce, Senate Committee on Banking, Housing and Urban Affairs, *Export Administration Act,* 98th Cong., 1st Sess., Hearings, February 3, 1983, p. 54.

42. Ibid., p. 87.

43. Testimony of William von Raab, Commissioner, U.S. Customs Service, Senate Committee on Banking, Housing and Urban Affairs, *Export Administration Act,* 98th Cong., 1st Sess., Hearings, February 3, 1983, pp. 111–115.

44. Testimony of Theodore L. Thau, Senate Committee on Banking, Housing and Urban Affairs, *Export Administration Act,* 98th Cong., 1st Sess., Hearings, February 3, 1983, p. 114.

45. Testimony of William von Raab, Commissioner, U.S. Customs Service, House Committee on Foreign Affairs, Subcommittee on Economic Policy and Trade, *Export Administration Amendments Act of 1983,* 98th Cong., 1st Sess., Hearings, March 1, 1983.

46. Interview with William von Raab, Commissioner, U.S. Customs Service, Washington, D.C., November 17, 1983.

47. Interview with William Rudman, director of the Office of Strategic Investigations, U.S. Customs Service, Washington, D.C., October 25, 1983.

48. Interview with special agent, U.S. Customs Service, Washington, D.C., November 18, 1983.

49. Interview with William Rudman, Washington, D.C., October 25, 1983.

50. Interview with Special Agent, U.S. Customs Service, Washington, D.C., November 24, 1983.

51. Ibid.

52. Ibid.

53. Interview with senior official, U.S. Customs Service, New York City, January 7, 1984.

54. Interview with Patrick O'Brien, assistant regional commissioner for enforcement, Region II, U.S. Customs Service, New York City, December 7, 1983.

55. Testimony of Senator Sam Nunn, House Committee on Foreign Affairs, Subcommittee on International Economic Policy and Trade, *Extension of the Export Administration Act,* 98th Cong., 1st Sess., Hearings, April 13, 1983.

56. Testimony of Richard Perle, Assistant Secretary for International Security Policy, Department of Defense, Senate Committee on Banking, Housing and Urban Affairs, Subcommittee on International Finance and Monetary Policy, *Reauthorization of the Export Administration Act,* 98th Cong., 1st Sess., Hearings, March 2–April 14, 1983, pp. 188–189.

57. Interview with former State Department official, Virginia, November 17, 1983.

58. Testimony of Lawrence J. Brady to the House Armed Services Committee, Research and Development Subcommittee, *Hearings to Amend the Export Administration Act, 1969,* 96th Cong., 2nd Sess., Open hearing, May 23, 1979.

59. Interview with former Commerce Department official, Washington, D.C., November 23, 1983.
60. Ibid.
61. Interview with Rauer Meyer, former director of the Office of Export Administration, U.S. Department of Commerce, Virginia, December 6, 1983.
62. Interview with Richard Perle, Washington, D.C., November 16, 1983.
63. Interview with former Commerce Department official, Washington, D.C., November 23, 1983.
64. Ibid.
65. *Federal Register,* vol. 47, p. 9044, March 3, 1982. U.S. Department of Commerce, International Trade Administration, Order Temporarily Denying Export Privileges to Piher Semiconductures, S.A., Avda San Julian, s/n, Apartado Correos 177, Granallers (Barcelona), Spain, and related companies, signed, February 25, 1982.
66. U.S. Department of Commerce, International Trade Administration, order amending temporary denial of export privileges, signed, April 8, 1982. *Federal Register,* vol. 47, p. 16819, April 20, 1982; U.S. Department of Commerce, International Trade Administration, order amending temporary denial of export privileges, signed June 2, 1982. *Federal Register,* vol. 47, p. 24765, June 8, 1982.
67. Report of Inspection, Compliance Division, Office of Export Administration, International Trade Administration. Prepared by Office of Inspector General, U.S. Department of Commerce, June 11, 1982.
68. Interview with special agent, U.S. Customs Service, November 5, 1983.
69. Interviews with senior employees and former employees, U.S. Customs Service, November, 1983.
70. Interview with senior official of U.S. Customs Service, December 7, 1983.

Chapter 7

1. Text of radio address of President Ronald Reagan, November 13, 1982. From the White House Office of the Press Secretary.
2. Remarks of the President on his departure from the South Lawn of the White House, November 13, 1982. From the White House Office of the Press Secretary.
3. Glenn Frankel, "Brookings Economist Says Soviets Can Circumvent U.S. Embargo Easily," *Washington Post,* July 31, 1980.
4. Richard Owen, "Pipeline Problems: Tough Challenge for Soviet Expertise," *The Times* (London), August 3, 1983.
5. *Technology and East-West Trade: An Update,* Office of Technology Assessment, Congress of the United States, Washington, D.C., 1983, p. 4.
6. Interview with Rauer Meyer, former director of the Office of Export Administration, U.S. Department of Commerce, Virginia, December 6, 1983.
7. Henry S. Reuss (Wisconsin), chairman of the House Joint Economic Committee, opening statement to the Joint Economic Committee, 97th Cong., 2nd Sess., Hearings, September 22, 1982.
8. David Shears, "Doubts in US on Reagan's 'Soviet Trade Curb Pact,'" *Daily Telegraph* (London), November 16, 1982, p. 1.

9. Report of the Senate Committee on Governmental Affairs, Permanent Subcommittee on Investigations, *Transfer of United States High Technology to the Soviet Union and Soviet Bloc Nations,* 97th Cong., 2nd Sess., November 15, 1982, p. 64.
10. *New York Times,* August 17, 1978, at 126. (microfilm edition).
11. Testimony of Miles Costick, president of the Institute on Strategic Trade, Senate Committee on Governmental Affairs. *Proposed Legislation to Establish an Office of Strategic Trade,* 96th Cong., 2nd Sess., Hearings, September 24, 1980, p. 148.
12. Testimony of James A. Gray, president of the National Machine Tool Builders Association, Senate Committee on Banking, Housing and Urban Affairs, Subcommittee on International Finance and Monetary Policy, *Reauthorization of the Export Administration Act,* 98th Cong., 1st Sess., Hearings, March 2, 1983, p. 365.
13. Interview with Theodore L. Thau, Salinas, California, December 28, 1983.
14. Caspar W. Weinberger, "Technology Transfers to the Soviet Union," *Wall Street Journal,* January 12, 1982, p. 32.
15. Interview with senior British COCOM delegate, London, October 4, 1983.
16. Testimony of James L. Buckley, Under Secretary of State for Security Assistance, Science and Technology, Department of State, Senate Committee on Governmental Affairs, Permanent Subcommittee on Investigations, *Transfer of United States High Technology to the Soviet Union and Soviet Bloc Nations,* 97th Cong., 2nd Sess., Hearings, May 1982, p. 156.
17. Interview with Richard Perle, Assistant Secretary for International Security Policy, Department of Defense, Washington, D.C., November 16, 1983.
18. Sarah Booth Conroy, "Amazing Feats of Kitchen Magic," *Washington Post,* October 5, 1980, p. E1.
19. Richard Cohen, "Politics, Foreign Policy, Economy — and Soufflés?" *Washington Post,* August 1, 1976, p. B1.
20. Robert G. Kaiser, "Behind-Scenes Power over Arms Policy," *Washington Post,* June 26, 1977.
21. Arthur M. Cox, *Russian Roulette — The Superpower Game* (New York: Times Books, 1982).
22. Robert G. Kaiser, "Behind-Scenes Power over Arms Policy."
23. Ibid.
24. Mary McGrory, "The Pentagon's Mr. T. K. Jones Shows Both Faces on the Hill," *Washington Post,* April 1, 1982.
25. Glenn Frankel, "U.S. Experts Debate Variety of Approaches to Soviet Successions," *Washington Post,* May 18, 1982, p. A16.
26. Interview with William Root, Virginia, January 6, 1983.
27. Interview with Fred Asselin, Washington, D.C., November 1, 1983.
28. Harold Jackson, "East-West Trade Chief Resigns in Anger," *The Guardian* (London), September 23, 1983.
29. *Technology and East-West Trade: An Update,* Office of Technology Assessment, Congress of the United States, Washington, D.C., May 1983, p. 64.
30. Interview with former Commerce Department official, Washington, D.C., November 20, 1983.
31. Interviews with senior Pentagon officials, Washington, D.C., November 1983–January 1984.
32. Interview with Richard Perle, November 16, 1983.

33. Interview with Richard Perle, November 23, 1983.
34. Testimony of Lionel Olmer, Under Secretary for International Trade, Department of Commerce, House Committee on Foreign Affairs, Subcommittee on Economic Policy and Trade, *Export Administration Amendments Act of 1983,* 98th Cong., 1st Sess., Hearings, March 1, 1983.
35. Interview with former Commerce Department official, Washington, D.C., November 28, 1983.
36. Confederation of British Industry letter and submission on the U.S. Export Administration Act; additional material received for the record. Senate Committee on Banking, Housing and Urban Affairs, Subcommittee on International Finance and Monetary Policy, *Reauthorization of the Export Administration Act,* March 1983, pp. 1181–1194.
37. Linda Melvern and Mark Hosenball, "U.S. Warns Britain to Stamp on High-Tech Smugglers," *Sunday Times* (London), June 19, 1983, p. 3.
38. Interview with senior British COCOM delegate, London, December 18, 1983.
39. Interview with British Customs official, London, October 6, 1983.
40. Ibid.; interview with British diplomat, Washington, D.C., October 20, 1983.
41. Interview with Richard Perle, November 23, 1983.
42. Interview with former U.S. Commerce Department official, Washington, D.C., November 20, 1983.
43. "Government Acts on U.S. 'Big Trouble' Warning," *Computer News* (London), January 12, 1984, p. 1.
44. *Hansard,* House of Commons debate, "New Technology," February 17, 1984, pp. 476–536.
45. Transcript, BBC Radio Four program, "Today," January 20, 1984.
46. Plasma Technology Ltd., letter to J. J. D. Ashdown, M.P., January 11, 1984.
47. *Hansard,* House of Commons debate, "New Technology," February 17, 1984, pp. 476–536.
48. "U.S. Trade Law: The Triple Threat. The Stifling of High-Technology Business." A memorandum by International Computers Ltd., 1984.
49. Ron Condon, "Geoffrey Pattie: Priming Industry with Defence Cash," *Scicon Software and Services Review,* First Quarter, 1984, pp. 8–18.
50. Interview with senior Defense Department official, Washington, D.C., January 14, 1984.

Chapter 8

1. "How Washington Put the Squeeze on Austria," *Business Week,* April 4, 1983.
2. "Mann der Kontraste," *Wochenpresse* (Vienna), April 12, 1972.
3. Ibid.
4. Ibid.
5. Background of Proksch and Wein can be found in *Trend* magazine (Vienna), November 1974; *Wochenpresse,* February 14, 1979; *Kurier* (Vienna), November 25, 1979; *Profil* (Vienna), November 26, 1979, p. 58; *Kurier,* December 29, 1979.
6. "Ich bin kein Spion," *Profil,* November 26, 1979, p. 58.
7. "Macht, Marx und Moneten," *Wochenpresse,* February 14, 1979.

8. Ibid.
9. "Der Tortenfresser," *Wie-Wo* magazine, March 1972.
10. *Wochenpresse,* April 12, 1972.
11. Proksch's TV appearance was on "Panorama" on Austrian television, as reported in "Also sprach Kirchhofer," *Kurier,* September 14, 1973.
12. The press accusations in Vienna began with *Wochenpresse* articles as early as February 1979 ("DDR-Spionage, Aussenstelle Wien") and continued sporadically into 1982.
13. "Geschichten vom Dr. Kreisky," *Die Presse* (Vienna), April 19, 1979.
14. "Der Herr von Sacher," *Trend,* November 1979, p. 186.
15. Ibid., "Pfneudls Praxis," p. 184.
16. Interviews with Peter Gopal, Sunnyvale, California, July 12, 1983, and November 21, 1983; interview with Douglas Southard, United States Deputy District Attorney, Santa Clara, California, July 11, 1983.
17. Documents and materials that were seized at the time of Gopal's arrest on September 28, 1978 by U.S. agents, portions of which were used in evidence during Gopal's subsequent trial, are currently held by Santa Clara County Court clerk. (Abbreviated hereinafter as "Gopal case: documents/materials, Santa Clara County Court.")
18. Interview with Peter Gopal, November 21, 1983.
19. Gopal case: documents/materials, Santa Clara County Court.
20. Ibid.
21. Interview with Douglas Southard, Santa Clara, California, July 11, 1983.
22. Interviews with Peter Gopal, Sunnyvale, California, July 12, 1983, and November 21, 1983.
23. Gopal case: documents/materials, Santa Clara County Court.
24. "Herr Proksch, sind Sie ein Ostspion und Waffenschieber?" *Kurier,* November 25, 1979, p. 5.
25. "Ich bin kein Spion," *Profil,* November 26, 1979, p. 58.
26. Ibid., p. 60.
27. Interview with Douglas Southard, Santa Clara, California, July 11, 1983. According to Peter Gopal, Sacher invited U.S. Department of Commerce officials to inspect his Vienna premises and equipment.
28. Gopal case: documents/materials, Santa Clara County Court.
29. Ibid.
30. Pfneudl is described as "Verwaltungsrat" in business registration records. See *Profil,* November 26, 1979, p. 56.
31. Statement of Douglas Southard, Deputy District Attorney, Santa Clara County, Senate Committee on Governmental Affairs, Permanent Subcommittee on Investigations, *Transfer of United States High Technology to the Soviet Union and Soviet Bloc Nations,* Hearings, May 1982, pp. 500–504.
32. Interviews with Peter Gopal, Sunnyvale, California, July 12, 1983, and November 21, 1983.
33. Interview with Peter Gopal, Sunnyvale, California, November 21, 1983. Gopal's motion for a new trial was denied on August 19, 1983; Superior Court document 70499, San Jose District Attorney's Office.
34. Interview with Peter Gopal, Sunnyvale, California, July 12, 1983.
35. "NBC Magazine," October 3, 1980.
36. Interview with Peter Gopal, Sunnyvale, California, July 12, 1983.
37. "NBC Magazine," October 3, 1980.

38. Interview with Peter Gopal, July 12, 1983. On BBC Television "Panorama," July 25, 1983, Gopal tried unsuccessfully to deny any business connection to Swiss companies.
39. Compilation of information mainly based on *Wochenpresse,* February 7, 1979, p. 5.
40. "Affäre Stiller: Vermutlich aus der BRD," *Profil,* December 3, 1979, p. 56.
41. Interview with Peter Gopal, Sunnyvale, California, November 21, 1983.

Chapter 9

1. Testimony of Dr. Lara H. Baker, Jr., Assistant Office Leader, International Technology Office, Los Alamos National Laboratory, University of California, to Senate Committee on Governmental Affairs, Permanent Subcommittee on Investigations, *Transfer of United States High Technology to the Soviet Union and Soviet Bloc Nations,* 97th Cong., 2nd Sess., Hearings, May 1982, p. 59.
2. United States District Court, Central District of California. *United States* v. *Anatoli T. Maluta, Sabina Dorn Tittel.* Court document, exhibit no. 1, no. 90-24-9D-19-127.
3. Biographies of FTO officials are published regularly in the Soviet magazine *Foreign Trade.*
4. United States District Court, Central District of California. *United States* v. *Anatoli T. Maluta, Sabina Dorn Tittel.* Court document, exhibit no. 1, no. 90-24-9D-19-129.
5. Anonymous letter dated June 20, 1977, Düsseldorf. In authors' possession.
6. Anonymous letter dated February 11, 1978. In authors' possession.
7. Based on the prepared statement of Fred Asselin, staff investigator, to the Senate Committee on Governmental Affairs, Permanent Subcommittee on Investigations, *Transfer of United States High Technology to the Soviet Union and Soviet Bloc Nations,* 97th Cong., 2nd Sess., Hearings, May 1982, pp. 366–425. All information in this section refers to this citation unless otherwise noted.
8. BBC television program "Panorama," July 25, 1983.
9. Prepared statement of Fred Asselin to the Senate Committee on Governmental Affairs, Permanent Subcommittee on Investigations, *Transfer of United States High Technology to the Soviet Union and Soviet Bloc Nations,* 97th Cong., 2nd Sess., Hearings, May 1982, p. 423.
10. Prepared statement of Theodore Wai Wu, Assistant United States Attorney, Criminal Division, Central District of California, to the Senate Committee on Governmental Affairs, Permanent Subcommittee on Investigations, *Transfer of United States High Technology to the Soviet Union and Soviet Bloc Nations,* 97th Cong., 2nd Sess., Hearings, May 1982, pp. 510–532.
11. Prepared statement of Dr. Lara H. Baker, Jr., to Senate Committee on Governmental Affairs, Permanent Subcommittee on Investigations, *Transfer of United States High Technology to the Soviet Union and Soviet Bloc Nations,* 97th Cong., 2nd Sess., Hearings, May, 1982, p. 343.
12. Testimony of Dr. Lara H. Baker, Jr., to Senate Committee on Governmental Affairs, Permanent Subcommittee on Investigations, *Transfer of United*

States High Technology to the Soviet Union and Soviet Bloc Nations, 97th Cong., 2nd Sess., Hearings, May 1982, p. 68.

13. Steve Johnson and Pete Carey, "Greed More Than High-Tech Spies Threatens US Military Security," a Mercury News Special Report, *San Jose Mercury News,* May 12, 1982, pp. 3A–4A.

14. Steve Johnson and Pete Carey, "Chip Thieves Play for High Stakes," a Mercury News Special Report, *San Jose Mercury News,* May 12, 1982, pp. 7A–9A.

15. Ibid.

16. "Counting the Chips," editorial, a Mercury News Special Report, *San Jose Mercury News,* n.d., 1983, p. 14B.

17. Statement of Douglas Southard, Deputy District Attorney, County of Santa Clara, to Senate Committee on Governmental Affairs, Permanent Subcommittee on Investigations, *Transfer of United States High Technology to the Soviet Union and Soviet Bloc Nations,* 97th Cong., 2nd Sess., Hearings, May 1982, p. 485.

18. Ibid., p. 483.

19. Testimony of Douglas Southard to Senate Committee on Governmental Affairs, Permanent Subcommittee on Investigations, *Transfer of United States High Technology to the Soviet Union and Soviet Bloc Nations,* 97th Cong., 2nd Sess., Hearings, May 1982, p. 148.

20. Statement of Douglas Southard to Senate Committee on Governmental Affairs, Permanent Subcommittee on Investigations, *Transfer of United States High Technology to the Soviet Union and Soviet Bloc Nations,* 97th Cong., 2nd Sess., Hearings, May 1982, p. 486.

21. Testimony of Douglas Southard to Senate Committee on Governmental Affairs, Permanent Subcommittee on Investigations, *Transfer of United States High Technology to the Soviet Union and Soviet Bloc Nations,* 97th Cong., 2nd Sess., Hearings, May 1982, p. 147.

22. Steve Johnson and Pete Carey, "From the Dump: Chips for Sale," a Mercury News Special Report, *San Jose Mercury News,* May 12, 1982, p. 12A.

23. Testimony of Douglas Southard to Senate Committee on Governmental Affairs, Permanent Subcommittee on Investigations, *Transfer of United States High Technology to the Soviet Union and Soviet Bloc Nations,* 97th Cong., 2nd Sess., Hearings, May 12, 1982, p. 146.

24. Statement of Douglas Southard to Senate Committee on Governmental Affairs, Permanent Subcommittee on Investigations, *Transfer of United States High Technology to the Soviet Union and Soviet Bloc Nations,* 97th Cong., 2nd Sess., Hearings, May 12, 1982, pp. 494–495.

25. Ibid., p. 490.

26. Christopher Simpson, "Electronics Underworld," *Computer World,* August 31, 1981.

27. Statement of Douglas Southard to Senate Committee on Governmental Affairs, Permanent Subcommittee on Investigations, *Transfer of United States High Technology to the Soviet Union and Soviet Bloc Nations,* 97th Cong., 2nd Sess., Hearings, May 12, 1982, pp. 484–485.

28. Christopher Simpson, "Electronics Underworld."

29. Testimony of Douglas Southard to Senate Committee on Governmental Affairs, Permanent Subcommittee on Investigations, *Transfer of United States High Technology to the Soviet Union and Soviet Bloc Nations,* 97th Cong., 2nd Sess., Hearings, May 12, 1982, pp. 151–152.

30. Ehud Yonay, "Mirrors for Moscow," *New West* magazine, September 1981.
31. Ibid.
32. BBC television program "Panorama," July 25, 1983.
33. Testimony of Douglas Southard to Senate Committee on Governmental Affairs, Permanent Subcommittee on Investigations, *Transfer of United States High Technology to the Soviet Union and Soviet Bloc Nations*, 97th Cong., 2nd Sess., Hearings, May 12, 1982, p. 154.
34. Interview with David Meisner, Exodus Project Manager, U.S. Customs Service, Los Angeles, January 4, 1984.
35. United States District Court for the Central District of California. Application for search warrant, *United States* v. *The residence/business of Robert Joseph Lambert*, doing business as Computer and Test Systems, located at 5671, Via Ceresa, Yorba Linda, California. Affidavit made by Dick Roberts, Special Agent, U.S. Customs Service, June 2, 1982.
36. Interview with David Meisner, Los Angeles, January 4, 1984.
37. United States District Court for the Central District of California. Application for search warrant, *United States* v. *The residence/business of Robert Joseph Lambert*, doing business as Computer and Test Systems, located at 5671, Via Ceresa, Yorba Linda, California. Affidavit made by Dick Roberts, Special Agent, U.S. Customs Service, June 2, 1982.
38. Interview with David Meisner, Los Angeles, January 4, 1984.
39. BBC Television program "Panorama," July 25, 1983.
40. Unless otherwise indicated, information in this section (pp. 173–182) comes from interviews with a senior U.S. Customs Service agent, San Francisco, November 22, 1983, and London, February 24, 1984.
41. Based on evidence for the defense presented at the first trial of II Industries Inc., Gerald M. Starek, Carl E. Storey, et al., United States District Court, Northern District of California, San Jose, January–February, 1977; testimony of Bernard Petrie (attorney for Starek and Storey), Starek, and defense witness Jack L. Melchoir, January 26–28, 1977.
42. United States District Court, Northern District of California, San Jose. Testimony of Bernard Petrie, January 26, 1977. See also Joe Frein, "No Conspiracy Intended," *San Jose Mercury News,* January 27, 1977, p. 6A.
43. Testimony of John D. Marshall, businessman, Santa Clara, California, to Senate Committee on Governmental Affairs, Permanent Subcommittee on Investigations, *Transfer of United States High Technology to the Soviet Union and Soviet Bloc Nations,* 97th Cong., 2nd Sess., Hearings, May 1982, pp. 71–73.

Chapter 10

1. Interview with special agent, U.S. Customs Service, Los Angeles, January 20, 1984.
2. Personal experience of one of the authors, September 1976.
3. Norman C. Davis and Seymour E. Goodman, "The Soviet Bloc's Unified System of Computers," *Computing Surveys,* June 1978, p. 114.
4. Interview with managing director of London-based computer services company, January 17, 1984.

5. Ibid.; interview with former head of London-based computer training companies, October 12, 1983.
6. Interview with managing director of London-based computer services company, January 17, 1984. Authors' inquiries of various record-keeping bodies for the American professional football leagues have found no trace of McVey.
7. Interview with managing director of London-based computer services company, January 17, 1984.
8. Details contained in a letter dated May 4, 1977, to McVey's associate Roy Gibson, in authors' possession.
9. United States District Court, Central District of California. *United States* v. *Charles McVey II, Rolf Lienhard, Yuri Boyarinov,* Grand Jury Indictment no: CR 83–188.
10. Telephone interview with senior NASA official, February 1, 1984.
11. Speech by Secretary of Defense Caspar Weinberger to the American League for Exports and Assistance, as reported in *Washington Times* and *Washington Post,* October 8, 1982.
12. Thomas O'Toole, "Customs Thwarts Soviet Attempt to Steal Camera," *Washington Post,* October 8, 1982, p. A16.
13. Pages 191–192 represent personal experience of one of the authors.
14. Interview with managing director of London-based computer services company, January 17, 1984.
15. Testimony of John Maguire, president of Software A.G. of North America, Senate Committee on Governmental Affairs, Permanent Subcommittee on Investigations, *Transfer of United States High Technology to the Soviet Union and Soviet Bloc Nations,* 97th Cong., 2nd Sess., Hearings, May 1982, p. 121.
16. Statement of Theodore Stewart Greenberg, Assistant United States Attorney, Eastern District of Virginia, to Senate Committee on Governmental Affairs, Permanent Subcommittee on Investigations, *Transfer of United States High Technology to the Soviet Union and Soviet Bloc Nations,* 97th Cong., 2nd Sess., Hearings, May 1982, p. 437.
17. Ibid., p. 438.
18. Ibid., p. 439.
19. Ibid., p. 440.
20. Ibid., pp. 442–444.
21. Ibid. Exhibit no. 3, pp. 449–452.
22. Testimony of Theodore Stewart Greenberg, to Senate Committee on Governmental Affairs, Permanent Subcommittee on Investigations, *Transfer of United States High Technology to the Soviet Union and Soviet Bloc Nations,* 97th Cong., 2nd Sess., Hearings, May 1982, pp. 129–142.
23. Ibid., p. 131.
24. Interview with David Cutner of Shea and Gould, New York City, December 6, 1983.

Chapter 11

1. Interview with former senior U.S. Department of Commerce official, Washington, December 2, 1983.

2. Interview with special agent, U.S. Customs Service, Washington, D.C., February 21, 1984.
3. Interview with Ericsson's spokesman, February 25, 1984.
4. Ray Joseph, Bennie van Delft, Sylvia Vollenhoven, "The High Life of Herr Millions," *Sunday Times* (Cape Town), November 27, 1983.
5. Telephone interview with Uwe Schumann, Hamburg, February 20, 1984.
6. "Tycoon in Espionage Probe," *Weekend Argus* (Cape Town), October 8, 1983.
7. Statement of Charles L. McLeod, Special Agent, U.S. Customs Service, Senate Committee on Governmental Affairs, Permanent Subcommittee on Investigations, *Transfer of United States High Technology to the Soviet Union and Soviet Bloc Nations,* 97th Cong., 2nd Sess., Hearings, May 1982, pp. 287–294.
8. Letter, dated October 17, 1980, ref: 23 (80)-14 RJR, from Kent N. Knowles, Director, Office of Export Administration, U.S. Department of Commerce, to Paul Hermann, president of Fabrik für Feinmechanik und Apparatebau, Bahnhofstrasse 39, 7742 St. Georgen, Schwarzwald, West Germany.
9. Interview with special agent, U.S. Customs Service, Washington, D.C., February 21, 1984.
10. This account is based on material broadcast by West German television's "Panorama" program on September 27, 1983.
11. Ibid.
12. Felix Kessler, "Crackdown on Transfers of Technology to the East Spotlights Dubious Deals," *Wall Street Journal* (European edition), January 27, 1984.
13. Telephone interview with Roger Urbansky, head of Technology Investigations Branch, U.S. Customs Service, Washington, D.C., February 3, 1983.
14. Telephone interview with Dr. Athol Harrison, Cape Town, February 21, 1984.
15. Pages 211–17 are reconstructed from interviews with a West German–based special agent of the U.S. Customs Service, February 6, 1984, and February 27, 1984.
16. Information from Lloyd's Register of Shipping, records of reported movements of M/V *Elgaren,* Swedish registered, home port, Gothenberg.
17. Telephone interview with U.K. Customs official, December 8, 1983.
18. "Sweden 'Freezes' Mystery U.S. Cargo," *Rand Daily Mail,* November 18, 1983.
19. Felix Kessler, "Crackdown on Transfers of Technology to the East Spotlights Dubious Deals."
20. Sune Olofson, "Sweden Gave in to U.S. Pressure," *Svenska Dagbladet,* December 6, 1983.
21. "DOD Officials Charge Commerce Mishandled VAX Case As Conflicting Reports Abound," *U.S. Export Weekly,* January 3, 1984, p. 491.
22. Telephone interview with Roger Urbansky, Washington, D.C., February 3, 1984; Felix Kessler, "Crackdown on Transfers of Technology to the East Spotlights Dubious Deals."

Chapter 12

1. *Congressional Record.* House of Representatives, 97th Cong., 2nd Sess., March 12, 1980, pp. H1822–1825.
2. The information is based on the following documents, released to authors in January 1984 by the U.S. Department of Commerce under the Freedom of Information Act: Correspondence between Bertram Freedman, Hearing Commissioner, Department of Commerce, and Cole, Corrette, and Bradfield, 17th St. N.W., Washington, D.C., March 1980–August 1981. Commerce Department letter ref. 23 (77) 3, January 23, 1980, to Franz Eggeling. *Federal Register,* vol. 45, June 30, 1968, p. 43818. *Federal Register,* vol. 32, May 13, 1967, p. 7223.
3. U.S. Department of Commerce documents: the orders denying export privileges on cases 478 (a) and 478, file case numbers 28 (74)–1. *Federal Register,* vol. 39, December 2, 1974, p. 42935. *Federal Register,* vol. 40, March 17, 1975, p. 13015. *Federal Register,* vol. 40, January 30, 1975, p. 6383.
4. U.S. Department of Commerce documents: the order denying export privileges on files nos. 23 (73)–2, 23 (73)–5, 22 (73)–1. Order conditionally restoring export privileges, Caramant GmbH, et al., September 30, 1975; German National Denied All Export Privileges, U.S. Department of Commerce press release, January 4, 1977. *Federal Register,* vol. 41, December 15, 1976, pp. 54787–54788. *Federal Register,* vol. 22, January 5, 1977, p. 1062.
5. U.S. Department of Commerce documents: file nos. 23 (72)–8. Related party determination order, no. 23 (72)–8. Order denying export privileges: files nos. 23 (72)–8, 23 (72)–3. *Federal Register,* vol. 41, July 20, 1976, p. 29895.
6. U.S. Department of Commerce documents: Order Extending Temporary Denial of Export Privileges, file no. 23 (71)–15; Order Denying Export Privileges, file no. 23 (71)–15; Notice of Related Party Determination, case no. 466; Order Conditionally Restoring Export Privileges, file no. 466. *Export Administration Report,* U.S. Department of Commerce, April–September 1975, Chapter 8, p. 75. *Export Administration Report,* U.S. Department of Commerce. April–September 1976, Chapter 7, p. 75.
7. Don C. Hoefler, "You Still Can't Fight City Hall," *Don C. Hoefler's Microelectronics News,* Silicon Valley, December 5, 1981, pp. 1–3.
8. U.S. Department of Commerce documents: Orders Denying Export Privileges for an Indefinite Period, file nos. 23 (66)–23, August 20, 1968.
9. Interviews with former directors of related companies, June/July 1983, and February 20, 1984.
10. Ibid.
11. Pages 233 et seq. are reconstruction based on interviews with senior U.S. Customs Service officials, New York, February 21, 1984.
12. "Chinese shopping list" in authors' possession.
13. Interview with Patrick O'Brien, director of general investigations, U.S. Customs Service, New York City, February 21, 1984.

Chapter 13

1. Interview with William Dougherty, Villa Park, California, February 3, 1984.
2. Mary Ann Galante, "The Spy Files: Bill Dougherty Takes on the CIA," *National Law Journal,* December 3, 1983.
3. Ibid.
4. Interview with William Dougherty, Villa Park, California, February 3, 1984.
5. Ibid.
6. Interview with William Dougherty, Villa Park, California, February 4, 1984.
7. Mary Ann Galante, "The Spy Files: Bill Dougherty takes on the CIA."
8. Ibid.
9. Interview with Federal Bureau of Investigation agents, Los Angeles, February 5, 1984.
10. Interview with William Dougherty, Villa Park, California, February 4, 1984.
11. Press release, U.S. Department of Justice, Federal Bureau of Investigation, Office of the Director, Washington, D.C., October 17, 1983.
12. Mark Nelson, "FBI Claims He Sold Crucial Data to Poles," *San Jose Mercury News,* October 18, 1983, p. 1.
13. David Willman, "Judge in Spy Case Known as Hard-Liner," *San Jose Mercury News,* December 18, 1983.
14. Glenn F. Bunting and Kevinne Moran, "Harper Was a 'Little Boy, Wandering Around Lost,' " *San Jose Mercury News,* October 30, 1983, p. 10A.
15. Interview with Albert Nelson, Los Angeles, February 4, 1984.
16. Ibid.
17. Kevinne Moran, " 'Big Man' Hugle," *San Jose Mercury News,* October 19, 1983, p. 20A.
18. Pete Carey, "Semiconductor Group Formed," *San Jose Mercury News,* August 2, 1970.
19. *Federal Register,* vol. 44, April 27, 1979, p. 24900.
20. United States District Court, Northern District of California. In re: Hugle International, Inc., bankrupt order sustaining objection to claim. Dated March 21, 1977. Signed Seymour J. Abrahams, Bankruptcy Judge.
21. United States District Court, Northern District of California. In re: Hugle International, Inc., Bankrupt, Report and Account of Receiver. Signed Jerome E. Robertson, Receiver, April 29, 1975.
22. United States District Court, Northern District of California. Hugle International, Inc., Bankrupt. Documents Attached to Proof of Claim. Receipt dated October 31, 1974, Warsaw.
23. Interviews with Peter Gopal, Sunnyvale, California, July 12 and November 21, 1983.
24. "Spy Suspect May Have Sold Our Top Secrets," *Computer News* (London), October 27, 1983, p. 1.
25. Interview with William Hugle, Paris, February 3, 1984.
26. United States District Court, Northern District of California. *United States* v. *James Durward Harper Jnr.* Affidavit signed by Allan M. Power, Special Agent, Federal Bureau of Investigation. Dated October 14, 1983, p. 5.
27. Ibid., p. 6.
28. Ibid., pp. 6–7.
29. Ibid., p. 9.

30. Ibid., p. 12.
31. Interview with Neal Schuler, Los Angeles, February 4, 1984.
32. Scicon press release, dated January 8, 1981, "British Company Invests in Silicon Valley."
33. Interview with Yvonne Halliday, press officer, Scicon, London, February 1, 1984.
34. Alicia C. Shepard, "Motive for Selling Missile Documents Unknown," *San Jose Mercury News*, October 18, 1983, p. 1A.
35. "California Gets Life Sentence in Espionage Case," *New York Times*, May 15, 1984.
36. Mark Nelson and Glenn F. Bunting, "High-Tech Workers Implicated in Spy Case," *San Jose Mercury News*, October 20, 1983, p. 1A.
37. Mark Nelson and David Willman, "At Least Six Aided Spying, Attorney Says," *San Jose Mercury News*, October 21, 1983, p. 1A.

Chapter 14

1. J. Edgar Hoover, director of Federal Bureau of Investigation, U.S. Department of Justice, "Why Reds Make Friends with Businessmen," *Nation's Business*, May 1962. Reprinted in Report of the House Select Committee on Export Control. *Investigation and Study of the Administration, Operation and Enforcement of the Export Control Act of 1949 and Related Acts*, 87th Cong., 2nd Sess., May 25, 1962, pp. 60–64.
2. Testimony of Secretary of State Dean Rusk, to House Select Committee on Export Control, *Investigation and Study of the Administration, Operation and Enforcement of the Export Control Act of 1949 and Related Acts*, 87th Cong., 1st Sess., Hearings, October 25–December 8, 1961, pp. 73–74.
3. U.K. Public Records Office. *F/O 371/106007 M3424/120, Confidential*, "Security Export Controls on Trade with the Soviet Bloc," R. S. Crawford, November 16, 1953, p. 1.
4. Ibid., p. 6.
5. U.K. Public Records Office. *F/O 371/10608 M3424/128, Secret*, Dunnett, U.K. delegation to OEEC, Paris to Rolleston, Foreign Office, London, November 18, 1953, p. 2.
6. Prepared statement of Dr. Stephen D. Bryen, Deputy Assistant Secretary for International Economics, Trade, and Security Policy, Department of Defense, to Senate Committee on Governmental Affairs, Permanent Subcommittee on Investigations, *Transfer of United States High Technology to the Soviet Union and Soviet Bloc Nations*, 97th Cong., 2nd Sess., Hearings, May 1982, p. 584.
7. Charles Higham, *Trading with the Enemy: An Exposé of the Nazi-American Money Plot, 1933-49* (London: Robert Hale, 1983), p. 116.
8. Letter dated February 9, 1961, from Secretary of Commerce Luther H. Hodges to Senator Thomas Dodd (Connecticut), quoted in Senate Committee of the Judiciary, Report of the Subcommittee to Investigate the Administration of the Internal Security Act and other Internal Security Laws, *Proposed Shipment of Ball Bearing Machines to the USSR*, 87th Cong., 1st Sess., February 28, 1961, p. 2.
9. Ibid., p. 6.
10. Ibid.

11. Senate Committee on the Judiciary, Subcommittee to Investigate the Administration of the Internal Security Act and Other Internal Security Laws, *Export of Strategic Materials to the USSR and Other Soviet Bloc Countries,* 87th Cong., 1st Sess., Hearings, October 23, 1961, p. 26.
12. BBC television program "Panorama," July 25, 1983.
13. Boris Kozhevnikov, "Export Control System of the USA," *Foreign Trade,* April 1983, pp. 42–46.
14. Interview with senior Pentagon official, Washington, D.C., October 31, 1983.
15. William Woodruff, *America's Impact on the World: A Study of the Role of the United States in the World Economy, 1750–1970* (London: Macmillan, 1975), p. 104.
16. Ibid.
17. Charles Higham, *Trading with the Enemy: An Exposé of the Nazi-American Money Plot 1933–49,* p. 116.
18. Ibid., p. 93.
19. Ibid., p. 99.
20. Charles Levinson, *Vodka-Cola* (New York: Gordon & Cremonesi, 1978), pp. 213–214.
21. Charles Higham, *Trading with the Enemy: An Exposé of the Nazi-American Money Plot 1933–49,* p. 175.

Chapter 15

1. James R. Ferguson, "Scientific Freedom, National Security and the First Amendment," *Science,* August 12, 1983, pp. 620–624.
2. Testimony, Dr. Jack Vorona, director of scientific and technical information. Defense Intelligence Agency, Department of Defense, to Senate Committee on Governmental Affairs, Permanent Subcommittee on Investigations, *Transfer of United States High Technology to the Soviet Union and Soviet Bloc Nations,* 97th Cong., 2nd Sess., Hearings, May 1982, pp. 110–121.
3. Testimony, Arthur van Cook, director of information security, Department of Defense, and chairman, National Disclosure Policy Committee, to Senate Committee on Governmental Affairs, Permanent Subcommittee on Investigations, *Transfer of United States High Technology to the Soviet Union and Soviet Bloc Nations,* 97th Cong., 2nd Sess., Hearings, May 1982, pp. 181–193.
4. Dorothy Nelkin, "Intellectual Property: The Control of Scientific Information," *Science,* May 14, 1982, p. 706.
5. Rosemary Chalk, "Security and Scientific Communication," *Bulletin of Atomic Scientists,* August–September 1983, p. 20.
6. Testimony, Joseph Arkov (assumed name of former Soviet engineer), to Senate Committee on Governmental Affairs, Permanent Subcommittee on Investigations, *Transfer of United States High Technology to the Soviet Union and Soviet Bloc Nations,* 97th Cong., 2nd Sess., Hearings, May 1982, pp. 27–37.
7. Rosemary Chalk, "Security and Scientific Communication," p. 19.
8. Letter to the U.S. Department of Commerce, from Genrad, Santa Clara, California, dated August 2, 1983.
9. Statement of Computer and Business Equipment Manufacturers Association,

Senate Committee on Banking, Housing and Urban Affairs, Subcommittee on International Finance and Monetary Policy, *Reauthorization of the Export Administration Act,* 98th Cong., 1st Sess., Hearings, March 2 and 16 and April 14, 1983, p. 229.

10. Testimony, James A. Gray, president of the National Machine Tool Builders Association, Senate Committee on Banking, Housing and Urban Affairs, Subcommittee on International Finance and Monetary Policy, *Reauthorization of the Export Administration Act,* 98th Cong., 1st Sess., Hearings, March 2, 1983, pp. 365–366.

11. *Export Control Regulation Could Be Reduced Without Affecting National Security,* report by the Comptroller of the United States, United States General Accounting Office, May 26, 1982, p. ii.

12. Mark Potts, "U.S. Seizes Equipment Illegally Sent to USSR," *Washington Post,* August 25, 1982.

13. Interview with Ron Hendron, international sales manager, Comtal, Pasadena, Los Angeles, January 1984.

14. Internal Comtal memorandum from Harry Andrews to Rolf Westgard, September 3, 1982, subject: Department of Commerce seizure of Comtal system.

15. Interview with former Commerce Department official, Washington, D.C., November 5, 1983.

16. Elias Castillo, "Apathy Can Shortcircuit the Most Complex Security System," *San Jose Mercury News,* October 21, 1981, p. 1A.

17. Armando Acuma, "Firm Was High on Soviets' Shopping List," *San Jose Mercury News,* October 18, 1983, p. 5A.

18. Elias Castillo, "Apathy Can Shortcircuit the Most Complex Security System."

19. Report of the Committee on Governmental Affairs, Permanent Subcommittee on Investigations, *Transfer of United States High Technology to the Soviet Union and Soviet Bloc Nations,* 97th Cong., 2nd Sess., November 15, 1982, p. 63.

20. Senator Sam Nunn during testimony to Senate Committee on Governmental Affairs, Permanent Subcommittee on Investigations, *Transfer of United States High Technology to the Soviet Union and Soviet Bloc Nations,* 97th Cong., 2nd Sess., Hearings, May 1982, p. 75.

21. *An Analysis of Export Control of U.S. Technology — A DOD Perspective,* report of the Defense Science Board Task Force on Export of U.S. Technology, February 4, 1976.

22. Text of speech by Bo Denysyk to the National Council for United States and China Trade, Washington, D.C., July 8, 1981.

INDEX